T0315098

REDESIGNING WORK

REDESIGNING WORK

A Blueprint for Canada's Future
Well-Being and Prosperity

GRAHAM LOWE AND FRANK GRAVES

UNIVERSITY OF TORONTO PRESS
Toronto Buffalo London

© Graham Lowe and Frank Graves
Rotman-UTP Publishing
University of Toronto Press
Toronto Buffalo London
www.utppublishing.com

ISBN 978-1-4426-4445-8

Library and Archives Canada Cataloguing in Publication

Lowe, Graham S., author
Redesigning work: a blueprint for Canada's future well-being and prosperity/
Graham Lowe and Frank Graves.

Includes bibliographical references and index.
ISBN 978-1-4426-4445-8 (cloth)

1. Work – Canada.   2. Work environment – Canada.   3. Quality of work life –
Canada.   4. Well-being – Canada.   I. Graves, Frank, 1952–, author   II. Title.

HD6957.C3L65 2016   306.3'60971   C2016-903171-3

University of Toronto Press acknowledges the financial assistance to its
publishing program of the Canada Council for the Arts and the Ontario Arts
Council, an agency of the Government of Ontario.

 Canada Council   Conseil des Arts
for the Arts   du Canada

 ONTARIO ARTS COUNCIL
CONSEIL DES ARTS DE L'ONTARIO
an Ontario government agency
un organisme du gouvernement de l'Ontario

Funded by the   Financé par le    Canadä
Government   gouvernement
of Canada   du Canada

To the tens of thousands of Canadians
who over the past several decades
have shared their opinions and experiences with us.

Contents

Preface

This book is about the future of work. Our goal is to outline a better working future for all Canadians, a future that meets their aspirations and needs. This is urgent. Our public opinion research identified a disturbing trend in the Great Recession's aftermath: Canadians increasingly believed that opportunities for middle-class progress, once the bedrock of our society, were rapidly disappearing. Individual effort, skill, and innovation no longer assured economic security or upward mobility. What's more, our parallel tracking of work trends before and after the recession showed the same arrested progress and, more disturbingly, a decline in the quality of work life. *Redesigning Work* argues that it is possible to counter these negative trends and create a more positive future. We outline how improvements in people's jobs and workplaces can raise the quality of life and strengthen the Canadian economy by unlocking the previously untapped potential of workers. That's how well-being and prosperity are linked.

Redesigning Work is intended to be a catalyst for the actions needed to build a better future for Canada's economy and society. Canadians view their future with considerable pessimism. Large majorities of Canadians see on the horizon declining living standards, a besieged middle class, an anaemic economy, a widening divide between haves and have-nots, and a reduced quality of life. We counter this bleak scenario with a blueprint for creating better jobs and workplaces.

This blueprint for the ideal future is grounded in what Canadians tell us they want. According to our analysis, this worker-defined vision for the future not only will lead to higher levels of well-being but also will stimulate the creativity and productivity Canada needs from its workforce for a thriving economy.

Prosperity and well-being go hand in glove; you can't have one without the other. Most commentators and experts would agree with this point. Yet surprisingly, a focus on people's daily work has been missing from the post–Great Recession media commentary and expert analysis of how to kick-start the economy and restore opportunities to achieve a comfortable middle-class living standard. *Redesigning Work* aims to fill this gap, offering constructive insights into how jobs and workplaces hold some of the keys to recovery. This is not about "reinventing" work. Rather, based on the extensive feedback we received from thousands of Canadian workers, we identify numerous practical ways that existing jobs can be made more motivating, rewarding, and productive. Our evidence paints an optimistic picture of the future of work, especially if employers and policymakers are willing to implement small changes that have the potential to make a big difference.

And there may be more will to act now than at any time in the last ten years. The federal election in October 2015 focused on the theme of restoring middle-class progress. Polls by EKOS Research Associates after the Trudeau Liberals' election victory show a spike in public optimism: people believe that the economic outlook can be improved. To be sure, the Canadian public laid a fairly bold wager on a new approach to the economy, eschewing a neoliberal model which seemed oblivious to eroding living standards and rising inequality. These bigger concerns are the backdrop for the book. Our focus is on people's daily work, arguing that more rewarding and engaging jobs are an essential component of any plan to restore prosperity.

As sociologists, each of us has spent our career (Lowe as a university professor and workplace consultant, Graves as a pollster and public opinion researcher) analysing how people's work experiences influence their thinking and behaviour. We've interpreted these work experiences on the wider canvas of social, demographic, and economic change. We believe that it is possible to design a better future using solid evidence about how individuals respond to the bigger forces affecting their working lives today.

Redesigning Work provides that evidence, using workforce surveys and public opinion polls conducted by EKOS Research Associates. The book's foundation is without a doubt the most extensive data-bank currently available of Canadians' work experiences, reactions to social change, and concerns about the state of the economy and labour market. In every chapter, we build our analysis and arguments on the rich and previously unpublished data EKOS has assembled through hundreds of surveys since the mid-1990s. These surveys describe through the eyes of individual Canadians the relentless forces shaping the world of work. And it's from the vantage point of Canadian workers that we have designed a blueprint for a better future of work. This is a future that the vast majority of Canadians want.

The topics we address in the book – public attitudes to economic change, workers' well-being, work motivations and values, workforce demographics, job skills and training, and how to design higher-quality work – have been of keen interest to us for over 25 years. *Redesigning Work* is the result of a long partnership that has evolved around these future-of-work issues.

EKOS's polls started tracking Canadians' reactions to massive shocks to the economy and the labour market in the early 1990s, during a deep recession and subsequent jobless recovery. Lowe drew on some of this research in an influential policy paper, *The Future of Work in Canada*, which he co-wrote in 1997 with EKOS researcher Gordon Betcherman. EKOS and Lowe teamed up in 2000 to design and conduct an extensive workforce survey, Changing Employment Relationships, resulting in Lowe's 2001 report entitled *What's a Good Job: The Importance of Employment Relationships* (co-authored with Grant Schellenberg). In 2004, we co-designed and conducted a survey of the Canadian workforce, Redesigning Work, to document early twenty-first-century workforce and workplace trends. This was a syndicated project sponsored by government and corporate clients, so the project's results had limited circulation – until now.

Then along came the global financial crisis and the Great Recession of 2008–9. EKOS polls tracked Canadians' reactions to the recession, but missing was a detailed picture of how all this economic turbulence had transformed people's work. Using the 2004 Redesigning Work project as a pre-recession baseline, we repeated most of the same measures in a 2012 survey of the Canadian workforce. We then had pre- and post-recession measures of key job and labour market indicators. Yet we remained concerned that what we picked up in the 2012 survey, Rethinking Work, may be transitory, especially given glimmers of economic recovery at the time. As we analysed the changes between 2004 and 2012, we wanted to know if the experiences and concerns about the future we documented in 2012 were a "new normal." So EKOS conducted a shortened version of the Rethinking Work survey in early 2015. Essentially it confirmed that what we documented in 2012 was, unfortunately, the new normal. We make extensive use of all these surveys in *Redesigning Work*.

EKOS conducts polls weekly, so we have the advantage of December 2015 results on some of the key trends that form the backdrop for *Redesigning Work*. If anything, these recent polling results confirm our view that reversing the deterioration of Canadians' quality of life and quality of work must be a national priority for employers and government policymakers. People's outlook for their own financial future and for the economy remains bleak. Three of four survey respondents at the end of 2015 believe that the economy is in recession. A large majority believes that fixing the economy must be the top priority for the federal government and its provincial counterparts. Workers are growing somewhat less confident that they have the skills and knowledge to be competitive in the labour market. And workers' sense of job insecurity rose slightly during 2015. What hasn't changed in the past several years is the view that a growing and optimistic middle class is essential for social progress – a view shared by 86 per cent of Canadians whom EKOS polled in late 2015.

This book explores ways to restore a real sense of middle-class prosperity and progress. One EKOS poll finding signals, for us, a readiness for the changes proposed in *Redesigning Work*. For the past several years – including the December 2015 poll – 80 per cent or more of Canadians polled by EKOS have agreed that "Canada needs a clearer plan or blueprint to restore a growing and optimistic middle class." That's where our idea for a blueprint for well-being and prosperity comes from: the many thousands of citizens responding to this question in EKOS polls. Indeed, we believe that all of the ingredients for a return to shared prosperity are in place. It is our sincere hope that the lessons we have learned from the evolution of Canadians' working lives can help point the way to renewal and growth.

Our partnership for this book is unique; neither of us would have produced the book without the other's involvement. The basic ideas are the product of our long association on the projects described earlier. Graves provided the evidence base for the book in the form of all relevant EKOS data and reports; Lowe did additional background research and wrote the book's text.

Many individuals contributed to this book. We especially want to thank the tens of thousands of EKOS survey respondents who have shared their opinions and experiences with us over the past several decades. We have dedicated the book to these individuals, who were generous to us with their thoughts and time. Without their cooperation and input, this book would not have been possible. At EKOS, Susan Galley contributed to the design of the Rethinking Work surveys; Jeff Smith provided the extensive data we mine in the book; and James McKee offered comments on an earlier draft of chapter 5. Participants at a number of conferences in Canada provided feedback on some of the findings and interpretations we present here. Jennifer DiDomenico, our editor at Rotman-UTP Publishing, offered constant encouragement and sound advice. Lori Johnson of Dragonfli Studio greatly improved the graphics. Barbie Halaby's careful copyediting made the book more readable. And while we relied on many sources for background research, one stands out as particularly helpful: the *Perry Work Report*, a weekly e-publication of the Centre for Industrial Relations and Human Resources Library at the University of Toronto. And finally, on a personal note, we owe a huge thank you to our families – especially our wives, Joanne and Susan – for their support, encouragement, and patience during what turned out to be a much longer project than we ever expected.

Graham Lowe
Kelowna, British Columbia
Frank Graves
Ottawa, Ontario
January 2016

REDESIGNING WORK

Introduction

There's no shortage of reasons to be pessimistic about the future. The boom-and-bust roller coaster of the past decade has reshaped Canadian society but not how Canadians want. The dynamics of the twenty-first-century economy have ruptured the late twentieth-century ethic of progress – the belief that opportunities for a middle-class life were widely available. The public now expects that living standards will decline in a stagnant economy and fewer young people will achieve the middle-class lifestyles of their parents' generation. If current trends continue unchecked, in 10 years Canadian society will have more inequality, less opportunity, and a reduced quality of life.

But the future doesn't have to unfold like this. While Canadians are living in an era of arrested progress and diminished expectations, many recognize the potential to achieve a healthier society and a stronger economy. That's why the October 2015 federal election was foremost about how to restore a sense of optimism about the future. So how can Canadians jump-start progress? Needed are fresh approaches to jolt the economy out of what business commentators have dubbed "the seven-year slump," describing the sputtering recovery since the Great Recession of 2008–9. As Bill Hammond, CEO of Hammond Power Solutions Inc. – a Guelph, Ontario, manufacturer of electrical transformers for industry – observes, "It has become clear that we are really dealing with a different kind of economic recovery than anyone has experienced since World War II."[1] Employers like Hammond share one thing in common with many experts, policymakers, workers, and others across the country: they are searching for new ways forward.

This book sketches one path towards a better future. We argue that redesigned jobs and workplaces can be a cornerstone for recovery, provided these changes support workers in being healthy, engaged, and productive. Conventional economic thinking says we need a prosperous economy in order to achieve higher living standards and a better quality of life. However, the extensive input we have received from thousands of Canadian workers suggests that a happy, healthy, and engaged workforce is a key enabler of prosperity. We show how better jobs and workplaces can lead to a more promising future – and outline actions to get us there.

Our well-being–prosperity blueprint offers an action guide for workers, employers, governments, unions, professional associations, non-governmental organizations, and other groups. This blueprint integrates three big issues: work, well-being, and prosperity. We illustrate how workers' job quality influences their overall quality of life, or well-being. We call this the "quality triangle" and it connects work improvements to bigger economic goals. The same workplace and job conditions that matter for quality of life also are critical for a thriving economy. When Canadians identify their work values and motivations, they are describing what's required for businesses to innovate and grow. That's how Canada can achieve a more prosperous future.

We invite others to join in a wide-ranging, action-oriented discussion about how to create better jobs and workplaces. This sort of dialogue happens all too infrequently. We hope that employers, workers, governments, and many other interested organizations will be convinced to join this discussion by our argument that Canadian's future quality of life depends, in large part, on finding solutions to present job and workplace challenges. Put simply, a critical step towards renewed prosperity is the redesign of work.

Key Questions

Economists, employers, industry groups, policy experts, journalists, and researchers have waded into the debate about how to kick-start the economy. All sorts of disparate issues get thrown into the mix, including how to address growing income disparities, adapt to an aging workforce, spark more innovation and entrepreneurship, and provide greater opportunities for women and recent immigrants. Often missing from these debates is the voice of workers. That's what we seek to provide in *Redesigning Work*.

As seasoned observers of labour markets and workplaces, we bring our own personal insights and professional expertise to bear on these national trends. But most important, we build our case for redesigning work around the work experiences, opportunities, and problems that thousands of Canadians have expressed as respondents to numerous workplace surveys and public opinion polls conducted by EKOS Research Associates. Using this unique source of evidence, we answer four key questions about Canadians' experiences, aspirations, and vision for the future:

1 What social and economic trends are expected to shape
   the country's future?
2 How have work experiences changed over the past decade?
3 What does the ideal future job and workplace look like?
4 How will achieving this vision contribute to improved well-
   being and prosperity?

Redesigning Work's contribution is to shine a bright light on one of the most fertile yet often overlooked venues for economic and social renewal – people's jobs and workplaces. The world of work, we argue, offers much potential to improve our quality of life in inclusive and sustainable ways. And the best way to unleash this potential is to ask Canadian workers – which is what we do in this book.

We can't resist one political comment: At the time of writing (November 2015), Prime Minister Justin Trudeau had made his international debut at a G20 meeting. In front of these other world leaders, he reiterated the newly elected Liberal government's commitment to "inclusive growth" that provides opportunities for all Canadians.[2] Swept into office on a wave of optimism and pent-up desire for change, the Trudeau government has committed to investing in infrastructure, building stronger communities, encouraging innovation, and helping young people succeed – all important steps to a more robust economy and fairer society. Only time will tell, of course. However, inclusive growth will remain a policy platitude unless all stakeholders are involved in finding and implementing solutions and all workplaces are the stage for action.

The Future of Work Revisited

> New technology, economic globalization, high unemployment, declining job security, stagnant incomes, polarized working time, and work-and-family tension – these define the new context of work for many Canadians. Not surprisingly, as we learn from poll after poll, the changing world of work is often accompanied by a growing sense of anxiety. These concerns are intensified by the lack of a clear understanding of where the future of work is headed.[3]

This comment rings familiar today. Yet it describes the state of work in Canada in the mid-1990s. The quotation comes from a 1997 public policy report, *The Future of Work in Canada*, which Lowe co-authored with EKOS economist Gordon Betcherman. EKOS provided the polling data that led us to conclude that a pessimistic mood enveloped Canadian workers, so much so that we called the mid-1990s mindset "the age of economic anxiety."

In the early 1990s, the economy had skidded into recession. Companies and the public sector responded with deep job cuts. Employers relied increasingly on outsourcing or temporary workers to reduce labour costs. A jobless recovery was driven by massive investments in new technology. As well, memories of the early 1980s recession were still fresh, with its media images of a "lost generation" of young graduates and the spread of "McJobs" as good manufacturing jobs were replaced by low-paid jobs in service industries. Analysts tried to make sense of this changing landscape of work, proposing two contradictory future-of-work scenarios: bleak predictions about the "end of work" versus an upbeat image of a nation of freelancers. By the end of the twentieth century, diagnosing work problems and conjuring up possible solutions became a growth industry.

Not surprisingly, the anxiety people felt about the changes swirling around them and threatening to disrupt their lives precipitated a heated debate about the future of work. This debate took place in a vastly different world. The Internet was a new thing, smartphones weren't invented yet, and most companies that dominate information technology today either didn't exist or were small niche players. China was only beginning to stir as an economic superpower. Threats to peace and security were ratcheted down in Western nations in the wake of the Soviet Union's collapse; no one could imagine the terrible events of 9/11 and the resulting "war on terror."

Three key points in *The Future of Work in Canada* still resonate. One is that the high level of "economic anxiety" was out of proportion with the facts about the labour market and workplace changes occurring since the 1970s. Second, the large-scale shift away from permanent full-time jobs that provided decent living standards was polarizing job opportunities and rewards, making the labour market a far more risky place for individuals. And third, there is nothing inevitable about the future of work. Better jobs and workplaces can be created, but it depends on decisions made by employers, workers, policymakers, and a host of other labour market organizations.

Looking into the future, we address fundamental questions about the kind of jobs, workplaces, and career opportunities Canadians want. The answers we provide are intended to help employers, workers, policymakers, and other labour market stakeholders to find new ways to make work more rewarding and productive.

Redesigning Work contributes to the ongoing debate about the future of work by documenting from the perspective of the thousands of Canadian workers we have surveyed the unrealized aspirations and untapped potential in the workforce. The country's future economic success, we argue, depends in large part on how effectively decision-makers respond to the challenges of a workforce that is rapidly aging, less satisfied and engaged than a decade ago, often struggling to find what they truly value in a job, and with considerable untapped potential to use their ideas to achieve organizational goals.

Indeed, leading organizations are constantly seeking ways to help their workforces be happy, healthy, and productive. But it's not enough for just the industry leaders to be doing this. The future imperative for all employers must be their people. Among the many experts who advocate this approach are researchers from Cornell University, who urge employers to "build organizational capabilities that support the innovation, collaboration and continuous learning essential for success in a complex, fast-changing environment."[4] The best way for employers to do this is by listening to workers' ideas, understanding their values and aspirations, and responding accordingly. And as we'll see in *Redesigning Work*, this is precisely what many Canadian workers want in their jobs.

Regarding the future of work, we have been influenced by the two approaches articulated by London Business School professor Lynda Gratton. The "default future" accepts the status quo because "no one is prepared to work together to take cohesive action or to change the status quo." As she puts it, "events outpace actions." In sharp contrast, the "crafted future" can result in better work in the future because "people are experimenting with ways of working, learning fast from each other, and rapidly adopting good ideas."[5] We argue that Canadians, on the whole, want a "crafted future," one that they can participate in designing and which is guided by what they want and need most in their jobs.

Why Redesign Work Now?

The case for improving jobs and workplaces rests on three main points:

- Canadians' quality of life depends on workers having positive day-to-day experiences in a job or career that offers reasonable financial security.
- Well-being contributes to a more engaged workforce, which then contributes to a more productive and innovative economy.
- Providing higher-quality work for more people will help to reduce labour market inequities.

Now is an ideal time to have a national dialogue about how to plan and implement improvements in work as a path to a better economic future. The most prominent reaction to the 1990s recession was a pervasive sense of job insecurity and concerns about the social consequences of high unemployment. Job creation was the number one public policy priority. Improving the quality of jobs was far down the agenda.

In the aftermath of the Great Recession, readers have good reason to think that job security is a pressing concern today across large swathes of the workforce. Layoffs or outright closures in 2014 included H.J. Heinz, Sears, Hallmark, Kellogg's, Potash Corporation, Encana, and Bank of Montreal. As *Canadian Business* magazine remarked, "The net effect is a recovery that feels more like the recession that preceded it."[6] The shutdown of 133 Target Canada stores, eliminating almost 18,000 jobs, and Future Shop store closures continued the trend.[7] In the six months prior to Target closing down, other retailers shut their doors and gave employees pink slips, including Sony, Mexx Canada, Smart Set, Jacob, Bombay, Bowring & Co., and Benix & Co.[8] Then in 2015, Alberta's energy boom went bust as oil prices plummeted. The Canadian Association of Petroleum Producers tallied over 35,000 job losses in the province's oil and gas sectors.[9]

Yet despite this bad news, Canadians are less concerned now about their job security than they were 20 years ago in the aftermath of the early-1990s recession. The national unemployment rate has hovered around 7 per cent of the workforce for the past several years, down from a high of 8.3 per cent during 2009, when the Great

Recession was in full swing. That compares with unemployment rates in the 11–12 per cent range during previous recessions in the 1980s and 1990s.[10] This is not to say that unemployment has receded into the background as a public worry. The fact remains that around one in four Canadian workers are worried about losing their job. However, other economic and social issues weigh more heavily on the public mind. Foremost are the prospects of declining living standards, income polarization, and a stalled economy for the foreseeable future. Overlaid on these worries is the reality of a slow decline in the quality of work over the past decade. Working Canadians on the whole are less satisfied and engaged at work, more stressed, and finding it more difficult to balance work with their personal life.

The Great Recession of 2008–9 accentuated other big forces that were already reshaping social and economic life. The downturn hit Canada at a time when our workforce was aging rapidly, lightning-fast technological advances were transforming workplaces, and changing employment conditions accentuated social inequalities.

David Foot, Canada's most famous demographer, predicts that while retiring baby boomers will slow economic growth, it's still possible for incomes to rise if the economy grows faster than the population – a big "if" to be sure.[11] Predictions about the impact of technological change in the digital era are no less dire than the 1990s end-of-work discourse. For example, the rise of companies like Uber, TaskRabbit, and Handy has spun out images of the emergence of a gig economy, where more and more workers – especially young ones – struggle to make ends meet as part of a virtual pool of on-demand labour performing digital piecework obtained via a smartphone app.[12] Guy Standing, a University of London professor, argues that just as in Britain and many other countries, "there is a new class whose voice will soon be at the centre of Canadian life. It is the precariat, the growing mass of Canadians who are in precarious work, precarious housing and hold precarious citizenship."[13]

These prominent trends – aging, new information technologies, precarious work – etch the contours of Canada's contemporary social landscape. Polling by EKOS Research Associates during 2014 and 2015 reveals Canadians' reactions to these and other trends.

Three out of four workers are "really worried" that Canada is becoming more divided into haves and have-nots. While we've lived with this worry for over two decades, inequality took on a sharper edge during the Great Recession because people connected it with declining living standards for the many and a spectacularly lush life for the few. Here's a snapshot of these views:

- 69 per cent of Canadian adults polled believe that Canada's middle class is shrinking.
- 47 per cent of poll respondents describe their households as "middle class" today, far less than the two-thirds who identified as middle class in the early twenty-first century.
- Looking ahead, 57 per cent of the Canadians surveyed expect the next generation to be worse off when compared with their overall quality of life today.

Enduring solutions to these complex problems need to be comprehensive and sustainable over the long term, with actions on many fronts. For our part, we take a more immediate and focused approach, looking for opportunities to improve what is familiar to Canadians and within their grasp to reshape – their work.

The quality of work life matters for society's overall well-being. Canadians are less satisfied with their lives now than they were a decade ago. And the fact that there has been no improvement in life satisfaction since the recession raises the distinct possibility that only a robust economic recovery will push the country back up to pre-recession levels of well-being. That's because today, worries about personal finances, a weak global economy, a divided society, and declining living standards all detract from life satisfaction.

One way to improve life satisfaction is to ensure that more people have decent work opportunities. Well-being is unequally distributed, mirroring inequalities in income and non-economic job rewards. The self-employed and permanent full-time employees have the highest life satisfaction. The unemployed and temporary and contract workers have the lowest, revealing the psychological costs associated with low incomes and unstable work.

Our Evidence

Our evidence comes from EKOS Research Associates' national public opinion polls and worker survey data collected over the past 20 years. These survey results enable us to provide an in-depth analysis of how Canadians experience work and the kind of future jobs and workplaces they want. We also are able to assess the impact of the 2008–9 recession on work attitudes, values, and experiences, using Rethinking Work surveys designed by the authors and conducted by EKOS in 2004, 2012, and 2015. And EKOS's tracking polls, which regularly ask the same questions, provide time-series data on work and economic attitudes going back 15 to 20 years.

The centrepieces are the 2004, 2012, and 2015 surveys. These three surveys enable us to compare workers' attitudes and experiences during a decade of transformative change in Canada's economy, society, and workplaces. Rethinking Work 2004 was conducted using EKOS's computer-assisted telephone interviewing (CATI) system. The field dates for this survey are August 24–October 7, 2004. In total, a random, stratified sample of 2,002 members of the labour force ages 16 and over responded to this survey. The margin of error associated with a sample of this size is plus or minus 2.2 percentage points at a 95 per cent level of confidence.

Rethinking Work 2012 and 2015 were conducted exclusively online using EKOS's unique, hybrid online/telephone research panel, Prob*it*. This panel offers exhaustive coverage of the Canadian population (i.e., Internet, phone, cell phone). Participants are recruited randomly using probability sampling; they do not opt into the panel themselves. All respondents to our panel are recruited by telephone using random digit dialing and are confirmed by live interviewers. Unlike opt-in online panels, Prob*it* supports margin-of-error estimates. We believe this is the only probability-based online panel in Canada. While panelists are randomly recruited, the survey itself excludes Canadians without Internet access.

The field dates for Rethinking Work 2012 are January 27–February 8, 2012. In total, a random, stratified sample of 2,891 Canadians aged 18 and over responded to the survey. The margin of error for this sample is +/−1.8 percentage points, at a 95 per cent level of confidence. Rethinking Work 2015 involved an online-only survey of 13,936 Canadians aged 18 and over, conducted between January 31 and February 10, 2015. The margin of error for this sample is +/−0.8 percentage points, at a 95 per cent level of confidence. The results of these 2012 and 2015 surveys can be considered generalizable to Canada's online population, which includes most of the workforce.

Three additional points about EKOS's methodology are pertinent:

1 All data are statistically weighted by age, gender, and region to ensure the samples' composition reflects that of the actual population of Canada according to Statistics Canada's estimates and census data.
2 The margin of error increases when the results are subdivided (i.e., error margins for subgroups such as region, sex, age, education).
3 Survey respondents have been sorted into one of two groups: currently working for pay in some capacity (including full-time, part-time, contractually or seasonally employed, temporary work, or self-employed), and unemployed but looking for work and have held a job in the previous 12 months. Full-time students are excluded from the workforce samples.

We also make use of EKOS time-series data, based on identical questions being asked in regularly conducted polls since the 1990s. For our longer-term tracking, any studies conducted before 2009 would have been done with CATI. From 2009 onwards, EKOS used either Probit online polls or interactive voice response (IVR) phone polls. Sample sizes vary from 1,300 to 13,854, with margins of error ranging between +/−0.8 and +/−2.9 percentage points, at a 95 per cent level of confidence for national estimates.

Chapter Outline

Chapter 1 makes sense of economic change through the eyes of workers. Concerns about falling living standards and a more divided society are pervasive. We document that the "good jobs–bad jobs" distinction, prominent since the 1990s, no longer describes the complexities and inconsistencies of people's work lives. We update this model of work by considering how non-economic job rewards have become polarized, an urgent problem that must be addressed in order to provide Canadians with greater opportunities for decent work. On a positive note, workers may be more receptive now to improving the quality of jobs than at any time during the past three decades.

Chapter 2 focuses on the well-being of the workforce and how it has changed in the past decade. For us, well-being means happy and healthy workers. Canadians' quality of work has been declining. Well-being in society can improve only if employers, supported by governments and with the active participation of workers, address three things: job satisfaction, stress, and work-life balance. While improving incomes is a long-term goal for society, we identify immediate steps that can improve work-life balance, reduce job stress, and boost job satisfaction. Doing so will not only raise the well-being of the workforce, it also will contribute to business success.

Chapter 3 examines what motivates workers to go to work, which we argue is the prerequisite for an engaged workforce. What most motivates workers is having great co-workers, having challenging work to do, and being able to help others and make a difference. Pay is less important as a motivator than these three intrinsic job conditions, although better pay would make workers look forward to work more. A more engaged workforce will have multiple benefits for employers, workers, and society. Achieving this goal requires changes to the psychological, social, and economic dimensions of work – changes that are clearly articulated by workers.

Chapter 4 explores Canadians' work values. Rarely do employee surveys probe into values, so this chapter fills a significant gap in our understanding of the workforce and how it is changing. Value differences across age groups have more to do with a person's life stage than their generation. The most valued job characteristics are a workplace free of harassment and discrimination and work that provides a sense of pride and accomplishment, is challenging and interesting, and provides economic security. Closing the gaps between what workers consider important in a job and what they actually have will lay the foundation for more innovative, productive, and engaging workplaces.

Chapter 5 looks at the implications of an aging workforce for the future of work. By reducing the effects of age differences on work opportunities and rewards, employers will lessen generational inequity. Employers can respond to the needs of an increasingly diverse workforce by introducing more flexible and customized approaches to work schedules, employment arrangements, and career paths. Public policy can promote the continued employment of older workers through active aging policies and age-neutral human resource strategies, including training and development. We show how flexibility is a powerful concept for redesigning work and retirement in ways that benefit workers, employers, and society.

Chapter 6 addresses how to unleash workers' existing capabilities and develop their potential to contribute in the future. Canada has a highly educated workforce, so we are definitely "punching below our weight" when it comes to productivity, innovation, and skill use. There is untapped potential for workers to contribute more of their skills and knowledge in their jobs, assume more responsibility, take initiative, and learn how to do their jobs better. However, Canadian employers underinvest in workplace skills, and workers downplay the importance of human capital. We argue that whether employees can apply their capabilities in their jobs comes down to how managers decide to design work systems.

Chapter 7 sketches out a blueprint for achieving the goals of improved well-being and prosperity. We combine the views, experiences, and values of Canadians from EKOS surveys into a vision for the future of work. This vision describes four dimensions of a great job: working relationships, tasks performed, the work environment, and economic rewards. By integrating EKOS survey evidence about work experiences, well-being, engagement, and values, we identify promising opportunities to strengthen overall quality of life, the quality of people's work experiences, and the quality of working conditions.

Chapter 8 pulls together suggestions we have made through-out the book as a guide to action. We know from EKOS polls that Canadians are ready to consider bold actions to make their work lives better. And we also know that a good number of the workers we surveyed already have what we describe in chapter 7 as a great job. Now it's up to more people and organizations – particularly industry and public policy leaders – to acknowledge the urgency of making these changes and then build momentum that can move us towards a more optimistic future.

1 How Economic Change Affects Canadians

The twenty-first century has so far been an economic roller-coaster ride for Canadians. We hurtled from strong growth and the lowest unemployment on record in the middle of the first decade into a global financial crisis and the Great Recession of 2008–9. We're still struggling through an anaemic recovery. And in 2015 the collapse of oil prices took the wind out of Alberta's once-booming energy economy, with dampening effects felt across the nation.

These are turbulent times indeed, raising crucial questions about how economic change has affected Canadians. What has been the impact on people's work lives and more broadly on society? Looking at these transformations through the eyes of Canadians, how have individuals experienced what's been happening to their society and where do they think it is headed? This chapter provides some answers.

We start by describing the big trends that are transforming work. Then we turn our attention to how Canadian workers have experienced the ups and downs of the economy over the past several decades. The two changes that most concern Canadians are income polarization and declining living standards. We link these to an erosion of job quality, a trend with roots in the late twentieth century that was accentuated by employers' responses to the Great Recession of 2008–9. Here we set the stage for exploring in later chapters how to design better work.

There's no doubt that economic change is reshaping society in some unsettling ways. In the wake of the Great Recession, income inequality and declining living standards have become flashpoints, sparking public outrage along with much media attention. The Occupy Movement was a grass-roots response to growing social inequality marked by a rapid redistribution of wealth to the top 1 per cent. But the challenge for most people now is maintaining or attaining a decent living standard. Shoring up the middle class was a prominent issue in Canada's 2015 federal election, with each party suggesting different ways to do this, from tax cuts and credits to subsidized day care and better pensions.

There is pressure on governments to alleviate inequality and increase opportunities. One way to do this is by nudging employers to create secure, decent-paying jobs. But this is a long-term project; what can be done more immediately? Our response is to look at ways to improve the overall quality of their work, defined more broadly to include economic, social, and psychological work rewards. That's why it is critical, we argue, to expand current discussions of job quality beyond income and encompass social and psychological features of work that are essential for individuals' well-being. Doing so will help to identify opportunities to improve jobs and workplaces in ways that benefit workers, employers, and society.

Transforming Work

Let's start with an overview of the relentless forces transforming work. The labour market plays a pivotal role in this regard. That's where people find or create employment opportunities, earn incomes, and achieve the social and psychological rewards of work they value. And the quality of those work opportunities and experiences are directly influenced by employers' human resource practices, how organizations put new technology to use, the rise of new industries and decline of old ones, governments' employment policies, and demographic changes in the workforce – particularly as it ages and becomes better educated.

The Good Jobs–Bad Jobs Divide

Labour markets in many countries have become more polarized. This is clearly evident in the rise of what's called "precarious" employment – a trend that has social and political implications on a global scale.

The International Labour Organization (ILO) estimates that only one in four workers worldwide have a stable employment relationship. Among countries where data is available, there have been more part-time than full-time jobs created since 2009 (when the Great Recession ended in most places).[1] Guy Standing calls the global "precariat" a "class-in-the-making," whose economic instability makes it angry, anxious, and alienated.[2] As American academic Andrew Ross observes, "precarious livelihoods" are becoming more common around the world as a result of labour instability and growing divisions between a high-wage professional class of knowledge workers and a multitude of temporary, migrant, and other low-wage workers.[3]

The rise of precarious work is most visible in the United States. Sociologist Arne Kalleberg uses the "good jobs–bad jobs" dichotomy to describe how over the past four decades in America, changes in employment systems have bred greater inequality and insecurity.[4] Working conditions have become more polarized. Even full-time jobs are now more precarious, all because of employers' quest for a more flexible workforce in response to relentless competitive pressures and outdated employment regulations by government.

MIT economics professor Paul Osterman and policy analyst Beth Shulman propose raising pay for low-wage workers in the United States to at least two-thirds of the median wage. This is a policy response that should interest governments, argues Osterman, because the social costs associated with poor living standards and being unable to fully participate in society are much greater than any modest pay raises for those at the bottom rung of the income ladder. They conclude that in America, "it is possible to redesign 'bad' jobs so that they are better."[5] However, other prominent economists argue that some industries and communities will not be able to absorb minimum wage jumps to this level.[6]

Recent trends in US job creation, job losses, and income distribution confirm that an elite of well-educated knowledge workers in professional, technical, and management roles have benefited most from the digital technology revolution under way. According to economist David Autor, the expanding elite now make up the top 10 per cent of American households. There's also growth at the bottom of the labour market, where less-educated workers provide a range of in-person, retail, or manual services that are difficult to send abroad.[7] And middle-skill and average-income jobs in sales, production, repair, manufacturing, and office work are disappearing.

Turning to Canada, research by TD Economics shows that this country is on a different trajectory than the United States when it comes to job polarization. The US labour market has polarized as a result of job growth at the top and bottom of the skills distribution, but not in the middle. Canada, in contrast, has seen movement "up the skills curve" in terms of job creation over the past decade and a relative decline in medium- and low-skilled jobs – with skills and income being closely related.[8] Among experts, competing explanations for growing inequality and its resulting social stresses focus on poverty, the growing 1 per cent at the top, and middle-class decline. With no consensus on causes, no clear policy solutions have so far crystallized.[9]

The average Canadian has felt the impact of labour market change. EKOS polls document that fewer consider themselves to be middle class today than at the beginning of the century. In 2002, 67 per cent of Canadians described their household as middle class (choices were poor, working class, middle class, or upper class), dropping during and after the recession to 47 per cent in 2014. This mirrors the United States, where 62 per cent considered themselves middle class in 2002, down to 46 per cent in 2014. When EKOS asked Canadians in 2015 about their personal financial situation, 37 per cent said they have fallen behind in the past year, while only 17 per cent had moved ahead (the rest stayed the same). In short, Canadian society has reached a point where moving down is more common than moving up in terms of living standards.

A Twenty-First-Century Digital Precariat?

New technology is a driving force behind these changes. Indeed, speculation is rife that digital technologies will reinvent work, giving rise to a global pool of workers who rely on smartphone apps and the Internet to pick up little pieces of work. Uber exemplifies this emergent gig economy, turning the traditional taxi business upside down by using an app to connect customers directly with drivers, whom it treats as independent contractors, not employees.

Internet-based crowdsourcing platforms enable companies to farm out bits of work to the lowest bidder anywhere in the world. Amazon's Mechanical Turk service pays humans (known as "turkers") a tiny wage of between 1¢ and $1 to complete small tasks that can't be delegated to a computer, such as transcribing audio recordings or screening inappropriate photos for social network sites. A journalist who tried this out concluded that "Turkers represent the Wild West of the crowdsourcing work force" because there are few rules or protections for these digital freelancers.[10]

There is lots of debate now over how far the "sharing economy" can advance before tripping up on its own limitations.[11] Advocates claim that crowdsourcing expands opportunities, so that anyone with a smartphone and the requisite skills can find work. Critics argue that decent full-time jobs could be replaced by apps that farm out piecemeal tasks for tiny sums. More ominously, according to the *Harvard Business Review*, the twenty-first-century "hyperspecialization" of work poses "new social challenges, such as the possibility of exploitation as work quickly finds the cheapest takers."[12] Uber's fights with municipalities who want to ban it and with drivers who want the rights of employees are among the many regulatory and legal challenges that crowdsourcing companies face.[13]

Predictions about the impact of digital technology on work are reminiscent of the future-of-work debates in the 1990s. Back then, doomsayers such as Jeremy Rifkin envisioned a dystopian future in which computers replaced humans. Rifkin predicted that "more sophisticated software technologies are going to bring civilization ever closer to a workerless world."[14] Optimists in the 1990s, such as career guru William Bridges, saw a silver lining in the "dejobbing" of organizations. Bridges proclaimed that "*the job* is not going to be part of tomorrow's economic reality."[15] He foresaw work increasingly performed by freelancers with no attachments to an employer.

Strains of these debates echo today. Evoking Rifkin, some Uber watchers expect that its freelance drivers will soon be displaced by self-driving cars, which also could decimate the traditional taxi business. Then there's the prediction by the Bank of England's chief economist that robots could replace 95 million jobs in the United Kingdom and the United States, mostly those in sales, service, administrative, and skilled trade occupations.[16] The current version of dejobbing is the smartphone-enabled gig economy. The difference today is that rather than raising overall living standards, the digital revolution has enriched an elite of knowledge workers who make, manage, or use new technologies. Interpreting these occupational shifts in the United States, economist Tyler Cowen makes the dire prediction that the top 10 to 15 per cent of America's workers will thrive in the digital knowledge economy, while most of the rest will become a permanent underclass.[17]

What's Happening to Jobs in Canada?

To understand how these trends affect Canada today, it helps to look back. The term "McJobs" became a popular stereotype in the wake of a hard-hitting recession in the early 1980s. It described "burger-flippers" and other minimum-wage, part-time, low-skilled, service-sector jobs that college and university grads were backed into by a tough labour market. Some readers will remember the economic pain of that era: interest rates over 20 per cent and double-digit unemployment. McJobs were harbingers of a working future characterized by seismic industrial and occupational shifts, above all the steady decline of blue-collar factory jobs that provided decent wages and benefits and the rise of low-wage service jobs. Look around your local mall and big-box stores and you'll see how these predictions unfolded.

The recession of the early 1990s had a more profound impact on work than the Great Recession of 2008–9. It was the jobless recovery from this downturn that promoted debates, previously noted, about the "end of work." By the close of the twentieth century, ominous signs in Canada's job market prompted many analysts to reflect on the future of work.

And we did, conducting a major study of the Canadian workforce to understand how employment relationships were being rewritten by new technology, globalization, the shift to knowledge-based industries, and the spread of precarious forms of work. In *What's a Good Job?*, the study's report, we argued that employee-employer relationships were weakening, undermining individuals' quality of work life as well as organizational performance.[18] So-called "permanent" employment was less secure, precarious jobs were on the rise, and more workers were becoming freelancers.

Taking stock of these changes 15 years later, we see more continuity than we might have expected in the split between permanent and contingent work. However, job quality has continued to erode and add to labour market polarization – but in ways that blur the lines between what traditionally were thought of as "good jobs" and "bad jobs." We'll now briefly highlight these job trends.

Part-time Work

Part-time work has been a prominent – and consistent – feature of Canada's job scene for a quarter century. Each recession bumped up part-time employment to a slightly higher level.[19] Around 12 per cent of employees were in part-time jobs in 1976. The early-1980s recession bumped the part-time rate up to 17 per cent, and it held steady there until 1990, when another downturn led employers to prefer part-time over full-time workers. Part-time jobs accounted for about 19 per cent of all employment into the twenty-first century, so it's not a recent employment practice. Even during the boom years of 2004–6, part-time jobs accounted for just over 18 per cent of all employment. During the recent recession, the rate inched up only slightly to just over 19 per cent.

Some people seek out part-time work; others are pushed into it by necessity. Since the 1990s, roughly 1 in 4 part-timers say they are in this sort of job because of personal preference – underscoring the need for flexible employment options.[20] Another 1 in 10 part-timers are caring for children, so they don't want full-time work. This number has declined as the workforce has aged. And for decades, students have been a ready source of part-time help. Students held 26 per cent of part-time positions in 1997, increasing only slightly to 29 per cent in 2015.

Involuntary part-time employment gets to the heart of job quality. If a person is stuck in a part-time job but wants to work full-time, the result is wasted human resources. Part-time work as a form of underemployment was built into the job market decades ago. Indeed, it was a bigger problem in the 1990s during the jobless recovery, when the involuntary part-time employment rate peaked at 31 per cent of all part-timers. During and after the Great Recession, it was lower (between 27 and 28 per cent) and little changed from pre-recession boom years.

Precarious Work

Precarious work is the bottom tier of a two-tiered labour market, according to some analysts. It signals a shift away from full-time "permanent" employment with a single employer, which was "standard" during the quarter century of unabated expansion after the Second World War.[21] Basically, "standard" refers to stable and secure jobs that provided a decent living. In contrast, "non-standard" work describes a variety of casual, contingent, or contract jobs, or short-term work assignments obtained through staffing agencies. The rise of precarious employment has put the well-being of more workers at risk.[22]

There are now over two million Canadians in temporary jobs, about half of whom are contract workers. Temp positions pay less than equivalent permanent jobs and don't provide benefits. Commentators are quick to draw sweeping conclusions. One newspaper headline proclaims "Canada's shift to a nation of temporary workers," which suggest a fundamental restructuring of Canada's job market.[23] The article quotes a 25-year-old Torontonian who had hopped from job to job 12 times: "I've been literally living paycheque to paycheque."

To help make ends meet, some workers caught in precarious employment piece together various contract or part-time positions into the equivalent of a full-time job. We have in mind a Kelowna yoga instructor on a month-to-month contract who also cuts hair part-time. But the practice of holding multiple jobs is not widespread, accounting for 5 per cent of the workforce since the 1990s – again, not a twenty-first-century trend.[24]

The growth of temporary jobs outpaced permanent ones during all recessions since the 1980s. But the same thing happened during prosperous times too.[25] Even so, temporary jobs accounted for 13 per cent of all employment during the past decade, up from 11 per cent in 1997 – hardly a huge increase.[26] In short, employers have long relied on a flexible, low-cost pool of temps or contract workers.

According to Statistics Canada, 73 per cent of the workforce is an employee in a "permanent" full-time or part-time job.[27] Basically, these are jobs that do not end on a specific date. However, there's no guarantee that a permanent job won't disappear if employers restructure or downsize. Just think of auto-sector jobs relocating from Ontario to Mexico, job losses from business failures such Target, and layoffs by Alberta's energy companies triggered by the collapse in oil prices.

The flip side is that 12 per cent of employees are in non-permanent jobs (the rest, as the next section documents, are self-employed). These contract, limited-term, seasonal, or casual workers form part of an on-demand, flexible pool of labour that employers draw on as dictated by business conditions. The employee-employer relationship is weak, with no long-term commitment or security. Increasingly, this non-permanent workforce is managed by temp agencies, a booming business that matches employers' needs with available temps. Digital freelancers, like the Uber drivers described earlier, are still only a tiny slice of this contingent labour pool.

The Self-employed

So far, we've focused on employees: those workers who have some kind of employment contract with an employer, however tenuous that may be. In another corner of the labour market are the self-employed. By 2015, the self-employed made up 15 per cent of Canada's workforce – a share that has been consistent this century, showing no change during or after the recession.[28] So in a workforce of 17.9 million, 2.75 million are self-employed – more than in temporary or contract positions.

The self-employed are very diverse. Close to 70 per cent of all self-employed (10.5 per cent of the entire workforce) have no employees. Basically, these solo self-employed are another source of temporary labour. *The Economist* magazine commented on the similar situation in Britain: "Being self-employed is, for many people, a dignified way of describing the loss of full-time employment."[29] Self-employment jumped by 67,000 individuals during the Great Recession, only to fall by 56,000 during the recovery. This suggests that self-employment is a safety valve for employees who are downsized or who retire without sufficient savings and so need to keep working.[30] It also provides opportunities for older employees seeking new challenges and others who want independence they can't get as an employee.

Working conditions and job rewards are more diverse for the self-employed than for employees. At one end of the spectrum are owner-operators of small or medium-sized businesses – from local fast-food franchises to family-owned manufacturing firms. Many lawyers, accountants, doctors, dentists, chiropractors, and real estate agents also are self-employed. These well-paid professionals can reap significant tax advantages by working this way, especially if they incorporate or set up a professional services firm.

At the other end of the spectrum are the marginal self-employed, eking out a sporadic low-income existence, which often requires patching together bits of precarious work. These are the house cleaners and home day-care operators, typically women and often recent immigrants or Canadian-born workers with no post-secondary education. These sorts of freelancers would be fortunate to earn as much as $30,000, which is the threshold set by the Canada Revenue Agency for collecting GST. Some (nobody has an exact count) operate in the cash-only unregulated "grey" economy, like the house-cleaner, child-minder, or grass cutter you may have used.

To recap, we've seen that concerns about fewer and worse jobs have been an evolving story since the early 1980s. This against a backdrop of three recessions, the rapid advance of new technologies, and global markets. The picture of Canada's job market we have sketched shows more continuity than change, at least in the distribution of workers between the various forms of standard and non-standard work. What this means for job quality has, however, been the subject of intense scrutiny and debate, as we will now see.

Changing Job Quality

The Great Recession pushed job quality into the spotlight. The CIBC–World Markets employment quality index has drawn much public attention in this regard.[31] The CIBC index tracks part-time employment, self-employment, and the distribution of full-time paid employment by compensation level. By early 2015, this index had fallen to a record low. The assumption is that part-time jobs and self-employment offer inferior wages and benefits compared with full-time jobs. Critics have pounced on the index, claiming that job quality is more complex and multidimensional.[32] Regardless, the CIBC index has succeeded in putting job quality on the public agenda. It raises, but doesn't answer, the crucial question of what can be done to improve job quality – which is our focus in this book.

The rise of part-time jobs and self-employed freelancers fits the definition of precarious work widely used by commentators. The most thorough investigation of precarious work in Canada is a study led by Wayne Lewchuk, a professor at McMaster University.[33] Conducted between 2002 and 2007, it doesn't document the aftermath of the Great Recession. However, its conclusion – that the lines have become blurred between permanent and precarious employment – applies today, as we will show. Instability has become a common feature of so-called "permanent" positions because of weaker commitment from both workers and employers. And while the popular image of temporary or contract work is that it detracts from a person's health and well-being, that's not what the research team found in a survey of Toronto-area workers.

In short, the long-standing dichotomy between precarious and permanent jobs may no longer fit twenty-first-century labour market realities. The converse of not having enough work is having too much. This contrasting perspective on what's happening in people's work lives focuses on those in full-time jobs, which covers most of the workforce. Since the 1990s, Linda Duxbury of Carleton University's Sprott School of Business and Chris Higgins of the Richard Ivey School of Business have been tracking work-life balance. Results from the latest survey have identified a new and troubling trend: "Now we are moving into the concept of intensification, the idea that there is too much to handle – too much at work, too much at home, too much in total."[34]

Our review of labour market trends suggests that Canada is not becoming a nation of part-timers, freelancers, or contingent workers. The proportion of workers in these types of jobs has been fairly constant over the past several decades. However, the nature of all these jobs has changed in ways that could threaten job quality. What's needed now is a ground-level view of how individual Canadians have experienced economic change, particularly its impact on their jobs and quality of life.

The Paradox of Twenty-First-Century Work

The above overview of labour market trends is a broad-brush one. Now we will add important highlights, profiling who is in different types of jobs based on Rethinking Work 2015 survey results. Using a wider range of job quality indicators than what is available from Statistics Canada or other studies, the picture of the labour market that emerges is more nuanced than images of a growing precariat or of bad jobs displacing good jobs.

Here's a quick demographic overview of what the labour market looks like, based on respondents to Rethinking Work 2015:

- The chance of being self-employed increases sharply with age. While only 6 per cent of workers under 35 years of age are self-employed, this jumps to more than 30 per cent among workers aged 55 and over.
- Around two-thirds of workers under the age of 55 are in full-time permanent positions. And part-time, temporary, contract, and seasonal work tends to be concentrated fairly evenly among younger (under 35) and older (over 55) workers. The reasons for this vary. Young people may be juggling work and school or having a tough time landing a secure job. Older individuals heading into retirement may prefer the flexibility of short-term or part-time work.
- As a sign of things to come in the knowledge economy, many temp, contract, and seasonal workers are better educated (i.e., have a university degree) than the self-employed and full-time employees.
- Men are more concentrated in full-time jobs or self-employment, while women are more concentrated in part-time or other forms of contingent work (patterns that are well known).
- Whether a worker immigrated to Canada or was born here is not related to their labour market location.

Keeping in mind these demographic profiles, what about the day-to-day work experiences of Canadians who occupy different locations in the labour market? Here's a quick comparative summary based on some of the Rethinking Work 2015 quality-of-work and well-being indicators, which chapters 2 and 3 will examine in more depth:

- Full-time employees have the highest incomes (most earning more than $60,000 annually), the self-employed are spread across the income spectrum, and about half of part-time and contingent workers earn less than $40,000 annually (20 per cent reported an annual income of less than $20,000).
- Full-time employees have the highest levels of job stress, whereas low job stress is reported by the self-employed and workers in contingent positions.
- The self-employed experience the highest overall job satisfaction and life satisfaction. In contrast, individuals in part-time and contingent positions are the least satisfied with their jobs and lives.
- The self-employed are most likely to look forward to work each day, and full-time employees are least likely to feel this way, even less so than part-time or contingent workers.

Canadians in full-time continuing jobs may have to trade off well-being – in the form of high stress and low engagement – for a decent income. In contrast to negative portrayals of the self-employed, it turns out that this group is happier and more motivated than full-time employees, which for many labour market analysts remains the touchstone for a "good" job. Often overlooked is that self-employment provides flexibility, autonomy, and personal fulfilment – key features of high-quality work. Indeed, we often hear HR managers in large organizations ask, "What can we do to encourage our employees to feel more like they are self-employed?" In other words, how can employees feel a greater sense of "ownership" over their jobs?

To summarize, we've identified a basic paradox of the twenty-first-century job market. On one hand, the income and security of a full-time job is highly sought after and seen by many experts as the benchmark for a good job. Yet on the other hand, there are certain aspects of non-standard work – particularly the flexibility, autonomy, variety, and self-direction– that can contribute to better-quality work and life. A major challenge for policymakers and employers today is striking the right balance between these different job features.

How Canadians Experienced Economic Change

The labour market is where working Canadians' experience economic change. Now that we know the prominent features of the twenty-first-century job market, we can shed much-needed light on how Canadians have experienced large-scale transformations affecting their work life. We do this by mining several decades of EKOS Research Associates' polls that provide time-series data. The trends established by these polls show how workers have reacted to the rapid and unpredictable changes in the socio-economic landscape. And they set the stage for designing better work.

Reduced Economic Anxiety

Canadians' feelings of economic security have undergone dramatic swings in the past two decades. But perhaps surprisingly, the Great Recession did less to undermine economic security than did the previous recession in the early 1990s. Whatever other work-related problems still exist – and there are plenty – Canadians have become less concerned about the chances of losing their job.

We know this from EKOS polls, which regularly asked working Canadians whether they agree or disagree with the statement "I think there is a good chance I could lose my job over the next couple of years." Compared with the mid- to late 1990s, when over 40 per cent of those polled felt insecure in their job, this number has declined through early 2015, fluctuating in the 20 per cent to 25 per cent range (see Figure 1.1). Stated positively, today more than half of those employed are confident that they will not lose their job in the near future. This reaction to job market churn meshes with Statistics Canada's conclusion that Canadian workers were more at risk of being laid off during the recessions of the 1980s and 1990s than during the 2008–9 downturn.[35]

Public concern also has moved away from the number of jobs available to the quality of those jobs. Back in the 1990s, many Canadians shared Rifkin's concerns about "the end of work" as a result of

Figure 1.1. Perceptions of job insecurity

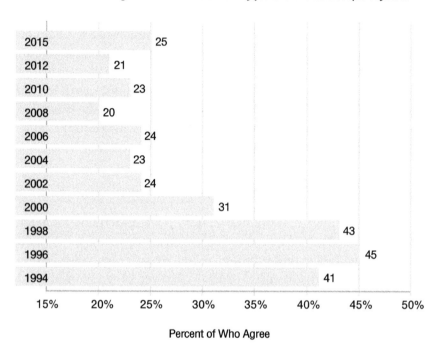

Q. Please rate the extent to which you agree or disagree with the following statement: *"I think there is a good chance I could lose my job over the next couple of years."*

Percent of Who Agree

Employed Canadians.

technology-induced mass unemployment. A 1998 EKOS poll asked this of a representative sample of Canadian adults: "Many people are talking about the 'end of work' or at least a very serious and permanent shortage of jobs. How likely do you think this 'end of work' thesis is?" Two in five respondents considered this scenario likely. Yet when the same question was asked again in 2012, just 25 per cent of respondents bought into the "end of work" scenario, while close to half considered it an unlikely prediction of the future.

Persistent Concerns about Inequality

Given that Canadians' worries about the "end of work" have receded in the twenty-first century, what is top-of-mind for the public
today? As we will see, there is growing concern about the erosion of
the middle class. In the public mind, the comfortable living standard that so many aspired to no longer can be taken for granted.

Canadians were concerned about society becoming more divided
and unequal long before the global financial crisis and the Great
Recession. In 1996, EKOS asked working Canadians to what extent
they agreed or disagreed with this statement: "I really worry that
we are moving to a more divided society of haves and have nots"
(see Figure 1.2). At the time, just over 80 per cent of respondents
were worried about this issue. No doubt this was a reaction to what
people were personally experiencing in their employment or seeing
all around them: a growing number of family members, friends, and
neighbours who were being excluded from paid work altogether or
pushed to the margins of the workforce into a twilight zone of job-
lessness and financial insecurity.

Anxiety over social inequality abated during the booming middle
of the next decade, but only slightly: 70 per cent of workers polled
during this expansionary period agreed that Canadian society was
becoming more divided. The Great Recession provided further con-
firmation that the post–Second World War social contract, based on
an understanding that economic growth would bring plenty of opportunities to improve one's living standard, had been rewritten.
By 2015, over three in four EKOS poll respondents agreed with the
"more divided society" view.

That's why books like French economist Thomas Picketty's *Capital
in the Twenty-First Century* have received so much media attention.
Picketty claims that wealth has grown faster than income and is
ever-more concentrated in the hands of the owners of capital.[36] His
book became an instant bestseller, remarkable for a dense, 670-page
economic treatise. The educated middle and upper middle classes
who bought the book wanted to know what can be done to smooth

Figure 1.2. Perceptions of polarization

Q. Please rate the extent to which you agree or disagree with the following statement:
"I really worry that we are moving to a more divided society of haves and have nots."

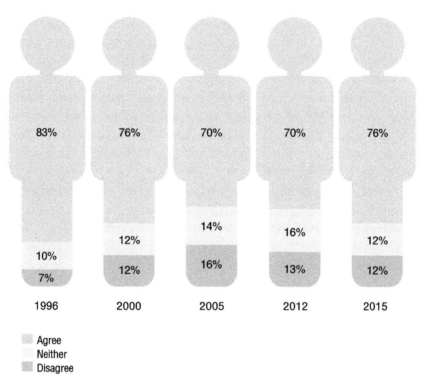

Employed Canadians.

capitalism's rougher edges and curb its excesses. Picketty is among a growing chorus of experts who articulate a popular sentiment today. As a recent EKOS poll found, fully 71 per cent of Canadian adults surveyed agreed that "almost all economic growth or progress over the past twenty years has ended up in the hands of the upper one percent."[37]

Although the public has expressed worry about inequality for the past 25 years, the dynamics driving this trend are different now. The risk of becoming unemployed was much greater in the 1990s than today. A bigger risk now is descending into the swelling ranks of the working poor, not the ranks of the unemployed.[38] These are trends that predate the Great Recession. Even before the Great Recession, the ranks of the working poor were growing. For example, Toronto experienced a 42 per cent increase in its working poor between 2000 and 2005, despite a strong economy.[39] And the Organisation for Economic Co-operation and Development (OECD), an international economic think tank, documents that the income gap in Canada between the top and bottom 10 per cent of income earners has widened since the 1990s. However, Canada is one of the few industrialized countries in which disposable income inequality did not increase during the Great Recession.[40]

Media coverage of a super-rich global elite only accentuates the average person's sense of relative disadvantage. Financial journalist (and member of Parliament) Chrystia Freeland calls this elite twenty-first-century plutocrats, a global club of billionaires that critics blamed for the financial crisis.[41] EKOS polling shows that a middle-class lifestyle is receding for the average Canadian. As we showed earlier, less than half of Canadians now describe themselves as middle class. And with the Great Recession slowing income growth, many people feel they are falling behind.

Canadians Look into the Future

Having now tracked workers' reactions to the recent ups and downs of the economy, let's look ahead. How do Canadians view their economic future? EKOS polls answer this question, showing that more than six years after the Great Recession ended, a sluggish recovery has cast a pessimistic mood over the country.

Canadians have scaled back their personal financial outlook. When the economy was humming in the first few years of this century, many expected their financial situation to improve, or at least stay the same. A 2003 EKOS poll found that 43 per cent of workers expected their personal financial circumstances to improve over the next year or so. When the same questions were asked after the Great Recession, in 2011 and 2015, this optimism had waned, with only about 30 per cent of survey respondents in each year expecting improvements.

The state of the global economy influences how Canadians judge their own prospects. Taking this broader perspective, a 2015 EKOS poll found that just over half of respondents are worried that the world economy is headed for 10 years of poor performance.

Given this pessimism, it will not come as a surprise that most workers foresee lower living standards in the future. When EKOS asked respondents in 2015 if they agree or disagree that "today's young Canadians can expect to have a lower standard of living than their parents," three out of five agreed with this prediction. Canadians are not alone in this regard. Surveys by the Pew Research Center in the United States and Europe also find that most adults in these countries expect the next generation will be worse off.[42] This troubling indicator of the public mood is related to perceptions of an increasingly divided society.[43] Today's young generation, in the eyes of most Canadians, will be at the losing end of this polarization.

In short, EKOS polls tell us that Canadians are worried about reduced opportunities for maintaining a decent quality of life. This thinking marks a reversal of conventional wisdom during the 1950s, 1960s, and 1970s, when a growing economy offered many workers and their families a steadily improving living standard. Expanding opportunity for a middle-class life was deeply engrained in the public consciousness. And it has taken decades of economic upheavals, the latest the Great Recession, to make this goal more difficult to achieve.

Personal Reactions to Economic Change

How would Canadians react if economic stagnation became the "new normal"? To answer this, EKOS asked Rethinking Work 2015 respondents what they most likely would do "if you were sure that there was going to be a prolonged downturn in the economy with low economic growth and high unemployment." Half of those surveyed would "hunker down." In other words, they would delay retirement, put off major purchases, work harder to try to maintain their living standard, or adopt other "keep your head down" economic survival tactics.

To summarize, Canadians' reaction to transformations in the economy and labour market is a blend of pessimism and optimism. Pessimistically, people are worried about income inequality and lower living standards – strong warning signs for the future. And based on how people define their socio-economic status, the middle class has shrunk over the past decade. But other public views provide grounds for optimism. The early-1990s recession was more traumatic for Canadians than the Great Recession. Canadian workers today are less anxious about job loss and technology-induced mass unemployment. They feel more in control of their economic future. And while half of the workforce would cope with a prolonged downturn by "hunkering down," almost as many would try to improve their work situation either through training, moving, or finding a better job. These behaviours show resilience in the workforce and are signs of a healthy labour market.

Our own personal experiences support an optimistic interpretation. We recall doing dozens of presentations in the 1990s on "the future of work" for a variety of audiences, including senior government policymakers, business executives, workers, and members of the public. All these groups shared a sense of despair about the future. In contrast, the mood at presentations we gave during and after the Great Recession was quite different. Often, business and government decision-makers wanted to talk about how to help workers develop the resilience they would need to thrive in uncertain times. This more positive and proactive reaction gives us hope that Canadians' working lives can be improved.

Images of a Darker Future

Another insight emerging from EKOS polling data is that workers' concerns about polarization, declining living standards, and a bleak economic outlook are widely shared. Our statistical analysis of the Rethinking Work 2015 survey answers about economic insecurity and inequality found that these perceptions vary remarkably little by a workers' labour market location or demographic characteristics.[44]

Specifically, EKOS's tracking of reactions to economic and social change shows that the self-employed are very similar in their views to full-time employees. Furthermore, part-time or contingent workers are only slightly more concerned about the future than the self-employed or full-time employees in permanent jobs. The limited prospects faced by many contingent workers do not result in heightened concerns about the direction Canadian society is headed. Specifically, about 75 per cent of self-employed and full-time employees agree that Canada is becoming more divided between haves and have-nots, a view shared by 80 per cent of contingent or part-time workers. And just over 60 per cent of workers in all these labour market locations anticipate lower living standards for the next generation. Interestingly, older workers are just as worried about social divisions and falling living standards as are younger workers.

In summary, the public's outlook for Canada's future is one of diminished prosperity. The consensus is that a more divided society with lower living standards and slower economic growth lies ahead. To emphasize how pervasive this view is, consider the fact that only 6 per cent of Rethinking Work 2015 respondents disagreed with these predictions.

Conclusion

This chapter explored how successive economic shocks have transformed work. By viewing the impact of the global financial crisis and the Great Recession of 2008–9 historically, we have arrived at some important conclusions. For one, the recent recession had a less traumatic psychological impact on Canadians than the recession of the early 1990s. Canadian workers are actually less concerned today about the prospects of losing their job than they were 20 years ago. And they also are less overwhelmed now by larger economic forces, feeling more in control of their economic future.

These EKOS findings may have a silver lining, given the underlying resilience of the workforce as people cope with and adapt to the economic headwinds of recent years. And they also suggest that Canadian workers, employers, and policymakers may be more receptive now than after the recessions of the 1980s and 1990s to improving the quality of existing jobs.

Our survey evidence reveals as well countervailing trends in public opinion, which could stand in the way of improving work. Two issues weigh heavily on people's minds today: the growing gap between haves and have-nots and the diminished prospects for young people to enjoy a better living standard. Channelling these public concerns into a search for realistic solutions will, among other things, require a more complete understanding of how employers' human resource practices – particularly how workers are provided with opportunities to contribute and are fairly rewarded – can help to reduce this gap. Furthermore, the expectation of declining living standards for the next generation raises the issue of generational equity within workplaces. These are prominent themes in the chapters that follow.

Many Canadian workers foresee an economy that won't return to robust growth any time soon. To prevent this from becoming a self-fulfilling prophesy within Canada, it's important to explore realistic solutions on many fronts. A critical focus in this regard is how we design jobs and workplaces. Yet this has received little attention, despite holding considerable potential for improving business success and the well-being of the workforce. A prominent theme in coming chapters is that successful efforts to redesign work must address the economic, social, and psychological dimensions of job quality. This approach moves beyond the well-worn distinction between "good" and "bad" jobs, highlighting the diverse work experiences and trade-offs Canadians make to achieve what they want from a job.

For us, the current focus on income polarization and middle-class decline are economic symptoms of a wider problem. Canadian society, in our view, is being polarized by more than just income and wealth. Opportunities for a decent quality of work and life also are unequally distributed, more so today than in the past, but not along clear-cut lines based on one's job type. But exactly how is this happening and what are the consequences for workers? To answer this question, the next chapter shows how worker well-being is a defining feature of a quality job – and a productive workplace.

2 Happy, Healthy, and Productive Workers

The remote Himalayan kingdom of Bhutan used to elicit chuckles from economists for striving to improve its "gross national happiness." Bhutan was unique among countries because it measured progress by the happiness of its citizens, rather than by its economy's gross domestic product (GDP, the sum of all goods and services a nation produces). It's now clear that Bhutan was ahead of the curve in pursuing this goal. While economics hasn't shaken off its reputation as the "dismal science," as nineteenth-century Scottish writer Thomas Carlyle labelled it, economists can't get enough of happiness these days. As many economic studies demonstrate, there's more to a society's well-being than its GDP.

Building on this insight, we focus on how the quality of work life contributes to a society's well-being. What's troubling for us is that the quality of work has been sliding backward in Canada. Evidence from the Rethinking Work surveys sound the alarm in this regard. We document rising levels of job stress, work-life conflict, and job dissatisfaction over the past decade. These work problems detract from individuals' quality of life, measured by overall life satisfaction – a widely used indicator of happiness. Unless these trajectories are reversed, employers will face mounting costs in terms of health benefits, absenteeism, turnover, and dissatisfaction.

We argue that a worker's well-being depends on having a satisfying job and a healthy work environment. Happy people are more productive, so as organizations perform better, so does the economy. That's the clear message from the World Economic Forum: "We should all care about well-being because it helps produce other good things that we care about – happier workers generate better performance for companies; happier people have more successful families and create more harmonious communities."[1] In other words, happy employees are indispensable for economic prosperity. That point alone is a powerful incentive for employers and policymakers to implement solutions to the ebbing quality of work.

We also examine how people's individual work experiences and job conditions help to explain their concerns about the future direction of Canadian society. In this regard, we provide the first analysis in Canada (at least to our knowledge) of how individuals' perceptions of big socio-economic trends are connected to the quality of their work life.

With this, we expand the national discussions about inequality and decline. As we saw in chapter 1, most Canadians do not think their lives are getting better. EKOS polls confirm that economic concerns about income inequality and stalled living standards outweigh media headliners such as climate change, the environment, or terrorism. However, in this chapter we discover, lying beneath this economic surface, patterns of inequality in how psychological and social features of work are distributed. These non-economic rewards of a job have become the new currency for a growing number of workers in the twenty-first-century knowledge-based economy – much sought after and highly motivating.

Measuring Happiness

In 2015, the World Happiness Report, first published in 2012, observed, "Increasingly happiness is considered a proper measure of social progress and goal of public policy."[2] Governments at all levels are using happiness data to inform their policy and program decisions. Happiness is important for sustainable development, a concept which balances a society's economic, social, and environmental objectives. Well-calibrated tools measure a country's happiness. The World Happiness Report's approach is to measure life evaluations on a 0-to-10 scale, with 10 being the best possible life. Canada scores 7.427, just behind top-ranked Switzerland, Iceland, Denmark, and Norway, which score slightly above 7.5.

Quality-of-life indices, another approach, combine a wide variety of data on what life is like for citizens. For example, the Economist Intelligence Unit (EIU) developed its "Where to Be Born Index" to rank countries on the opportunities they provide a child for a happy, safe, healthy, and prosperous life.[3] The EIU combines people's subjective assessments of their satisfaction with life as well as measures of crime, per capita income, trust in public institutions, life expectancy, unemployment, and more. Canada ranks ninth on the 2013 index, behind Switzerland and Australia (first and second respectively), the Nordic countries, Singapore, New Zealand, and the Netherlands. The EIU rankings are influenced by three sets of factors: ones that can't be changed (geography); those that slowly change (demographics); and ones that can be changed (public policies and the economy). The last set of factors is our focus in *Redesigning Work*.

The "Better Life Index," created by the Organisation for Economic Co-operation and Development, offers a complementary approach. This economic think tank sponsored by richer nations publishes a *How's Life* report, presenting a range of well-being indicators. The OECD answers the question "how's life?" by combining a basket of national indicators tracking things that matter in people's daily lives. Included are security, education, housing, work hours, healthcare, leisure, the environment, income distribution, and subjective well-being. Canada outranks most of the other 35 countries included in the OECD's Better Life index.[4] According to the index, Canadians rate their lives at 7.6 on a scale from 0 to 10, which is above the OECD average of 6.6. The OECD's conclusion: while there's more to a successful life than money, rising income and education levels contribute to the overall sense of well-being in a country.[5]

Canadians' quality of life is above average compared with other nations. Surely we have the potential to do better. For this to happen, we need better information about how working conditions and quality of life are linked. None of the quality-of-life indices incorporate direct measures of how people experience their jobs or their working conditions. The OECD index includes work-life balance, measured by the amount of time the employed population spends on sleeping, personal care, leisure, and time socializing. Canadian workers have less time for leisure, socializing, and personal care than workers in other countries. Yet the Better Life index stops short of assessing how workers are affected by work hours, or other job features for that matter. The result is a blind spot in our understanding of what influences the quality of life – which this chapter illuminates.

Happy Employees Drive Business Success

The well-being indices we've reviewed are especially helpful for comparing countries. But they don't tell us what we need to know about variations in well-being within Canada or more importantly within the workforce. Nor do they tell us how work experiences influence well-being. To grasp the importance of subjective well-being – or happiness – for economic prosperity, we need to look inside workplaces. What we find is that happy employees improve the bottom line, which in turn contributes to a more productive and prosperous society.

Researchers at the University of Michigan's Center for Positive Organizational Scholarship describe happy employees as "thriving." As they explain, "We think of a thriving workforce as one in which employees are not just satisfied and productive but also engaged in creating the future – the company's and their own."[6] Employees thrive in jobs that give them a sense of purpose and room to develop their potential. Successful companies such as Costco, QuikTrip, and Trader Joe's understand that low costs, excellent customer satisfaction, and strong financial performance depend on positive employee work experiences – or in other words, happiness.[7] Zappos, the online shoe retailer, has applied research on happiness to how the business is run.[8] And Plasticity, based in Waterloo, Ontario, uses the latest technology to help companies track and improve employee happiness on a daily basis.[9]

Behavioural economists have conducted experiments to determine if happy employees are more productive. The answer is yes. According to Andrew Oswald and his colleagues at the University of Warwick, England, their experiments on employee happiness and performance suggest that "if well-being boosts people's performance at work, this raises the possibility, at the microeconomic level and perhaps even the macroeconomic level, of self-sustaining spirals between human productivity and human well-being."[10] The researchers call this the "Google effect" because the high-tech company's efforts to raise employee satisfaction have been shown to improve productivity and generate innovative ideas.

Well-being is positively contagious. Gallup researchers examined well-being levels in 105 different work teams.[11] In a team environment, the well-being of each employee can enhance, or reduce, their fellow team members' sense of well-being. This is a two-way relationship, with each team member's well-being dependent on how other team members are feeling on any given day. Supervisors have a big influence; employees whose supervisors have "thriving" well-being were themselves more likely to be thriving in the future. In sum, how you feel contributes to the collective well-being of your co-workers. And when collective well-being is high in a workplace, so is productivity, loyalty, and employee health.

Well-Being in Canada Is Slowly Declining

Yet happiness levels in Canada are declining. The Canadian Index of Wellbeing provides some evidence of this.[12] The index combines 64 indicators, covering everything from life expectancy and affordable housing to education, air quality, and income. The index dropped by 24 per cent as a result of the Great Recession. What's more, during the 17-year period from 1994 to 2010, Canada's GDP rose by 29 per cent, with quality of life lagging far behind, increasing by only 6 per cent.

There's a notable omission in the Canadian Index of Wellbeing: Canadians' subjective assessment of their quality of life. EKOS's polls provide this missing piece of information by tracking Canadians' assessment of their overall satisfaction with life. EKOS measures Canadians' overall satisfaction with life using a 1–10 rating scale, where 1 is very dissatisfied and 10 is very satisfied. Research has confirmed that life satisfaction and happiness are equally reliable gauges for the well-being of societies.[13] With such a finely calibrated measurement scale, small changes are noteworthy.

According to EKOS's polls, about three in four Canadians were very satisfied with their lives in 2015 (see Figure 2.1). This is consistent with Canada's standing in the international rankings of well-being just described. International comparisons show how we stack up against other nations. But they don't answer a vital question: whether Canadians' sense of personal well-being has been shaken by the economic and labour market changes outlined in chapter 1.

To address this point, Figure 2.1 compares life satisfaction ratings in 2005, when the economy was growing and strong, with 2015, which captures the effects of the recession and a weak recovery (results from a 2012 poll are identical to 2015). The fact that the very satisfied group (7–10 on the scale) dropped during this period from 77 to 74 per cent signals a move in the wrong direction, and it is consistent with the decline in the more broadly based Canadian Index of Wellbeing during the recession. And more people are reporting being very dissatisfied with life (1–4 on the scale), rising from 6 per cent in 2005 to 11 per cent in 2015.

It is no surprise that turmoil in labour markets and workplaces would be reflected in people's assessment of their life satisfaction. Recall that Canadians reacted to the Great Recession with growing concerns about a bleaker economic future. These economic worries are related to levels of life satisfaction. Individuals who are optimistic about the economic future are also more satisfied with their life. However, we can't say from the EKOS data which comes first. Does well-being lead to a brighter outlook or the other way around? Both are plausible explanations.

Figure 2.1. Changes in life satisfaction, 2005–15

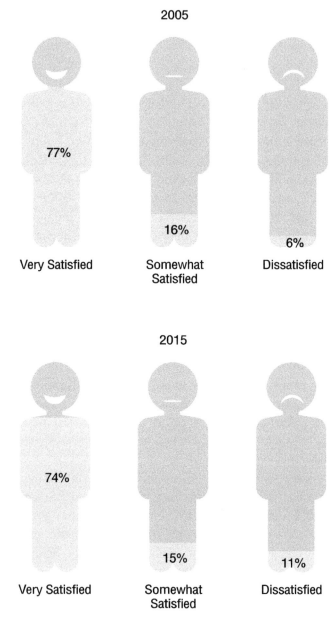

Canadian adults.

What we can confirm is that the more concerned people are about their economic future, the lower their life satisfaction. Canadians who have the following fears about the future have significantly lower life satisfaction than those who don't harbour these concerns:

- Expect their personal financial situation will get worse over the next year.
- Worried that Canada is moving to a more divided society of "haves" and "have-nots."
- Concerned that today's young people will have a lower living standard than their parents.
- Worried that the world economy is headed for 10 years of very poor performance.

It is not fear of job loss that leads individuals to expect their financial situation to worsen. Rather, people who are worried about bigger issues – a weak economy, declining living standards, and greater social inequality – are most likely see themselves at the losing end of these mega-trends, regardless of how secure their job might be.

Who Are the Most and Least Satisfied Canadians?

Digging deeper to identify opportunities to achieve well-being, we profile the social groups with the highest and lowest life satisfaction (see Figure 2.2). At first glance, income and happiness seem to go together. Well-educated knowledge workers in high-paid jobs are content with their lives. So are individuals in dual-income households.

But there's more at play in patterns of life satisfaction. Consider the fact that residents of Quebec and the Atlantic provinces are more satisfied with their lives than higher-earning Albertans. And while baby boomers are among the most satisfied, so are some of the Gen Xers (35- to 44-year-olds), even though they are at an earlier career stage and earn less than boomers.

A person's location in the labour market is a good predictor of life satisfaction. The self-employed score highest (75 per cent very

Figure 2.2. Demographic profiles of high and low life satisfaction

Characteristics of Rethinking Work 2015 respondents who have **High** life satisfaction:	Characteristics of Rethinking Work 2015 respondents who have **Low** life satisfaction:
• University graduate	• High school graduate or drop-out
• 35-44 years and 55+ years	• 45-55 year olds
• Live in Quebec and Atlantic provinces	• Live in Ontario
• Self-employed	• Unemployed
• High income (> $100,000)	• Low income (< $25,000)
• Dual-income household	• Single income household
• Children under age 18 years living at home	• No children living at home
• Manager or professional	• Sales and service or semi/unskilled manual worker
• Self-employed and full-time permanent employees	• Unemployed

Canadians in the labour force, Rethinking Work 2015. All group differences are statistically significant ($p < 0.05$).

satisfied), which is notable given the wide income distribution in this group. Full-time employees in permanent jobs have similar life satisfaction (73 per cent). The least satisfied are the unemployed – only one in three say they are very satisfied with their lives overall. Temporary and contract workers do somewhat better (53 per cent), and part-timers better still (62 per cent) – but both fall well below the self-employed or full-time employees.

Individuals who have low-quality jobs or limited human capital or who are jobless are generally dissatisfied with their lives. So do Ontario residents compared with those living in other regions of

Canada – which may reflect the decline in manufacturing. Individuals with low incomes or those living in single-income households – in other words, those who are struggling financially – are also at the bottom of the life satisfaction scale.

Two further observations about the distribution of life satisfaction: First, when we compare different age groups, 45- to 54-year-olds report lower well-being than older or younger Canadians. As we will see later, this can be explained in large part by the stresses experienced by people at this life stage. Second, there are no significant differences in life satisfaction between men and women or between immigrants and those who are Canadian-born.

So far, we've made some connections between well-being and a person's type of work. As a next step, let's consider how specific work experiences are related to well-being (see Figure 2.3).

Positive experiences at work improve one's overall quality of life, while negative work experiences detract from it. Specifically, three out of four workers who are very satisfied with their life are also satisfied and engaged when it comes to their job. The same can be said for less than a third of workers with low life satisfaction. More than half of workers with high life satisfaction have manageable levels of work stress, compared with 30 per cent who are dissatisfied with their lives. The same goes for work-life balance. One in three of the group with high life satisfaction experienced an improvement in work-life balance over the past few years, whereas only 8 per cent of the dissatisfied group reported this positive change.

So far, we've linked each of these factors on their own to an individual's life satisfaction. For a more comprehensive view of what most affects well-being, we used statistical tools that take all the demographic, labour market, and job quality factors and the perceptions of the future discussed earlier into account at the same time.

It turns out that a person's well-being depends, above all, on having a decent job and a positive financial outlook. High life satisfaction depends on having a high-quality job: being satisfied with your job, being able to balance your work with the rest of your life, and having manageable work stress. Also important are a decent income,

Figure 2.3. Life satisfaction related to quality of work life

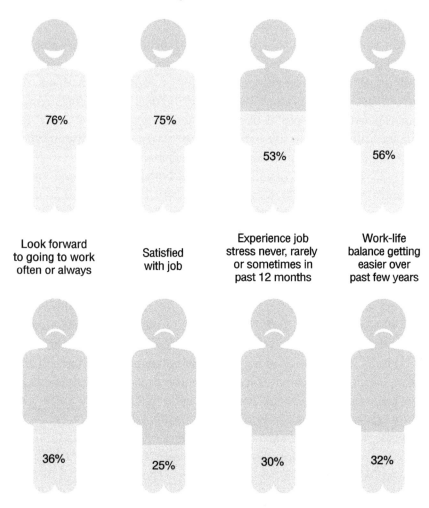

High Life Satisfaction

76%	75%	53%	56%
Look forward to going to work often or always	Satisfied with job	Experience job stress never, rarely or sometimes in past 12 months	Work-life balance getting easier over past few years
36%	25%	30%	32%

Low Life Satisfaction

Canadians in the labour force, Rethinking Work 2015. All group differences are statistically significant ($p < 0.001$).

having a knowledge-based occupation, and feeling optimistic about one's personal finances and the world economy. Personal characteristics (age, gender, immigrant status, or residence) don't help to explain who is satisfied or dissatisfied with their life, after considering job quality and perceptions of the future.[14] In short, the winners in the well-being stakes are people in satisfying and healthy jobs, financially comfortable knowledge workers, and economic optimists.

Raising incomes or generating more knowledge-intensive jobs are important longer-term strategies to improve national well-being, as we discuss in chapter 7. For now, employers can get their hands on three big levers that influence workers' well-being: work-life balance, job stress, and job satisfaction. All of these issues are already being addressed by professionals in human resources, wellness, and occupational health and safety. To encourage further action by these leaders and others, the rest of this chapter considers how Canadian workers are doing in terms of job stress and work-life balance – key indicators of job quality. The next chapter looks at job satisfaction as part of a broader discussion of what motivates and engages workers.

Deteriorating Quality of Work Life

Canadians are experiencing deterioration in their quality of work life. We've reached this conclusion based on Rethinking Work survey results, which show a rise in work-life imbalance and job-related stress between 2004 and 2015 (see Figures 2.4 and 2.5).

Over the past decade, the proportion of workers reporting that work-life balance has become harder to achieve jumped from 34 to 48 per cent. Those experiencing job stress "often" or "always" rose from 38 to 52 per cent. Surely we would be surprised if the Great Recession had no impact on workers' stress and work-life balance. Yet it remains troubling that by 2015, more than half of the workers we surveyed were dealing with high levels of job stress and finding it harder to balance their work and family/personal life.

Job stress and work-life conflict go hand-in-hand. Our evidence shows a strong link between high levels of job stress and difficulties

Figure 2.4. Work-life balance, 2004 and 2015

Q. Do you find that balancing your work and family or personal life has been getting easier or harder over the past few years?

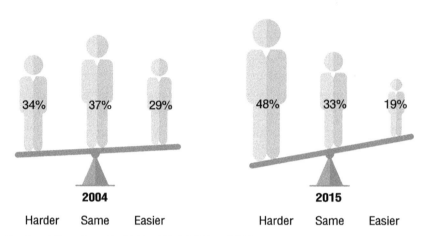

Employed Canadians. Rethinking Work 2004 and 2015.

Figure 2.5. Experiences of job stress, 2004 and 2015

Q. In the past 12 months, how often did you experience stress in your job?

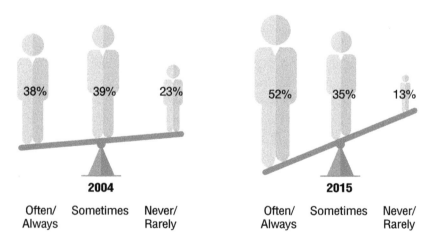

Employed Canadians. Rethinking Work 2004 and 2015.

achieving work-life balance. Stress also takes a toll on an individual's health in ways that increase healthcare costs for the public healthcare system and for employers. Specifically, many respondents to Rethinking Work 2015 who reported high job stress also said that in the 12 months prior to the survey, this stress had caused them mental and physical health problems. National well-being can't improve without addressing the workplace causes of stress and imbalance.

We Work Harder for the Money

Lying behind these rising levels of stress and work-life imbalance are fundamental changes in the nature of work. For many workers, job demands, time pressures, and performance expectations have been ratcheted up in the twenty-first century. As we've already noted, the overall thrust of these changes is what experts call "work intensification."

Work intensification has a variety of causes. These include corporate downsizing, a "doing more with less" response to a weak economy, pressure to work longer hours, the ubiquity of mobile technology that makes it easy for more people to work from anywhere at any time, and the high job performance expectations that some knowledge workers impose on themselves. These trends were clearly evident during and after the Great Recession. According to a Towers Watson global survey, which included 155 Canadian firms, most employers had concluded that their recessionary cost-cutting had a negative impact on employees' workloads, stress, and engagement.[15]

More-demanding work has become the norm for some, but not for all. This underscores the great paradox of the twenty-first-century labour market noted earlier – that workers have either too much to do or too little. At the other end of the work continuum from knowledge workers who are stressed out by excessive job demands are over 1.3 million unemployed people and many others who are underemployed. These individuals are stuck in part-time, temporary, contract, or seasonal jobs that don't provide an adequate income or career opportunities.

What's also new in the post-recession era is that financial worries have become more acute for many Canadian families. This certainly has contributed to the public concerns about personal finances and declining living standards we've documented using EKOS polls. According to a report from the Vanier Institute for the Family, the recession left many families caught in a near-impossible financial juggling act as they face higher debt loads, less savings, and unpredictable earnings.[16]

Work Hours and the Quality of Life

Longer work hours are a clear sign of work intensification. And as we'll see, weekly work hours are related to job stress and work-life imbalance.

The Rethinking Work 2015 survey provides an interesting perspective in this regard. On one hand, there is no difference in work-life balance experiences when we compare workers whose usual workweeks are less than 30, 30–40, or more than 40 hours. This suggests that people have adjusted their personal and family lives to their regular job hours. On the other hand, working longer hours definitely increases a worker's exposure to job stress. Specifically, 43 per cent of those whose usual workweek is less than 30 hours report experiencing job stress "often" or "always." This jumps to 56 per cent among those who put in more than 40 hours per week.

Overtime adds to work hours stress. There are two kinds of overtime work, paid and unpaid, which have very different economic and legal implications. For hourly paid unionized workers, overtime is good money because their union contracts guarantee an overtime premium of one and a half to twice their usual wage rate. Others workers aren't so fortunate: part-timers, temps, and contract employees have no negotiating power, so they have to settle for their hourly wage with no premium added when working extra hours.

Many hourly or salaried employees who put in hours above a 40-hour workweek (or 44 hours, depending on where you live in Canada) are entitled to be paid for that work under provincial or federal employment standards legislation. Managers and some professionals are exempt from overtime requirements, which partly explains the higher stress levels among knowledge workers.

Unpaid overtime can lead to a sense of unfairness among employees. Yet many feel powerless to do anything about it. That may be changing, however. In the past few years, employees at two Canadian banks – CIBC and Scotiabank – launched class actions against their employers, alleging that they were expected to work extra hours without compensation to complete routine banking tasks.[17] These lawsuits, one of which has been settled in favour of the employees, could cost the banks hundreds of millions of dollars in unpaid wages, plus legal fees and any damages awarded by the courts.

Against the backdrop of these broad working-time trends, Rethinking Work 2015 shows how overtime affects stress and work-life balance. The conclusion is clear: while paid overtime is not associated with elevated levels of job stress or work-life imbalance, working unpaid overtime is. Around 60 per cent or more of Rethinking Work respondents working unpaid overtime report high levels of job stress and work-life conflict.

It makes sense that people who work paid overtime choose to do so and accept the trade-off of having to cope with added work hours for more income or future time off. Given public concerns about declining living standards, the opportunity for paid overtime may be welcomed by some workers, especially those at the lower end of the pay scale. But the unpaid overtime scenario is starkly different. What's both stressful and disruptive to personal and family life is feeling compelled – either by your employer or by yourself – to essentially work for free.

Unpaid overtime is more common than paid overtime.[18] Surely this deserves the attention of decision-makers responsible for employment policies, both in government and in businesses. One in five employees work overtime in a typical week and more than half of this extra work time is unpaid. In other words, at least 1 in 10 workers are donating free time each week to their employer.

Even though illegal, this off-the-books work is built into the economy. Unpaid overtime is further evidence of the unfairness that has become a feature of the twenty-first-century labour market. Because unpaid overtime involves no financial or leisure time rewards, there's only a downside. Whether it involves pulling out your laptop late at night and working at the kitchen table, constantly being tied to your business smartphone, or having to come in early or stay late, the potential cost of unpaid overtime is reduced well-being.

Looking Backward into the Future

Both of us recall with some nostalgia when, back in the 1970s, a popular university course was "The Sociology of Leisure." There were even Leisure Studies programs and degrees at some Canadian universities. Futurists at the time predicted that computers – which then were "mainframes" occupying entire floors of office buildings – would give the economy a huge boost because workers would be able to produce more in less time. So for sociologists, the big challenge facing society back then was helping people find useful ways to fill their expanding leisure time. One expert put it succinctly: "The technological advances of post-industrial society have created unprecedented opportunities to escape the necessities of daily toil."[19]

The rising living standards and unbridled optimism of the 1970s stand in marked contrast to the troubled mood of post-recession twenty-first-century Canada. The 1970s visions of a leisure society were inspired by the notion that technology would give workers more choice over how they spend their time. Yet the basic insight underpinning the idea of a leisure society can be applied to workplaces today. The key point made by leisure society advocates is that personal and societal benefits will flow from giving workers more control over their time and activities. In today's workplaces, this idea is the key to solutions for job stress.

Reducing Job Stress

Employers can improve the overall quality of work life for employees by alleviating the causes of stress. Indeed, more employers now recognize the need for action to reduce stress. Canadian employers rank work-related stress as their top employee health concern.[20] And they are far from alone in this regard. A global wellness survey also flagged stress as the leading health risk that prompts employers to invest in employee wellness programs.[21]

We know a lot about what causes work stress and what must be done to reduce it. Hundreds of studies confirm that people feel under stress when their job demands exceed their resources to respond to these demands.[22] High psychological job demands – urgent deadlines, too much work, unclear roles, competing or conflicting goals – and a low level of control over these demands increases a person's exposure to what researchers call "job strain," which is the main cause of work stress.

Many studies document that job strain is bad for workers' health and costly for employers.[23] Stressed-out employees report more fatigue, depression, low motivation, headaches or stomach problems, and unhealthy coping behaviours such as increased smoking, alcohol consumption, and poor nutrition – all symptoms that can be expensive for employers. The chronic experience of job strain has been linked to degenerative disease processes, such as heart disease, as well as depression, diabetes, asthma, migraines, and ulcers. Among knowledge workers, persistently heavy job demands can result in burnout, a psychological state in which people feel mentally exhausted, cynical about their work, and professionally ineffective. In short, solutions to job stress must address these underlying causes in the workplace.

To spur action, employers need to think about the costs of job stress. Basically, unhealthy workers are less productive and an added burden on employer-sponsored health benefit plans. Here's a quick overview of what academic research tells us about how stress can damage workers' health and well-being:

• Stress can lead to long-term disability. Long-term disability claims can be reduced by better regulating workers' job demands and providing them with more say over how they do their jobs.[24]

- Job stress contributes to neck and shoulder disorders. Prevention strategies for musculoskeletal problems also must consider workers' exposure to the psychological risks that increase stress, in addition to physical or ergonomic causes of these disorders.[25]
- Job strain is significantly associated with hypertension. Hypertension, or high blood pressure, is a risk factor in heart disease, coronary artery disease, strokes, aneurysms, and chronic kidney disease.[26]
- Stress resulting from job strain, job dissatisfaction, high effort-reward imbalance, organizational downsizing, and economic recession reduces our body's natural defences against sickness and disease by disrupting the body's immune responses.[27]
- Job stress has a negative spillover effect on leisure time activities. Cumulative job strain can lead previously active individuals to become inactive, which over time can result in a deterioration of their overall health.[28]
- A meta-analysis of 169 job stress studies concluded that an employee's job performance is negatively influenced by the presence of job stressors.[29]

Rethinking Work 2015 also identifies work-to-family conflict as another major source of stress. High levels of work-family conflict also impose costs on employers. Many studies confirm that work-life conflict can contribute to dissatisfaction with life, psychosomatic symptoms, depression and other forms of psychological distress, use of medication, alcohol consumption, substance abuse, clinical mood disorders, clinical anxiety disorders, and emotional exhaustion. These costs include turnover, low morale, and increased absenteeism.[30]

We would like to wrap up this discussion on an upbeat note. Workplaces can be made more productive by reducing job stress. This requires changes to improve the basic ingredients of a high-quality job. In this scenario, an employee with challenging job de-mands but who has the autonomy to make decisions, appropriate job resources, and support from their co-workers and supervisor to manage these demands is more likely to experience well-being and fully contribute to company goals.

Promoting Workplace Wellness

Introducing comprehensive worksite health promotion is a proven strategy for helping employees alleviate job stressors and attain work-life balance. The goal of these "wellness" initiatives is to enable employees to improve their overall well-being, which is a positive state of mental and physical health. Indeed, the benefits of comprehensive wellness programs are extensively documented.[31]

Although stress may be a symptom of the need for such an approach, it is not the only pressure on employers to find better ways to make workplaces healthier. Employee absenteeism costs are rising.[32] The aging workforce will strain future drug, disability, and other employee health costs. Lost productivity in workplaces accounts for about one-third of the annual $51 billion cost of mental illness in Canada.[33] And in a global knowledge-based economy, employers can't afford to let an unhealthy workplace reduce an employee's potential to contribute their energy and ideas.

Employers will be better positioned to find solutions if they view employee wellness as a strategic business advantage. A first step is to embrace a broader view of employee health, defining wellness as a complete picture of a person's quality of life, encompassing their physical, psychological, and social well-being. Wellness focuses on positive states of being, not just the absence of illness, disease, or injury – although this too is a goal. Wellness is promoted, whereas illness, disease, and injury are prevented.

Yet according to a Sanofi Canada Healthcare Survey, only 40 per cent of employees report that their employer offers programs to promote health and wellness.[34] Similarly, a Conference Board of Canada survey of large employers found that only around one in four had a comprehensive wellness strategy that addresses health risks and the underlying causes of well-being and productivity.[35]

Ingredients of Effective Wellness Initiatives

The big question for management is not whether to introduce a wellness program but how to design, implement, and evaluate it to achieve the best outcomes in terms of improved employee well-being, reduced health benefit costs, and improved productivity. A recent review of numerous studies in this area identified common success factors for employer-sponsored wellness strategies:[36]

- The corporate culture promotes wellness as a means of enhancing employees' quality of life, not just to reduce costs.
- Leaders and employees are motivated to support wellness initiatives and to improve their overall health.
- Corporate policies and the physical work environment encourages employees to participate.
- Programs adapt over time to the changing wellness needs of employees.
- Community health organizations partner to provide support, education, and treatment.
- Technology facilitates health risk assessments and access to wellness education.

A major challenge faced by many wellness initiatives is how to encourage employees to take advantage of available resources, supports, and programs. These range from employee assistance programs, nutrition advice, fitness programs and facilities, health risk assessments, counselling, and online mental and physical health resources. However, a review of workplace health promotion programs found a median participation among eligible employees of only 33 per cent.[37]

That's why successful worksite health promotion strategies actively involve employees. When employees participate in designing, implementing, and monitoring worksite wellness initiatives, they take greater ownership for their overall health, safety, and well-being. The key to a successful wellness strategy is following basic principles for building healthier organizations:

- Consult with employees.
- Involve them directly in the design process.

- Be open to a wide range of solutions.
- Evaluate the impact, learn from changes, and make improvements.

Effective wellness strategies empower employees to improve their own working conditions. A broadly representative worksite wellness committee (WWC) can do this. Indeed, WCCs play a critical role in the successful implementation of programs.[38] WWCs are able to respond to worksite needs, directly shaping how corporate wellness goals are achieved. It is at the local or worksite level – not the corporate level – that changes required to improve employee well-being occur.

Psychologically Healthy and Safe Workplaces

Increasingly, workplace health promotion is focusing on mental health issues. Canadian employers have a new resource that can help to guide actions in this area: the National Standard of Canada for Psychological Health and Safety in the Workplace (the Standard).[39]

A partnership between the Mental Health Commission of Canada and the Canadian Standards Association (CSA), the Standard provides resources for identifying, assessing, and reducing psychological health risks in the workplace. Stress and work-life imbalance are among these risks – as we have documented. Although the Standard is voluntary, legal experts predict that courts, tribunals, and arbitrators will take it into account when determining an employer's responsibility to provide a psychologically healthy workplace.

The Standard is intended to be easily implemented by employers. It can be built on existing occupational health and safety (OH&S) management systems many employers already have. Its approach to risk and needs assessment, planning, implementation, evaluation, leadership, and continuous improvement will be familiar to OH&S professionals. In this regard, the Standard offers an opportunity to develop an integrated approach to health promotion, safety, and employee engagement. This is consistent with experts' recommendation that companies develop more coordinated programs in human resources, OH&S, and wellness.[40]

The Standard offers employees and managers free workplace assessment resources, including an employee survey called Guarding Minds @ Work.[41] These tools can identify the underlying causes of stress in job design, work systems, relationships, and organizational processes. This is the first step to making the workplace psychologically healthy. Among workplace factors that the Standard assesses are many of the causes of work stress and work-life interference we've discussed, including job demands, workload, and influence on decisions.

The Standard is no magic bullet. However, it does map out the kinds of actions employers, unions, professional associations, and community mental health partners can take to improve workers' overall quality of life. Because the Standard is voluntary, we don't know exactly how many organizations have adopted it or what success they have had reducing stress, work-life imbalance, and other symptoms of an unhealthy workplace. But it has generated considerable interest. The Standard has the most downloads of any of the CSA's many standards – a good sign of interest. There are 41 organizations participating in a Mental Health Commission of Canada study to learn how the Standard is being implemented. And hundreds of organizations have completed the Guarding Minds @ Work survey to assess the workplace.[42] All of this action speaks to the opportunities at hand to design better work.

Conclusion

Our starting point in this chapter was how life satisfaction is a key indicator of a society's well-being. We then expanded this perspective on happiness by including the quality of people's jobs and work experiences. Our broader approach to happiness has important implications for policymakers and employers about how best to improve Canada's quality of life.

Well-being is influenced not only by big economic trends, but also by people's experiences in the labour market and the workplace. Workers who are satisfied with and engaged in their jobs, who can manage the daily stresses of work, and who are able to integrate their work with the rest of their life are happier and more productive. That these workers tend to be managers, professionals, or self-employed individuals with good incomes adds another dimension to inequality: the quality of work life. Just like incomes in Canada, the less tangible benefits of a job are unequally distributed.

EKOS surveys reveal that the same people in the top tiers of the labour market have more optimistic views about the future. Knowledge workers are more positive about their personal financial outlook and the direction of the world economy. This state of mind will, no doubt, make these workers more receptive to change, both in workplaces and in the economy. Ironically, those workers who could benefit most from workplace improvements – the less-educated, less-skilled, underemployed, or unemployed – have adopted a "hunker down" mentality that could actually make them more change-averse, even if they might benefit from those changes.

One of the big concerns affecting those workers who don't fall into the more privileged sectors of the labour market is family care and how the costs and logistics of family care affect their ability to manage daily stress, hold secure jobs, and achieve a decent quality of life. A national family-care strategy would be a welcome public policy solution for many workers with families. Promised by a succession of governments since the 1980s, with a focus on childcare, an updated policy would have to include families who care for seniors and other dependent adults. The Trudeau Liberal government has committed to develop in cooperation with the provinces, territories, and indigenous communities a comprehensive framework for providing affordable, accessible, and good-quality childcare. However, three big hurdles could stand in the way. Agreement has to be reached on a national childcare strategy, the scope must be widened to other types of care families provide, and appropriate resources need to be allocated. Assuming these hurdles can be overcome, there could be help coming for workers with family care responsibilities.

Governments can take steps to improve the quality of work life for disadvantaged groups in the labour market. Better monitoring and enforcement of employment standards legislation could cut down on abuses such as unpaid overtime. Expanding occupational health and safety legislation to accept a wide range of psychological health risks as causes of stress-related injury or disability would push more employers to take action to get at the sources of stress. There's movement in this direction. Quebec and Ontario have introduced anti-bullying and harassment legislation focusing on workplaces. And BC amended its occupational health and safety act to cover mental disorders resulting from stress caused by bullying, harassment, or other workplace conditions.[43]

There are also what Canadians might consider more "radical" solutions. The city of Malmo, Sweden, launched an experiment to see the effects of a six-hour workday on employees' health and performance.[44] At first glance, this looks like a post-industrial version of the leisure society. More accurately, it's a good health promotion idea given that reduced work hours is recommended by public health experts. Municipal workers in the study group will be compared with their co-workers who continue to work the normal seven-hour day. Results from this study could shape the future of Sweden's family-friendly approach to work.

Even more ambitious is the New Economics Foundation's (NEF's) proposal for a 21-hour workweek as the new norm, either on a weekly basis or spread out over the year if people choose to work longer hours but for shorter periods of time.[45] The NEF, a think tank in Britain, sees the shorter workweek as central to a sweeping agenda for social change. It considers a 21-hour workweek essential "to address a range of urgent, interlinked problems: overwork, unemployment, over-consumption, high carbon emissions, low well-being, entrenched inequalities, and the lack of time to live sustainably, to care for each other, and simply to enjoy life." While provocative, this is impractical, especially in Canada, where many households depend on two incomes and workforce aging could reduce the workforce in the coming decade.

Still, examples like these encourage Canadians to consider fresh approaches to a better future. That's the only way to break free of a workplace status quo that for many people is not optimal. Employers in particular should find many reasons in our discussion so far to design healthier organizations. A healthy organization is successful in business terms and sustainable in people terms because it supports worker well-being as a means to higher performance.[46] The goal is a motivated and engaged workforce – which is the topic of the next chapter.

3 Engaged Workers

Employee engagement has become the holy grail of twenty-first-century human resource management. *Canadian HR Reporter*, the profession's leading national publication, featured over 500 articles on engagement in the past three years alone. One of us recently gave a talk at a conference on healthy organizations, attended by senior managers from many of the largest companies and public employers in Canada. All of these organizations have strategies for achieving higher levels of workforce engagement. And all conducted regular employee engagement surveys to track progress towards this important human resource goal.

Like a growing number of corporate leaders, those at the conference believed that engaged employees are loyal, committed, and dedicated to doing excellent work. Academic studies back this up. Having an engaged workforce positively influences an employer's retention, attendance, and reputation as a good place to work.[1] Experts also agree that engagement translates into how well people perform their work roles.[2] That's why employee engagement has become a priority for many employers across Canada and other advanced industrial nations.

In this chapter, we offer a unique perspective on engagement that provides new insights for corporate and public policy decision-makers. We go beyond other studies of engagement in three ways:

- Providing an integrated view of job satisfaction and motivation, because both are central to understanding engagement. We are guided here by a key conclusion from decades of workplace research: workers feel more engaged when they are satisfied with their work and motivated to do it.
- Giving workers a voice by seeking their direct input about what motivates them and how it could be improved. Engagement surveys conducted by employers don't take this approach, so we provide new insights in this regard.
- Profiling engagement in the entire workforce by including in our analysis contract, temporary, and self-employed workers, in addition to employees. These "non-employees" account for about 15 per cent of the Canadian workforce, yet there is little research on their work experiences.

Rarely are the voices of workers heard in the voluminous academic and practitioner literature on engagement. Workers' perspectives on what's needed to better engage them is a critical piece of the well-being and prosperity puzzle, which this chapter provides. Chapter 2 showed that a person's health and happiness is influenced by their work experiences. In this chapter, we go further by documenting that satisfied and motivated workers are exactly what employers need for business success – and what a strong economy needs.

Feeling Engaged

Engaged workers derive a sense of well-being from their jobs. Words like "vigour," "dedication," and "absorption" are used to describe feelings of work engagement. Arnold Bakker, an expert on work engagement at Erasmus University in the Netherlands, observes that when employees are engaged, "they put their selves in their work by doing it the best way they could."[3] And they stay engaged by taking initiative and improving how their work is done. As Bakker puts it, they "are bursting with energy."

Engagement is at the positive end of the work experience continuum. Burnout is at the negative end.[4] Engaged workers perform their jobs better than their non-engaged co-workers because they experience positive emotions at work, are healthier, actively create their own job resources, and positively influence their team members to feel engaged as well. As one expert concludes, "work engagement is an important indicator of occupational well-being for both employees and organizations."[5]

Engagement also includes cognitive and behavioural aspects of how people perform their work roles. When someone looks forward to going to work they feel motivated and ready to act on this feeling. Psychologists call this "autonomous motivation." It results in superior job performance, greater satisfaction, and higher well-being. Autonomous motivation requires tasks to be interesting, challenging, and important – the opposite of performing trivial and boring tasks in a regimented environment.[6]

Leading employers, such as Google, have cultivated a highly engaging work environment.[7] With about 600 employees in Canada, Google was ranked #1 on Great Place to Work Institute Canada's list of the best large and multinational workplaces in the country.[8] Google Canada's engineering manager, Stergios Anastasiadis, explains that the company designs jobs and work environments to stimulate creativity and innovation. "We're not here to ride a wave, we're here to create them," he explains.[9]

At the mention of Google, readers may think of its impressive perks – a putting green, massages, free gourmet food, walking desks, and campus-style facilities – as expensive practices imported from deep-pocketed Silicon Valley firms. But they would be missing the low-cost approaches that it uses to inspire employees. These practices include having peers assess each other's performance, weekly team meetings where everyone contributes to goal-setting, and giving employees the autonomy to pursue ideas that one day could become breakthrough technologies.

Protegra Inc. is a Winnipeg-based software company – tiny compared to Google – recognized as one of the best small and medium employers in Canada. Its employees are self-motivated. The company has done away with a traditional business hierarchy and eliminated most job titles. Its culture empowers employees to collaborate with each other and with clients.[10] Protegra and similar employers are doing just what experts advise: motivating employees by giving them lots of freedom and responsibility.[11]

Work motivation is central to an understanding of workers' behaviour and workplace dynamics. Ever since Frederick Herzberg's seminal 1959 book, *The Motivation to Work*, managers have viewed motivation as a key piece of the job performance puzzle.[12] For Herzberg, workers are most satisfied and motivated when they experience achievement, recognition, challenge, responsibility, influence, and meaning and purpose through their work. These motivators arise from the nature of the work itself.

Job satisfaction also deserves our attention in this chapter. Long before engagement became an HR priority, social scientists plumbed the depths of job satisfaction. What's more, job satisfaction impacts firm performance and human resource costs through turnover, absenteeism, withdrawal, organizational citizenship (i.e., discretionary behaviours not part of an employee's job description), job performance, and workplace civility.[13]

Measuring Engagement

There's no standardized measure of engagement. To varying degrees, employee surveys usually examine its rational, emotional, and behavioural components.[14] Rethinking Work measures the cognitive and behavioural aspects of engagement, which are essential for workers to feel involved, enthusiastic, and energized about their jobs.

Engaged workers invest themselves in their jobs.[15] Workers who feel passionate about their work, energized by it, and immersed in it perform their roles much better than their co-workers who lack these experiences. It's difficult to imagine someone providing outstanding customer service, producing a quality product, or putting patients or students first if they reluctantly drag themselves into work each day.

Taking this perspective on engagement, the Rethinking Work surveys probed how motivated workers feel at the start of each workday. This is a basic behavioural marker of being energized at work. The question asks, "How often do you look forward to going to work?" Survey participants were presented with four response options: never, rarely, often, and always.

Complementing this is a measure of job satisfaction. It gets at the rational aspect of engagement: whether a worker likes their job relative to what else could be available to them. The question asks: Overall, how satisfied are you with your job? Survey participants were presented with five response options: very dissatisfied, dissatisfied, neither dissatisfied nor satisfied, satisfied, and very satisfied.

Feeling motivated is what sets an employee up to do a good job and fully contribute to their organization's goals. A satisfying day at work makes a person want to return the next day. It's this positive cycle of motivation and accomplishment that needs to be promoted through better work design.

Growing Job Dissatisfaction

The EKOS Rethinking Work surveys asked a global job satisfaction question, which researchers use to gauge overall quality of life. This job quality indicator declined between 2004 and 2015, from 71 to 63 per cent. We also detected growing discontent. Considerably more Rethinking Work respondents told us that they are very dissatisfied or dissatisfied with their job in 2015 than they did in 2004 (9 per cent in 2004 versus 18 per cent in 2015) (Figure 3.1). This trend should raise a red flag for employers and policymakers because it reveals an expanding minority of workers whose overall assessment of their work is negative.

A further concern is that employees are far less satisfied than the self-employed. Indeed, satisfaction rates among full-time permanent employees are at 63 per cent, compared to a 77 per cent rate

Figure 3.1. Overall job satisfaction, 2004 and 2015

Q. Overall, how satisfied are you with your job?

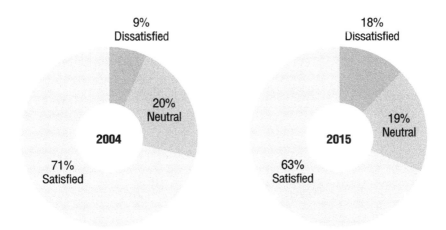

9%
Dissatisfied

18%
Dissatisfied

20%
Neutral

2004

19%
Neutral

2015

71%
Satisfied

63%
Satisfied

Employed Canadians. Rethinking Work 2004 and 2015.

among self-employed. Even more worrisome is that only around half of part-time employees and contract workers (including temp, term, and seasonal workers) are satisfied with their jobs. And at least one in five is dissatisfied.

Being satisfied with your job is a basic requirement for your overall well-being. Indeed, hundreds of studies confirm that job satisfaction is related to an employee's mental and physical health.[16] Basically, job dissatisfaction poses a significant risk to mental health, leading to problems such as burnout, low self-esteem, anxiety, and depression. At the positive end, high job satisfaction is associated with mental and physical well-being. Recall from chapter 2 that you can't be really satisfied with your life if you aren't happy with your job.

Job satisfaction and work motivation are linked. More than four in five of the Rethinking Work respondents who look forward to going to work also reported high levels of job satisfaction. And close

Figure 3.2. Looking forward to going to work, 2004 and 2015

Q. How often do you look forward to going to work?

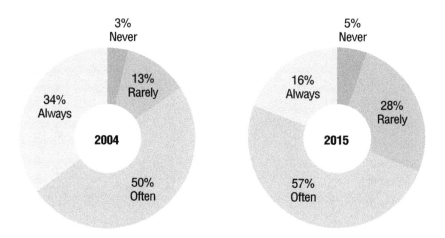

Employed Canadians. Rethinking Work 2004 and 2015.

to nine in ten respondents who are satisfied with their jobs also are motivated to go to work each day. Furthermore, 60 per cent of workers report high levels of both motivation and job satisfaction. This means that the quality of work life and motivation needs improvement for two out of every five workers in Canada.

Less Motivation

Declining job satisfaction reveals that all is not well in the nation's workplaces. A useful complement is a behavioural measure of how engaged an individual is in their work, asking how frequently they actually look forward to going to work. This gets directly at worker motivation, which we argue is a precursor to being engaged while doing your work.

Worker motivation also has declined in the past decade (Figure 3.2). In 2004, 34 per cent of survey respondents always looked forward to going to work, compared with only 16 per cent who felt this way in 2015. This group of what employers would call "highly engaged" workers has shrunk by more than half. The most obvious explanation for this lies in the workplace transformations triggered by the Great Recession.

Knowledge workers stand out as being the most motivated. Managers and professionals are very motivated, as are university-educated and high-income workers. And workers in administrative, clerical, sales, and personal service jobs are the least motivated. As we will show, these occupational differences boil down to the more positive work experiences associated with the knowledge-based work performed by professionals and managers. The self-employed are far more motivated than employees. This benefit of being your own boss is consistent with other indicators of positive well-being among the self-employed, noted earlier.

There are only a few notable demographic differences. Why workers in Quebec are the most motivated and those in Ontario the least can only be subject to speculation. Similarly, the older people get, the more motivated they feel about work. You might expect older workers to feel worn down or even jaded about their work. But not so, according to our evidence. Chapter 5 explores how employers and policymakers can harness older workers' motivation.

Workers' Perspectives on Motivation

Declining worker satisfaction and motivation surely is a problem we need to solve. To frame these solutions, we asked a wide cross-section of workers to describe in their own words what motivates them now and what could motivate them more in future. The Rethinking Work 2012 survey asked the following questions:[17]

- What is the one thing about your job that contributes the most to making you look forward to coming to work?

- If you could change one thing about your job that would make you look forward to coming to work more often, what would that change be?

Workers welcomed the chance to express what inspires them and what changes could inspire them more in their jobs. Respondents got right to the point, usually writing a sentence or two. To analyse responses to each question we sorted them by common themes, which describe Canadian's positive work experiences.[18] In chapter 7, we consolidate these perspectives into a collective vision of a great job.

What Makes People Look Forward to Work?

An ongoing challenge for HR professionals and managers is figuring out how to enable employees to feel more engaged in their jobs. The workers we surveyed provide helpful insights in this regard. After reviewing all the written responses to the question of why people look forward to going to work, we identified 20 distinct themes (see Figure 3.3).

"It's the People I Work With"

The social and psychological rewards of work stand out as big motivators and what differentiates great jobs from not-so-great ones. The most common reason people look forward to work is their co-workers. This accounts for one in five answers to the question. Some respondents simply stated that they looked forward to work because of "co-workers" or "collegiality." But most stated that the positive relationships they have with their workmates energize them at the start of a workday. Words like "friends," "fun," "enjoy," and "great" describe these co-worker relations.

Here are some typical statements of how good co-workers contribute to a positive work experience:

Figure 3.3. What makes you look forward to coming to work?

Q. What is the one thing about your job that contributes the most to making you look forward to coming to work?

1.	The people I work with	21%
2.	Challenging, interesting and varied work	17%
3.	Helping customers/clients/society	11%
4.	Pay	9%
5.	Relationships with customers/clients	8%
6.	Enjoy the work	7%
7.	Getting a sense of accomplishment or satisfaction	5%
8.	Using my education, skills or creativity	4%
9.	Having autonomy, control, responsibility or input	3%
10.	I love my job	3%
11.	The work environment or culture	3%
12.	The work schedule or hours	2%
13.	Being self-employed/my own boss	1%
14.	Being able to work from home	1%
15.	My contributions are valued/recognized	<1%
16.	My boss or the company management	<1%
17.	Doing healthy work	<1%
18.	Getting out of the house	<1%
19.	Travel	<1%
20.	Success and career advancement	<1%
	Other comments	3%
TOTAL		**100%**

Employed Canadians. Rethinking Work 2012. Based on 1,743 discrete responses provided by 1,302 survey respondents.

- I work with great people, so I look forward to seeing them every day.
- Enjoying the company of the people I work with and zero drama that could cause tension between us.
- The sense of working together in collaboration with others and socializing with coworkers.
- The people I work with [are a] good crew and sticking together is everything. Morale, morale, morale!

The characteristics of a business affect workplace relationships. Smaller workplaces tend to have closer personal relationships. As one respondent put it, "It is a small business so it feels like working with friends." Furthermore, the comments we received also highlight the important role of camaraderie in knowledge-based organizations. Here is what two knowledge workers said in this regard:

- I work in a creative field with people who are enthusiastic, intelligent, well-informed and interesting to be around.
- [I work with] clever, competent people in a positive environment where I'm granted enough autonomy to be effective.

These comments describe the ideal future workplace: friendly, creative, and collaborative. In this future workplace, capable co-workers support each other to do their jobs well. People don't go to work just to socialize, although that's a side benefit. Rather, having supportive relations with our immediate workmates is what helps us to succeed in our own job. Being in the same location isn't a necessity in this regard. The most motivated self-employed and contract workers cultivate good working relationships with their business partners, contacts, and clients.

Challenging Work

Second only to excellent workplace relationships is having challenging work. This theme describes 17 per cent of the answers we received. It is at the core of what psychologists call intrinsic work rewards. Basically, intrinsically rewarding work is personally interesting, meaningful, and stimulating. It feeds your mind, allows you to realize your potential, and gives you a sense of accomplishment. These job characteristics reflect the nature of the work itself.

These characteristics are distinct from pay and benefits, what psychologists call extrinsic rewards. This distinction between intrinsic and extrinsic rewards explains why the level of pay itself is rarely a major source of job satisfaction. It's the inner dynamics of the work that matter most in a quality job.

We were struck by how many workers are motivated by the daily challenges of their job, doing different things, having new projects and interesting tasks to work on, solving problems, and simply being intellectually stimulated. Some respondents gave additional details about what makes their work especially challenging and interesting. Consider the following:

- There's always something new in my job. I am a mortgage broker so each new appointment is interesting.
- Every day I work with others who are facing living with an acquired disability. My time with them is so rewarding.
- Finding new ways to execute the projects I work on.
- The variety of work and the knowledge that my contribution matters.
- Technically challenging and always changing.

These comments describe meaningful work – the opposite of a boring, repetitive, or routine job. Work becomes challenging when you are doing a good job, feeling like you're making progress, problem solving, succeeding, doing better, or helping others. It's also the excitement of something new. One respondent looks forward to work because of the "change, creativity, and challenge that comes from a new prospect at the beginning of a project." Another respondent explained that his work gives him a sense of purpose: "My job is field technical work, so every day is different, and there are challenges to overcome on every job. This makes the work interesting and enjoyable to do, giving a sense of accomplishment at the end of the day."

Helping Others and Making a Difference

We've seen how some survey respondents find meaning in their work because of the personal gratification it provides, whether problem solving, starting a new project, or helping a customer or client. Indeed, this latter point – helping others – is the focus of the third most common type of motivation for looking forward to one's work on a daily basis. The "helping others" theme includes 1 in 10 of the responses we received.

Feeling like your job is helping others and making a difference is fulfilling. This isn't restricted to the "helping professions" in healthcare, social work, or teaching. Workers in many sorts of customer or client service roles experience the satisfaction of doing "good" by helping people. For others, what matters is knowing that their contributions to corporate goals will help society. Some workers refer to "helping" or "making a difference." Naturally, the way in which people feel their work helps others will depend on their job. Here are some descriptions of the different ways workers feel helpful:

- At times my experience develops novel advances for society at large.
- Being able to help my coworkers with their work concerns.
- Being able to make a difference in the lives of people.
- Being able to help the sites I work with resolve their problems.
- Contributing to the safety and wellbeing of others.
- Feeling that I make a contribution to my team and the company.
- Knowing that our organization is making a difference.

Some workers provided more details about how making a difference motivates them to want to go to work each day. Again, what's interesting is how people in diverse jobs across the public, private, and non-profit sectors explain the importance of this aspect of their work:

- Making a difference in the lives of children; making an impression and teaching them things that they will have with them for life.
- I feel that the work I do contributes to a better future for the environment as a whole and is fiscally responsible at the same time.
- In each home where we clean a furnace or carpets, it feels really great to know that they will be healthier and happier.
- Risk Management and Loss Prevention provide an environment where public safety can be improved, with an end result that generates personal and professional satisfaction.
- I work at a charitable organization so knowing that I'm helping people makes me look forward to coming to work.
- I work with the poor, so I know that the work I do makes the world a better place.

To recap, Canadian workers look forward to going to work if they have great co-workers, are presented challenging tasks and are able to make a difference by helping others. Designing these characteristics into jobs is a sure way to achieve a highly engaged workforce. And it's not just one of these features that engages workers. Sometimes, it is a combination of factors that make a job engaging:

- I like my duties, enjoy the challenges every day and like my co-workers.
- The people I work with and for. I'm fortunate to work at a job that is a great fit … it allows me to do what I love while feeling I am making a difference in the world.
- The people I work with and the challenge of the job.
- The people I work with, the feeling of making a difference.
- Really enjoy working with the staff on the floor and enjoy helping my clients.
- There are always challenging problems to solve and people to help.

- I am a teacher, so the job brings new challenges every day and I enjoy working with my students.
- The challenge of helping people in distress and the professional people I work with.
- Contributing to society. Feeling ownership over my job. Doing something that I can feel good about at the end of the day.
- I lead a great team and we're making a difference in people's lives.

These statements aren't rationalizations justifying how people spend their work days. Rather, they express the deeper personal connections individuals have with their work. Many – but certainly not all – workers want to contribute to a larger purpose and will measure the worth of their job this way.

Other Motivators (Pay Isn't a Big One)

The three themes just reviewed – co-workers, challenging work, and helping others – account for close to half of all the reasons Rethinking Work 2012 respondents gave for being motivated about their work. The three themes that ranked next highest – pay, relationships with customers or clients, and enjoying the type of work – only account for about a quarter of all responses.

Money is not a big motivator. Indeed, less than 10 per cent of survey respondents mentioned pay as the main motivator for going to work. As decades of job satisfaction research shows, pay can be a source of dissatisfaction but rarely is a major source of satisfaction in a job.

Yet looking at how people describe the importance of pay highlights a distinction between those who are working to make ends meet – "pay the bills" as some respondents commented – and those for whom a decent wage is a means to other ends. Here are typical responses from the former group:

- Being able to pay bills and provide my family a warm home, food and enjoyment.

- At least I have a job to go to, pays more than EI [federal government Employment Insurance] would.

The workers in the other group are in better jobs that offer non-economic rewards. While these workers also consider money to be an important, it is not the main source of motivation. Their responses are different:

- Knowing I get a good paycheck at the end of the day for a job important to society.
- It makes my living better – i.e., I can enjoy life because I make a good salary that I use to spend on activities that I like (having a house, going out for a good dinner, travelling … etc.). So I guess the answer is: Money.

While relationships with co-workers is the top-ranked reason people look forward to work, relationships with customers or clients was mentioned by about 8 per cent of respondents. These two themes illustrate how important social relationships are in today's workplaces.

Most comments included some variation of "customer satisfaction," "relationships with clients," or "dealing with the public." To elaborate, one respondent described "gratification when a customer is happy" as what makes him look forward to work. Others described the satisfaction of working with specific groups, such as children, students, seniors, patients, or young people. Still others described how their relationship with customers is a basis for rewarding work and, moreover, a successful business:

- I do telephone sales and am good at establishing relationships with my customers. They say they are calling me for counselling rather than products, but I always sell them something. I look forward to helping my customers solve problems.

Experiencing enjoyment through work is another theme, accounting for 7 per cent of all responses. Some workers are motivated at the start of their workday because they simply enjoy what they do. This enjoyment can come from the type of work itself, feeling fortunate to be in one's chosen line of work, or from the contributions one is able to make.

- I enjoy sharing the knowledge I have with my clients.
- I enjoy the buying that is part of my business.

A smaller group used even more effusive language, stating that they "love" their job or are "passionate" about what they do. However, employers should note that this high level of enthusiasm accounts for a mere 3 per cent of responses to the survey question. This despite the fact that a good number of Canadian employers want their employees to feel "emotionally invested" in their job.

Rethinking People Practices

Combing through the comments provided by Rethinking Work 2012 respondents, we also compared what these workers said with those things considered important engagement "drivers" by HR professionals, senior managers, and policy and workplace experts. What we discovered invites a rethinking of some prominent people practices.

Human resource professionals place a lot of emphasis on employee recognition programs. Yet very few respondents mentioned being recognized or valued for their contributions as the most important reasons for wanting to go to work. It's not that recognition is unimportant. Rather, the question asks for the *most* important thing, so that's the frame of reference for interpreting Figure 3.3. Furthermore, it is likely that many of our respondents get positive recognition from their peers, given the importance of good co-worker relations.

Policymakers and economists advocate more investments in learning and skills development as a route to economic growth – a recommendation we endorse in chapter 6. While these investments contribute to a more engaged and productive workforce, very few responses to the survey question (4 per cent) mentioned being able to learn, use one's education or skills, or be creative as their primary work motivator.

Only 2 per cent of responses referred to a flexible schedule or a convenient commute to and from work. Despite much publicity around telework, few respondents mentioned being able to work from home as a primary motivator. While flexible arrangements or telecommuting may be nice to have for some workers, these changes won't trump the top three work motivators described earlier. The same goes for having a healthy workplace, which very few respondents mentioned as a specific motivator for them.

Chapter 2 showed that job stress results from a lack of control over job demands. So it's revealing that only 3 per cent of responses said that having autonomy or control was the main source of work motivation. Given the high level of job stress in the Canadian workforce, we expected workers to give more emphasis to this aspect of their job. The implication for advocates of psychologically healthy workplaces is clear: more effort must go into raising awareness of the importance of these job factors for worker well-being.

Finally, having a great boss is not a big motivator. Perhaps respondents included their supervisor or manager within their network of co-workers when they identified great co-workers as a big motivator. This has implications for the future. As work becomes more collaborative, horizontal working relationships will eclipse hierarchical ones. Some traditional management functions – feedback, coaching, and professional development – will increasingly be provided by supportive co-workers.

Finally, conspicuously absent in Figure 3.3 is any mention of the American version of success. Hardly anyone in the Rethinking Work 2012 survey said what made them look forward to work each day was the opportunity to climb the career ladder, get ahead, or, put bluntly, "be successful." It seems that Canadians are inclined to define success at work in terms of doing well at challenging tasks or solving problems in ways that help others.

Making Workplaces More Motivating

Our discussion so far has highlighted the positive features of people's jobs and workplaces. But we know there's much room for improvement. About half of Rethinking Work 2012 respondents look forward to work "often" and 23 per cent rarely or not at all. So we now will outline the job and workplace changes that could lead to a more motivated workforce.

Rethinking Work 2012 asked respondents to describe one change in their job that would make them look forward to work more often. Workers are quick to identify opportunities to improve their working conditions in ways that would achieve higher engagement levels. Higher engagement, it seems, is a goal shared by both workers and employers. As for the least motivated members of the workforce, more efforts must be made to reach out to these disengaged workers. Applying some of the insights offered by engaged workers about work motivators is the place to start.

More Income and Security

Higher pay is the most frequently mentioned change that would make people look forward to work more often, accounting for 17 per cent of responses to the question (see Figure 3.4). This fits the economic picture we sketched in chapter 1 of stagnant incomes and concerns about declining living standards. That pay is the top-ranked change is a contrast to the lesser importance people gave it as a positive motivator. Why the discrepancy?

Many respondents to the question listed "more pay" or "a higher wage" with little explanation. Some of these people have already told us that they enjoy the challenge of their jobs or their co-workers or customers. So more remuneration would make them look forward to coming to work "more often." But comments by respondents who are struggling to keep up financially provide valuable insights about what's behind declining living standards. Here are some of those comments:

Figure 3.4. What job change would make you look forward to coming to work more often?

> **Q.** If you could change one thing about your job that would make you look forward to coming to work more often, what would that change be?

1.	Pay	17%
2.	Change hours or schedule	12%
3.	Better boss/management/leaders	11%
4.	Relationships/culture/work environment	8%
5.	Workload/pressure/stress	7%
6.	Job security/stability	6%
7.	Red tape/paperwork/bureaucracy/processes	6%
8.	Commute/travel time	5%
9.	Resources/staff/equipment/facilities	5%
10.	Customers/clients	3%
11.	A different role/job/field/company	3%
12.	Responsibility/autonomy/input	3%
13.	Challenging/interesting/meaningful work	2%
14.	Nothing	2%
15.	More productive coworkers	2%
16.	Recognition/feedback/appreciation	2%
17.	Benefits	1%
18.	Career advancement/development/training	1%
19.	Respect/fairness	1%
20.	Government regulation	<1%
21.	Work-life balance	<1%
22.	Healthier/safer	<1%
	Other reasons	2%
TOTAL		**100%**

Employed Canadians. Rethinking Work 2012. Based on 1,635 discrete responses provided by 1,342 survey respondents.

- A raise. It has been 11 years due to a bankruptcy restructuring.
- I used to be a computer engineer who made a decent salary. Now I make very little and scramble for clients.
- [As a single parent] I would welcome some financial security in my life.
- More money, or at least assurances that my salary will not be affected by workplace slowdowns and forced unpaid days off.
- My wage. It's not enough to sustain my family nor provide any opportunity for saving.

A closely related theme is the need for more job stability and security, accounting for 6 per cent of responses to the question. These individuals need "job security," "a steady job," "more work hours," or some variation on the theme of a steady and predictable income. By comparison, those who mentioned pay explicitly focused on the amount of income they received. But ultimately it comes down to the same problem: an inadequate income and the resulting financial difficulties. Here are temporary and contract workers describing this predicament:

- I'm jumping from temp contract to temp contract these days. Finding any kind of work that lasts longer than a few months would be awesome.
- Knowing where my next contract is coming from instead of having to worry about whether I will have work when the current job is done.
- More stability. Knowing I have a job tomorrow and the next day and the next. It is difficult with contract work to plan.
- Find a job with security and benefits and just be an employee.
- That it was permanent rather than a contract job. The uncertainty about whether my contract gets renewed is an incredible source of stress.

Some self-employed people also raised income security as a problem. They expressed frustration at slow sales, difficulties recruiting clients, or unstable revenues. While the self-employed as a group are happier in their work than employees, we must not overlook the fact that for some, being your own boss is not necessarily a ticket to financial success.

Work Schedules and Hours

Better work schedules or hours ranks second as a priority change, making up 12 per cent of all responses to the question. What workers want in this regard is more control over when, where, and how long they have to work. This takes the form of a shorter workday, fewer days in the week, two days off in a row, or a later start time. In light of the high levels of job stress and work-life imbalance we documented in chapter 2, these would be welcome changes for many workers.

Comparing the comments about the two most beneficial changes brings into sharp relief the polarized nature of twenty-first-century work. In contrast to some of the pay-related comments seen earlier, which often come from workers who have too little work, a common thread in the "schedules and hours" theme is a desire for less work. Simply put, some people don't have enough work while others have more than they want. Here are samplings of the changes that workers in long-hour jobs would like to see:

- I work terrifically long hours, and always have. I would love to have a regular work day.
- Setting specific work hours and not working past 7:00 pm.
- The ability to take days off for personal reasons without being made to feel guilty about it.
- I would like more flex-time to see my kids' events at school and I would like to work from home.

These last two comments raise the problem of how to balance work with one's personal life. For some, the way to achieve more balance is to be able to work from home, which is an important flexibility option. For others, it's having more time off work for family, personal pursuits, or community volunteering. Or as one respondent explains, less work time will provide more energy for all of life's activities:

- I think if my work and life were more in balance, I would have more energy to look forward to coming to work. But currently, the amount of time I work (40–50 hours/week) means that I'm always left drained of energy to deal with the rest of my life – so I'm occasionally short on enthusiasm to go to work each day. If I were working less (e.g. part/time or maybe only 30 hours/week) I'd have time for everything else in my life and I'd look forward to it more.

And then there's shift work, from which a small number of respondents desperately want to escape. As two shift workers put it, "I hate shift work!" and "No more midnight shifts!"

Better Management

A common explanation among human resources professionals for turnover is that employees leave bosses, not jobs. So it's no surprise that more than 1 in 10 of the suggested changes have to do with better management. A number of respondents provided concise solutions in this regard, as in "a new boss," "better management," or "less supervision."

These cryptic statements target an employee's manager or management in general but don't outline specific changes that would lead to better people leadership in the organization. Other comments offer more detailed descriptions of the qualities employees want in a manager:

- A better manager that I could trust and that has the experience, skills and respect for employees to build a good work environment.
- I wish the senior management truly understood and valued the capacity of the employees and the ramifications of decisions that impact the employees but not them.

- I would like to report to someone who is more understanding and sympathetic.
- Less micro-management. Give me a job and let me do it without management over-supervising.
- Management that truly walked the talk about caring for their staff.
- A different supervisor, one that inspires me to do the best I can do and expects more from me.

It's also useful to know a respondent's organizational context, and some provided this. Here's what a teacher told us: having the principal realize that her controlling, micromanaging techniques, while successful in certain situations, greatly hinders an overall confident, successful, and productive environment. And a construction supervisor acknowledged an important need in his industry: "I'd like to see more emphasis placed on training for supervisors."

The last comment reveals awareness among some managers that they require better skills to succeed in their role. What management skills might that training provide? To answer the question, we need look no further than the changes suggested by respondents, which have to do with goal-setting, communication, feedback, integrity, empathy, mentorship, and trustworthiness – all basic people leadership skills.

Other Suggested Changes

The top three changes offered by our respondents – higher pay, improved hours or schedules, and better bosses – account for 40 per cent of all changes mentioned. Two additional changes each account for just over 7 per cent of the total: relationships and culture, and reducing workloads and stress.

Answers about workplace relationships and culture reflect the absence of the "great co-workers" who are a source of work motivation for many. Typical in this regard are calls for "less office politics," "more cooperation," "a more positive and supportive atmosphere," and "no back-biting or bickering." To further illustrate how relationships and culture can be improved, consider what some respondents answered:

- A kinder, more respectful workplace.
- A more social and friendly atmosphere with my co-workers.
- A more supportive work environment among my managers and colleagues.
- Attitude adjustments: More willingness to work together for the company goals.

Suggestions for reducing workloads and job stress get right to the point, such as "less pressure," "less extra work," "realistic deadlines," "reasonable expectations," "fewer demands," and "less stress." The specific changes that would make work less demanding vary according to the work setting. Here we compare a small business owner with an employee in a large healthcare organization:

- A full time assistant would be very helpful but unfortunately I cannot afford one. I have, however, just entered into an arrangement with another broker, which will allow me to use his back office for most of my "grunt work," which should make my life a lot easier and me much more productive.
- For [a large regional health service] to become more organized and to properly hire the right amount of people instead of having to do 4 peoples' jobs every day.

Other responses about changes to reduce work demands include the following:

- Less impacted by the current economic situation, allowing for adequate staffing and a more reasonable/defined workload.
- If I could just do my job and not have to take work home every night and go to work on the weekends too.
- That the company would stop pressuring us to sell, sell, sell, especially when it is not always appropriate for the clients.

Job security and stability is another theme. Recalling the concerns that labour market analysts have raised about precarious work, it is indeed interesting that only 6 per cent of all answers to this survey question raise this issue. For some workers, low pay and job insecurity go hand-in-hand. Yet for others, the lack of predictable and stable employment is the problem. For this latter group, a permanent job with predictable hours is a necessity:

- More stability. Knowing I have a job tomorrow and the next day and the next. It is difficult with contract work to plan beyond the short-term.
- That it is a permanent rather than a contract job. The uncertainty about whether my contract gets renewed is an incredible source of stress.

Reflecting on the same issue, several self-employed business owners said that for them, financial security would require more revenue and more customers, as well as clients who pay on time.

Just about as many comments (about 6 per cent of the total) had to do with an entirely different workplace issue: too much bureaucracy. Comments such as "fewer meetings," "fewer regulations," "fewer memos," and "less paperwork" reveal the obstacles that some worker face trying to do their jobs. Here's a sampling of some the changes that would address the problem of bureaucracy:

- "Administrivia" should be handled by clerical staff. The paperwork is daunting: forms, fee collection, notices, newsletters on top of all my marking, attendance, report cards!
- Reduce the amount of poorly conceived plans or programs I am expected to implement.
- Better organizational supports in place to help me do excellent work.

In sum, the seven change themes cover a wide range of workplace issues: pay, schedules, bosses, relationships, stress, security, and bureaucracy. Together, they account for two-thirds of all suggestions by Rethinking Work 2012 respondents that would make them look forward to coming to work more often.

The remaining themes cover issues as diverse as less commuting time and better equipment to benefits and career advancement. HR professionals will be struck by how little emphasis workers place on improvements in benefits, recognition, career development, and training as inducements to be more deeply engaged in their jobs. These programs are a focus of most HR departments today. Yet their contributions to work motivation may be minimal. Finally, it's revealing that a number of the least engaged workers took the time to let us know that nothing would make them look forward to work more.

Comparing the Two Lists

It's useful to compare the lists of biggest motivators and needed changes to see how some of the same themes end up with different rankings. Because respondents were at least moderately engaged already, it's understandable that the most important reasons they look forward to their jobs – good co-workers, challenging and interesting work – do not receive much mention as needing change. However, some of the lesser-mentioned motivators are related to the top-ranked changes.

Pay stands out in this regard because it is the fourth-ranked contributor to daily work motivation yet is the most frequently mentioned change needed. This is consistent with research in industrial psychology going back to Herzberg, which suggests that pay rarely is a direct source of motivation but will sow dissatisfaction if it is deficient. Flexibility is far down the list of factors contributing to work motivation, yet it is one of the top-ranked changes respondents would like to see. The same goes for bosses, who are barely mentioned as the main reason people look forward to work, yet better management is a recommended change. While very few respondents mentioned work-life balance specifically, we have seen that this was the desired result for many who want improved hours and schedules. Likewise, respect and fairness don't receive much attention on their own but are related to the larger themes of better management and more positive workplace relationships.

Bear in mind that these suggestions fit the parameters set by Rethinking Work 2012's questions about work motivation. The first question identifies those things that have the biggest positive impact on workers' daily motivation; the second question builds on this by asking for one improvement in a worker's job that would make them feel more motivated about work. This sequence of questions has identified key influences on engagement as seen through the eyes of our survey respondents. To reiterate an earlier point, we gave workers an opportunity to have a voice on this important issue – and they now have spoken.

Conclusion

Having listened to the many workers who described what motivates them to go to work, we can appreciate that the path to better jobs and workplaces takes us back to basics. Workers have told us that it's about the people they work with, the content of their work, and feeling they are helping others. And now that Canadians have shared their views on the major changes needed to improve work motivation, it's clear that decent pay, better hours and schedules, and sound people management also are basic requirements for a more engaged workforce.

The quality of work life has eroded during the past decade and, as a result, workers are less enthusiastic about going to work. To reverse these trends, employers need to pay more attention to ensuring that the preconditions for a satisfied, motivated, and engaged workforce are firmly in place. Employers are taking steps to strengthen the people-performance link, as they recognize that achieving higher levels of performance depends on a healthy and engaged workforce. The Rethinking Work findings presented in this chapter reinforce the importance of moving vigorously down this path. The kind of job that inspires Canadians to want to go to work each day – great co-workers, challenging tasks, being able to help people, and decent pay – also provides lots of opportunity for people to succeed in their role. Crucial in this regard is a culture that values employees, leaders who are committed to developing capable and healthy employees, and support systems that help people to excel in their jobs.[19]

Let's now tie together our previous discussion, in chapter 2, of worker well-being with these new insights about work engagement. A blueprint for the future of work must be grounded on the understanding that worker well-being and engagement are intertwined. For employers, this means finding synergies between the employee wellness initiatives discussed in the last chapter and strategies to make workplaces and jobs more engaging. Workers who feel energized to go to work and engaged while there will experience greater well-being than co-workers who are unmotivated and disengaged. Engaged employees have challenging jobs and excellent relationships with co-workers, supervisors, and customers or clients. These very same factors are essential for reducing workplace stress, improving work-life balance, and making jobs more challenging and interesting.

By inviting workers to tell us what motivates them in their jobs, we have added valuable behavioural insights into the sources of engagement. But we must not stop here if we want to fully comprehend the social and psychological dynamics of Canada's workforce in the post-recession era. To talk about motivation raises the question, why are workers energized by certain features of their work and not others? The next chapter provides answers, delving into what people value most in a job.

4 What Canadians Value in a Job

I'd like to be able to look back and identify places where my involvement meant something; something is going to be better at the end of it … It's about being able to connect to the bigger picture. Meaningful work for me is definitely being in a learning community. Exposed to new ideas and new information and new skills. It's work I can be proud of and that helps me increase the community of people I have around me with like-minded ideas.[1]

Brenna Atnikov

Brenna Atnikov had worked for more than a decade doing community development in Calgary and abroad. But she was searching for a way to make a bigger contribution, putting into action more of the ideas and knowledge from her BA in human and social development and master's in social work. So in 2012 she launched her own consulting business, Raven Conversations, specializing in stakeholder engagement. Brenna explains her career move this way: "for me, the way of figuring out meaningful work is figuring out what I am most curious about, and then participating in activity and work that helps me figure out the answers to those questions."[2] Brenna figured out that the route to meaningful work for her was through independent consulting in her hometown of Calgary. This career shift reflects Brenna's quest to do what she cares about most – helping others achieve positive change in their community.

Brenna's story illustrates the importance of work values. Ask yourself: What do I want most in a job? Is it money, security, personal fulfilment, making a difference, using your education, or something else? This question pinpoints your personal priorities for work. Not all Canadians are fortunate enough to have career options – think of the part-time barista who aspires to a kindergarten teaching career at a time when schools aren't hiring. Still, the job features we value provide guideposts for our work life.

In this chapter, we make the case that work values provide important insights into what makes people happy, motivated, and productive on the job. Often overlooked in discussions of work in Canada, values help define what's needed to achieve personal well-being and economic prosperity. What we value in a job reflects our basic wants, needs, and human potential. Later in the book, the work values we document here contribute to our vision of the ideal job and a blueprint for achieving a better working future.

Employers' HR policies and practices make assumptions about what's valued, often based on no evidence at all. Rarely do corporate employee surveys document values – an oversight that this chapter may convince employers to rectify. We contend that knowing what employees value provides employers with a useful yardstick for assessing how well people's jobs measure up to what they want. Addressing any gaps in this regard is an effective strategy for improving workforce well-being and engagement.

Our values perspective has important implications for employers and policymakers responding to a changing workforce. Work values have remained remarkably stable, despite public concerns about the negative economic and social trends in this era of arrested progress. While there are some big differences in work values based on workers' demographics, our evidence deflates claims that there is a huge generational values divide. In fact, there are wider differences in work values between women and men than across age groups. Work values vary depending on an individual's location in the labour market, but not in ways that the "good jobs–bad jobs" model would predict. More important are the distinct values held by well-educated workers – values which point to the kinds of jobs required for a strong knowledge-based economy.

We arrive at these and other conclusions by using the Rethinking Work 2004 and 2012 surveys to create a profile of 16 core work values.[3] Our analysis addresses four basic questions:

1 How have Canadians' work values changed since the early 2000s?
2 What's most important to Canadian workers in a job today?
3 How do work values vary across different groups in the workforce?
4 Do people's jobs meet their expectations as defined by their work values?

Revisiting the Meaning of Work

This chapter addresses an age-old topic: What is the meaning of work? Throughout history, humans have been fascinated by this existential question. Every civilization has articulated its own values on work, labelling some tasks as desirable, others as reviled. The ancient Greeks viewed physical work as a curse, which provided a justification for slavery and left the ruling classes free to leisurely pursue politics, the arts, and philosophy. Calvinists in pre-industrial Europe viewed hard work and deferred gratification as godly virtues – beliefs that contributed to the development of capitalism. And during the Great Depression of the 1930s, psychologists learned much about the importance of work for personal identity and well-being by studying what happens when unemployment deprives a person of the opportunity to work.[4]

The twenty-first century has renewed discussions about how the meaning of work is evolving. British writer Alain De Botton's philosophical investigation of the meaning of work took him to docks, biscuit factories, and science labs. He asks, "When does a job feel meaningful?" Here's his answer: "Whenever it allows us to generate delight or reduce suffering in others. Though we are often taught to think of ourselves as inherently selfish, the longing to act meaningfully in our work seems just as stubborn a part of our make-up as our appetite for status or money."[5] But as De Botton observes, a higher purpose in work isn't the exclusive preserve of surgeons or scientists. Even biscuit makers see how the snacks they produce contribute to society, if only in small ways.

Human resource experts and psychologists emphasize that as we find meaning in our work, we become motivated, inspired, and defined as unique human beings.[6] Dave and Wendy Ulrich, in their book *The Why of Work*, distinguish between work's inherent value, which gives meaning to life, and its market value, which provides tangible benefits to customers and shareholders. Companies that offer both kinds of meaning are "abundant organizations," because they provide "a work setting in which individuals coordinate their aspirations and actions to create meaning for themselves, value for stakeholders, and hope for humanity at large."[7] Doing meaningful work leads to more engaged and productive employees, more committed customers, and stronger financial results.

Economist Richard Florida argues that the rise of a creative class in the twenty-first-century knowledge economy has shifted work values.[8] According to Florida, the "creative class" consists of educated professional, technical, and artistic workers. This new class drives an information-based economy with its energy, ideas, and innovations. They value individuality, meritocracy (they are achievers who work hard to get ahead), diversity, and openness. Motivated by more than money, creative people won't settle for work that is "just a job." Some knowledge workers actively prefer freelance "gigs" because of the freedom, independence, and space to be creative. Well-educated creatives (like Brenna Atnikov) have the advantage of choice.

As work values evolve so do the sources of motivation. Writer Daniel Pink reconsiders the centuries-old "carrot and stick" thinking on what motivates workers. Now it is recognized that motivation primarily depends on "our innate need to direct our own lives, to learn and create new things, and to do better by ourselves and our world."[9] For Pink, this boils down to three principles of motivation, which essentially are values: autonomy (self-direction), mastery (get better at what we do), and purpose (be part of something larger). These three principles resonate for today's well-educated knowledge workers. This has work redesign implications. For example, Pink argues that organizations now have to be built not just for profit maximization, but for "purpose maximization" as well.[10]

So as you can see, we have waded into the sprawling terrain of what work means to us and why we are motivated to do it in the first place. It comes down to what we value. History shows that the values associated with work have been debated and reshaped through the centuries as societies evolved. There are a few nuggets we can take from commentators such as De Botton, the Ulriches, Florida, and Pink. First, the meaning we derive from our work defines who we are as humans. Second, meaningful work today can inspire us to pursue bigger goals and ideals tomorrow, for our own benefit and that of society.

Canadians' Changing Work Values

This discussion raises a key question: How have Canadians' work values been changing? In the past decade, the global economy has been transformed dramatically. During the first few years of this century, Canadians were experiencing one of the strongest economic booms in the post–Second World War era. Then came the economic tsunami of a global financial crisis and a deep recession. For many people, their job and economic circumstances changed between 2004 and 2012. How did this affect their work priorities? Would a tough labour market, corporate cutbacks, government belt tightening, and first-hand experiences watching family members and friends deal with job loss give people cause to reconsider their career goals and, more fundamentally, their work values?

We track changing values by comparing results from Rethinking Work 2004 and 2012 (see Figures 4.1 and 4.2). Both surveys asked respondents how important each of 16 basic job characteristics would be in deciding which job to take if they were looking for a new job

Figure 4.1. Work values in 2004 and 2012

Q. If you were looking for a new job today, how important would each of the following characteristics be in deciding which job to choose?

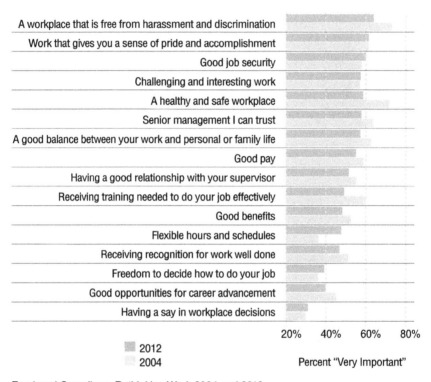

Employed Canadians, Rethinking Work 2004 and 2012.

today. Putting the two sets of results side-by-side, we are able to identify patterns of change and stability in work values during a period of economic boom and bust.

The biggest downward shifts in values occurred in three areas that have drawn considerable attention from employers and governments in the past decade: workplace health and safety, training, and a work climate free from harassment and discrimination. A couple of plausible explanations come to mind of why less value is placed on these factors in 2012. Employers may have made tangible

Figure 4.2. Changes in what's considered "very important" in a job between 2004 and 2012

Job characteristic	Percentage-point change 2004-2012
A healthy and safe workplace	-14
Receiving training needed to do your job effectively	-11
A workplace that is free from harassment and discrimination	-10
Senior management I can trust	-7
A good balance between your work and personal or family life	-7
Good opportunities for career advancement	-7
Good benefits	-6
Good pay	-5
Receiving recognition for work well done	-3
Having a good relationship with your supervisor	-3
Work that gives you a sense of pride and accomplishment	0
Challenging and interesting work	1
Good job security	2
Having a say in workplace decisions	3
Freedom to decide how to do your job	5
Flexible hours and schedules	11

-15% -10% -5%   0   5% 10% 15%

Employed Canadians, Rethinking Work 2004 and 2012.

improvements to these job features. If so, today's workers may be more inclined to de-emphasize such values, knowing they are more readily addressed. Or in a post-recession labour market workers may have diminished expectations, particularly about health and safety. Despite the initiatives we described in chapter 2 to promote psychologically healthy and safe workplaces, it is clear that governments, employers, and non-profit groups need to work harder to convince workers that these are critical workplace goals.

Recall from chapter 2 that work-life balance became more difficult to achieve between 2004 and 2012. Yet the proportion of respondents who place high importance on achieving good work-life balance declined during this period. Perhaps workers are adapting to the reality of more-demanding work and mobile technologies that keep them electronically tethered to their desk. However, advances in mobile and information technology – think iPhones, cloud computing, and "sharing economy" apps and collaborative software – can provide practical solutions to work-life balance through various forms of virtual work. The big increase in importance placed on flexible hours and schedules between 2004 and 2012 suggests that a growing number of workers see the potential to turn these new technologies to their advantage.

There are several other small but notable changes. In 2012, job security is slightly more important for workers, and benefits and pay slightly less. These changes are expected in a post-recession era as people become more willing to trade off better compensation for a steady income. Furthermore, the sorts of intrinsic work values that figured prominently in our discussion of motivation in the previous chapter show little change. In 2012 there was only slightly more importance given to having a job that provides challenge, decision input, and autonomy. This could reflect an aging workforce, because as we explain later, these are the sorts of things older knowledge workers look for in a job.

What's Important in a Job Today

For the rest of the chapter, we analyse results from the Rethinking Work 2012 survey in order to better understand post-recession work values (see Figure 4.3). What stands out is the priority placed on four job features: having a workplace free from harassment and discrimination; work that provides a sense of pride and accomplishment; good job security; and challenging and interesting work. For about 60 per cent of Rethinking Work respondents, these are very important considerations if they were looking for a new job today.

Figure 4.3. Work values in 2012

Q. If you were looking for a new job today, how important would each of the following characteristics be in deciding which job to choose?

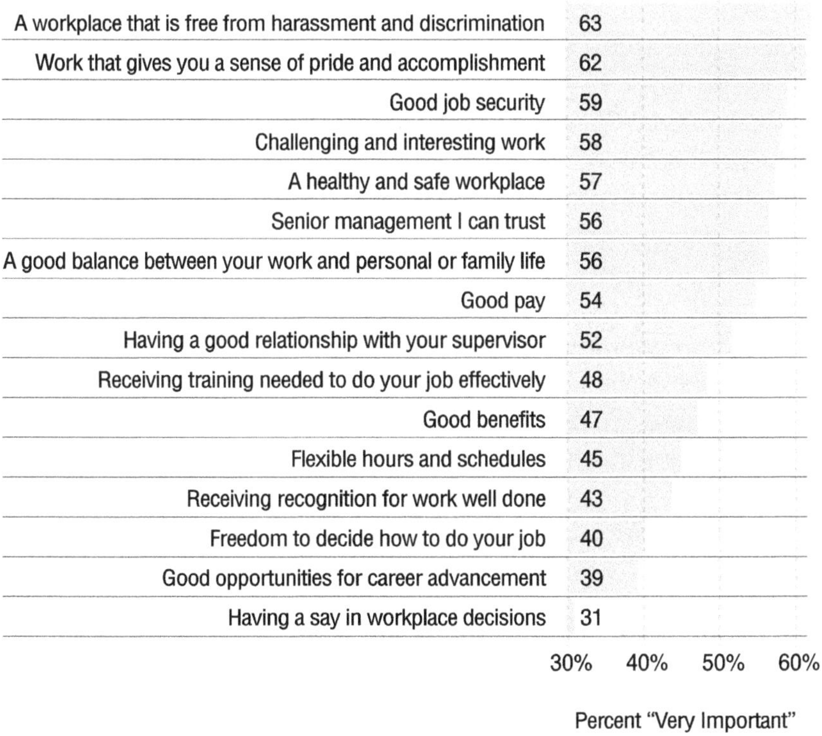

A workplace that is free from harassment and discrimination	63
Work that gives you a sense of pride and accomplishment	62
Good job security	59
Challenging and interesting work	58
A healthy and safe workplace	57
Senior management I can trust	56
A good balance between your work and personal or family life	56
Good pay	54
Having a good relationship with your supervisor	52
Receiving training needed to do your job effectively	48
Good benefits	47
Flexible hours and schedules	45
Receiving recognition for work well done	43
Freedom to decide how to do your job	40
Good opportunities for career advancement	39
Having a say in workplace decisions	31

30%   40%   50%   60%

Percent "Very Important"

Employed Canadians, Rethinking Work 2012.

Interestingly, there is only one economic aspect – job security – and it is considered more important than either pay or benefits. This may well be a reflection of a labour market in which work has become more precarious.

The strong desire for a workplace free from harassment and discrimination ties in with the comments workers provided in chapter 3 about how great co-workers are what makes them look forward to work. Stated positively, this value has to do with respectful relationships and fair treatment. These conditions are essential for a psychologically healthy workplace and for the positive co-worker relations that workers described earlier.

Indeed, it's a good sign that 63 per cent of respondents consider a harassment- and discrimination-free workplace to be very important. After all, positive workplace relations are the number one motivator for workers, as we saw in chapter 3. Recent initiatives such as the National Standard of Canada for Psychological Health and Safety in the Workplaces, discussed earlier, have heightened awareness about the harm that can be caused by bullying, harassment, discrimination, and other destructive behaviours. Canada's multicultural workforce has brought systemic discrimination against immigrants and visible minorities out into the open. Decades of policies and programs aimed at achieving greater gender equality have contributed to the fairer and more respectful treatment of women in workplaces. We now see that Canadian workers' values support further actions to address these problems.

Two other top-ranked values emphasize the intrinsic nature of the work performed, which as we've seen are also important motivators. A challenging and interesting job is a source of pride and feelings of accomplishment at the end of the workday. But so too is being recognized for your contributions. The same goes for having autonomy in how you do your job, a say in decisions, and career opportunities. Yet these are the least important things that respondents would look for in a new job. Indeed, about 40 per cent or less consider these characteristics to be "very important" in a job.

Our evidence lends additional support to the argument made by Daniel Pink, Richard Florida, and HR experts that people today want purpose and meaning from their work. Chapter 3 confirmed that meaningful work is a big motivator. But if this is the case, then why don't these same workers place similar importance on being recognized for their contributions or having the autonomy that allows them to find purpose and meaning? Among knowledge workers, we would expect that autonomy and decision input are an integral part of creative work. We will resolve some of these apparent contradictions later, when we look more closely at how specific demographic and employment groups are defined by distinct clusters of values.

The values ranking in Figure 4.3 has practical implications for employers. Despite all the efforts by HR departments to introduce recognition programs and to train supervisors and managers to provide this sort of informal feedback on a regular basis, it seems that employees are less interested in recognition per se than they are in getting a sense of personal pride and accomplishment from what they actually do in their job. Recognition programs and practices need to be recast to reinforce this sense of pride and accomplishment for both individual employees and for teams.

And a final point for both employers and policymakers to contemplate: To the extent that knowledge workers power the twenty-first-century economy, surely they require more latitude to decide how to do their jobs and should have opportunities to participate in workplace decisions. However, these two job features are considered "very important" by fewer than 40 per cent of our survey respondents. Also recall from chapter 3 that these two features are not important sources of work motivation. Perhaps this suggests an acceptance of deeply engrained top-down decision-making in larger organizations – a barrier to better jobs to be sure. Yet as we also pointed out in chapter 3, when employees are fully engaged, they experience a sense of ownership over their work and take initiative – which is hard to do unless autonomy and input are designed into their job.

Generational Differences in Work Values

Daniel Pink argues that as aging baby boomers face the end of their careers, and their own mortality, they will want more meaning from their work. Most of all, this has to do with "unrealized dreams" in their quest for purpose.[11] With huge numbers of boomers becoming seniors, we can expect more focus on purpose in work.

Pink's comment about purpose-seeking baby boomers raises the issue of generational differences in work values. This topic has captured lots of media attention and become something of a pre-occupation in management and HR circles. Most comparisons focus on the three generations in the workforce today: baby boomers (born between 1946 and 1965), Generation X (born between 1966 and 1979), and millennials or Generation Y (the children of baby boomers, born between 1980 and 1995).[12]

We devote the next chapter to generational differences in the workplace. For now, we focus on the work values of Gen X, millennials, and baby boomers. An accurate values profile of an increasingly age-diverse workforce will, in our view, help employers develop more effective recruitment, retention, and engagement strategies.

Our evidence shows that generational differences in work values often are overblown and misunderstood. Other research studies support this conclusion. As each generation ages and progresses through life stages, it loses some of the very features that labelled it unique in the first place. Historian Doug Owram's fascinating study of the baby boom generation shows that the "youth revolution" of the 1960s was over by 1975, "with the front edge of the baby boom approaching the magic age of thirty."[13] That's when it was time to get a job, so youth's anti-establishment values quickly ebbed.

Commentators today point out how millennials (also called Generation Y) differ from Gen Xers and baby boomers.[14] Millennials – children of baby boomers and the first to grow up with digital technologies and the Internet – are following the Gen Xers into the workforce. The arrival of millennials in workplaces has stirred up speculation about how they will shake things up. However, a study of millennials' impact on workplaces in 44 countries by PricewaterhouseCoopers (PwC), a management consultancy, discovered that these young workers want similar things from work as older generations, including steady employment with a few employers.[15] This counters one of the myths about millennial workers being serial job hoppers, unwilling to form lasting ties with one employer.

No question, millennials bring into the workplace a unique set of skills, interests, and experiences. These young people are information technology (IT) savvy, actively social networking, globally

oriented, and willing to travel – attributes that can benefit employers. For example, consumer electronics retailer Best Buy asked an
IT consulting firm to price a new employee Internet portal. When
a quote for several million came back, a group of young employees
assembled an informal team of developers and made the portal for
$250,000. Facing falling sales and profits, Best Buy is now looking
for novel ideas from the millennial generation employees to apply
the latest technology to marketing and sales.[16] This example illustrates younger workers' IT skills and an entrepreneurial flair, not
fundamentally different work values.

In short, we can't stereotype generations. A reminder of this is a
definitive study of work values by University of Alberta researchers. They compared Edmonton high school seniors in 1985 (Gen X)
and 1996 (Gen Y, or millennials), tracking how each graduating
classes' values changed between ages 18 and 25.[17] Both cohorts
highly valued intrinsic and extrinsic work rewards at age 18 when
they graduated. By age 25, the importance of intrinsic rewards had
increased somewhat for both groups. The importance of extrinsic
rewards increased only for the 1996 graduates, mainly because of
the more difficult job market they faced – not because of a distinct
Gen Y mindset about work. Furthermore, young people's work values change during the transition from school to work, regardless of
when they were born.

We agree with the academic researchers that so-called generational differences in work attitudes have more to do with a person's
stage in the life cycle than when they were born. A key insight from
Rethinking Work 2012 is that people's work values do vary by age,
but in more nuanced ways than a generational perspective suggests.

We analysed age-based variations in values by looking for differences between young (under age 35) and older (65 and over) workers, as well as three age groups in between. Our main comparison is
between the under 35s and the 55- to 64-year-olds – millennials and
boomers respectively (see Figure 4.4). The age group in between
represents Gen X, many of whom are mid-career and raising families. While most other analysts lump all baby boomers together, we

Figure 4.4. Millennial and baby boomer differences in job characteristics

Job characteristic	Percentage-point difference between 55-64 and <35 age groups
Senior management I can trust	21
Having a say in workplace decisions	20
Freedom to decide how to do your job	17
A healthy and safe workplace	14
Work that gives you a sense of pride and accomplishment	12
Having a good relationship with your supervisor	11
Good job security	11
Flexible hours and schedules	11
A workplace that is free from harassment and discrimination	9
Good benefits	5
Challenging and interesting work	4
A good balance between your work and personal or family life	2
Receiving training needed to do your job effectively	1
Receiving recognition for work well done	1
Good pay	-1
Good opportunities for career advancement	-18

-20% -15% -10% -5%   0   5% 10% 15% 20%

Employed Canadians, Rethinking Work 2012.

believe it is important to separately examine the 65-plus group because they make up a growing share of the workforce.

There are no statistically significant age group differences on 5 of the 16 work values we measure.[18] Workers of all ages place similar importance on having a workplace free from harassment and discrimination, job security, good relations with their supervisor, training, and recognition.

However, on five other values, there are notable differences between those under age 35 and their baby boom co-workers ages 55 to 64. Compared to younger workers, those aged 55 to 64 place far more importance on being able to trust senior management, a healthy and safe workplace, job autonomy, and having a say in workplace decisions. In contrast, younger workers place more importance on career advancement, which stands to reason given they are still in the early stages of their working lives.

HR professionals may find it particularly interesting that there are some differences in the work values held by 55- to 64-year-old workers and those 65 years and older. That's why it is important to distinguish between early and late baby boomers. The 65-plus group places greater importance on being able to trust senior management, job autonomy, and having a say. Employers who want to retain or recruit older workers will need to take these value differences into consideration. Rather than just trying to understand the aspirations of younger workers, employers now must pay attention to how values may change across all age groups, in particular the fast-growing 65-plus group.

Some values – particularly work-life balance, good pay, and benefits – are directly related to a person's stage in the life cycle. Gen Xers (35- to 44-year-olds) place by far the highest importance on having work-life balance (64 per cent consider it very important, well above the workforce average of 56 per cent). To explain this finding, we must consider Gen X's family situation. They are at a stage in life when raising children and paying a mortgage are the priority. Compared to other age groups, 35- to 44-year-olds are most likely to have partners or be married (75 per cent, compared to 46 per cent of those under age 35). And two-thirds of individuals (66 per cent) in this group have children under age 18 living in their household, in contrast with one-third of the 45- to 54-year-old age group. By contrast, millennials and 55- to 64-year-old baby boomers place the same importance on work-life balance, with about half considering it very important.

Flexible hours and schedules are more highly valued by boomers (55 and older) than by members of the millennial generation (under age 35). Furthermore, 35- 44-year-olds (Gen X) place the same importance on flexibility as do the boomers. Again, these value differences reflect a worker's life-stage needs. As just noted, Gen Xers are most likely to have young children to look after, while boomers may be providing care and support to elderly parents and, in some cases, grandchildren. And they may also seek flexible work arrangements as a transition into retirement.

Women and Men Value Different Job Features

We'll now look beyond age as a demographic influence on work values. Despite all the media attention given to generational differences in work values, there actually are more significant differences between men and women than between age groups. We reached this conclusion after discovering that men and women have statistically significant differences on 12 of 16 work values we measured in Rethinking Work 2012, compared with 10 among age groups.[19]

This should not surprise us. Social scientists have documented many ways in which men and women have different attitudes towards social, economic, and political issues.[20] The World Values Survey, perhaps the most extensive source of public opinion data, shows that there is a gender gap in political attitudes, with women tending to be more "liberal" or "left" than men on key issues, from taxation and the military to welfare and abortion. And in Canada, EKOS polling on federal election voting intentions found that women were less likely to vote Conservative than men.[21]

According to Rethinking Work 2012, women place more value than men on all but four of the work values tracked in EKOS polls (see Figure 4.5). There are no statistically significant gender differences when it comes to job autonomy (freedom to decide how to do your job), career advancement opportunities, good pay, and having challenging and interesting work. Women more highly value all other job features than do men on. However, these gender differences aren't huge. Indeed, it would overstate the case to claim that "men are from Mars and women are from Venus" when it comes to work values, to borrow the title of a popular book on couples' relationships.[22]

Figure 4.5. Gender differences in job characteristics

Job characteristic	Percentage-point difference between women and men

Job characteristic		
Freedom to decide how to do your job	1	
Good opportunities for career advancement	2	
Good pay	3	
Challenging and interesting work	4	
Having a say in workplace decisions	6	
Flexible hours and schedules	9	
Receiving recognition for work well done	9	
Work that gives you a sense of pride and accomplishment	11	
Good benefits	10	
Senior management I can trust	13	
Having a good relationship with your supervisor	13	
Receiving training needed to do your job effectively	13	
A good balance between your work and personal or family life	13	
A healthy and safe workplace	13	
Good job security	19	
A workplace that is free from harassment and discrimination	24	
	0 5% 10% 15% 20%	

Employed Canadians, Rethinking Work 2012.

Still, there is a consistent pattern that employers and HR professionals should be aware of when planning policies and practices. Women place greater importance than men do on having flexible hours/schedules and work-life balance, two issues that more directly impact the lives of women. After all, women still shoulder more family responsibilities. The biggest gender gap in work values has to do with a workplace free from harassment and discrimination. The fact that almost three-quarters of the women we surveyed place high importance on what essentially is a respectful and inclusive work environment – compared with half of the men surveyed – surely reflects the reality that it is women, more so than men, who bear the brunt of these uncivil behaviours in today's workplaces.

Several other gender differences stand out. Women seeking a new job place greater importance than men do on training, benefits, and job security. There also are less tangible aspects of a job which women view as more important than men. These reflect the nature of the work itself or the work environment and include recognition, supervisor relations, feeling a sense of pride and accomplishment, trust, a healthy and safe workplace, and decision input.

The gender differences in work values we have outlined fit what is already known about the gender gap in social and political attitudes. Women seem to favour the more intrinsic and, we might say, humanistic aspects of a job. Broadly, this fits political preferences, with women emphasizing social issues and men being more concerned about the economy. The one possible exception in this regard is the greater value women place on job security. On one hand, this could be interpreted as an emphasis on the economics of a job, given that there are proportionally more women part-timers and temporary workers. Yet on the other hand, it suggests that women are less willing to accept the risk of job loss than are men. This latter interpretation certainly fits with the overall gender difference in risk behaviour, with men taking greater risks than women in many areas of life.

Knowledge Workers' Distinct Values

In chapter 2 we discussed the concerns expressed by some analysts about the spread of low-quality precarious work. We countered that the post-recession labour market has more complex and nuanced patterns of inequality when both economic and non-economic factors are considered. We expand that argument here by asking a new question: What does a person's labour market location tell us about their work values? To answer, we compared the values of four labour market groups: self-employed; full-time permanent employees; part-timers; and those in precarious jobs (temporary, contract, and seasonal).

These four labour market groups place the same importance on work-life balance and deriving pride and accomplishment from one's work. The self-employed put high value on autonomy, which they likely have more of than employees. And self-employed and contract workers consider flexible schedules and hours to be more important than employees do. This suggests that some people choose to be their own boss or a freelancer because of the flexibility these work options offer. What's also intriguing is that precarious workers place the least value on job security, benefits, and career advancement. Have these workers lowered their expectations about those things contract work doesn't provide? Or did they choose this type of work because it fits their value scheme? After considering the demographic characteristics of precarious workers (age, gender, education), we tend towards the latter explanation.

To pursue this point about the role of demographics, education is especially important for explaining differences in work values. As people acquire more education, their career goals and job priorities change. Put simply, they raise their aspirations (see Figure 4.6).[23] Compared with those who have a high school diploma or less, university-educated workers place more importance on job autonomy and doing work that is challenging and interesting. These intrinsic features of a job may be viewed as luxuries by those whose work world is limited to low-paid, unstable, and dead-end jobs.

In the future there will be more well-educated workers and more knowledge-intensive industries – two trends that make it especially urgent to make work more intrinsically rewarding. Now we have solid Canadian evidence that backs up what commentators such as Richard Florida and Daniel Pink argue about the types of job conditions that appeal to knowledge workers. And we also have a prediction: as Canadians' educational levels continue to rise, so too will expectations for intrinsically rewarding jobs.

Figure 4.6. Differences by education level in job characteristics

Job characteristic	Percentage-point difference between university-educated and high-school-educated workers

Job characteristic	Value
Challenging and interesting work	16
Freedom to decide how to do your job	14
Good benefits	-7
A healthy and safe workplace	-11
Receiving training needed to do your job effectively	-15
Good pay	-16

-15%   -10%   -5%   0   5%   10%   15%

Employed Canadians, Rethinking Work 2012.

Turning to the economics of work, the highly educated also are better paid. This is because of the well-documented pay-offs from investing in a university education, measured by substantially increased lifetime earnings – a point we take up in chapter 6. Among survey respondents, 36 per cent of those with a high school diploma or less reported an annual personal income of $60,000 or higher, compared with 55 per cent of those with a bachelor's degree and 65 per cent of those with a graduate degree. Furthermore, more of the university-educated are permanent full-time employees, the sort of jobs that provide benefits. In other words, knowledge workers can afford to downplay the importance of job economics.

Similarly, other job features have become part of the standard employment package for knowledge workers in secure full-time employment. This adds another dimension to inequality. The better-educated Rethinking Work 2012 respondents place somewhat less importance on a healthy and safe workplace and training than less-educated workers do. Again, better-educated workers may already have these conditions and so end up taking them for granted.

Immigrants: A Source of Work Value Diversity

Today, workplaces have multiple sources of diversity.[24] Canada is among the most multicultural societies in the world, with a growing mix of ethnic, racial, religious, and linguistic characteristics in its population. The nation increasingly will rely on immigrants and the children of immigrants to meet future labour demands as baby boomers head into retirement.

Immigration is another demographic trend reshaping the workforce. Most of the workforce growth in the first decade of this century was due to immigration. The main sources of immigration are now Asia, particularly China and the Indian subcontinent, so most immigrants also are visible minorities. Statistics Canada estimates that the proportion of the Canadian population that are immigrants will increase from 20 per cent (in 2006) to 26 per cent by 2031, and by this time half of the population of Toronto and 44 per cent of Vancouver's will be immigrants.[25]

Despite the importance of immigrants to Canada's current and future workforce, their work values have received remarkably little attention. Rethinking Work 2012 sheds much-needed light on how immigrants value the 16 job characteristics we have been examining.

Because immigration is such an important source of diversity in our society and workforce, we might expect large value differences between recent arrivals and their Canadian-born co-workers. After all, immigrants' life experiences, cultural traditions, language, ethnic identity, and religion set them apart from the non-immigrant population. However, Canadian-born and immigrant workers share broadly similar work values. Overall, the differences that we do find are less pronounced than those based on age, gender, and education. Only 5 of 16 work values are significantly different between immigrants and non-immigrants, fewer than we found when comparing other demographic characteristics (see Figure 4.7).

Compared with Canadian-born workers, immigrants place more importance on job autonomy and work that is challenging and interesting. This may reflect their higher levels of education, compared with

Figure 4.7. Differences between immigrants and Canadian-born workers in job characteristics

Job characteristic	Percentage-point difference between immigrant and Canadian-born workers
Freedom to decide how to do your job	14
Good job security	14
A workplace free from harassment and discrimination	11
Challenging and interesting work	10
Good pay	4

0   5%   10%   15%

Employed Canadians, Rethinking Work 2012.

Canadian-born participants in Rethinking Work 2012. Immigrants also place greater value on having a workplace free from harassment and discrimination, which is understandable given that they often have been the targets of such behaviour. Furthermore, immigrants coming to Canada are striving to put down roots, get ahead, and provide opportunities for their children – goals that are consistent with the greater importance immigrants place on having a secure, well-paid job. Immigrants' emphasis on pay and security is what distinguishes them from equally well-educated Canadian-born workers, who may be more inclined to take these economic aspects of a job for granted. But in other ways, immigrants hold similar work values to Canadian-born workers.

To wrap up this discussion of labour market location and demographic differences in work values, here's a quick summary of our key points:

• Workers' demographic characteristics – age, gender, education, and immigration status – are more important in the values profile than labour market location. The differences we did find between full-time employees, the self-employed, and part-time or contingent workers have a lot to do with the demographics of these groups.

- A worker's stage in life goes a long way towards explaining the main age differences in work values.
- Focusing on generational differences in work values ends up with sweeping generalizations that don't reflect the diversity of life situations within the generations. Our discussion of 35- to 44-year-old Gen Xers and 65-plus baby boomers underscores this point.
- Work value variations have more to do with workers' gender than their age. Women place greater importance on intrinsic rewards, the work environment, and workplace culture than men do.
- Education is a values differentiator. University-educated workers seek the kind of job features – autonomy and challenge – that instil purpose in work and that also are vital for innovation and creativity.
- Immigrants also possess distinct values, emphasizing some of the work features important to women (security, a workplace free from discrimination or harassment) and well-educated workers (autonomy, challenge).

What's Most Important in a Job

So far, we have considered the relative importance that workers place on 16 core work values. To round out this picture of work values, it is helpful to focus on which of these values matter most to workers. To do this, Rethinking Work 2012 asked respondents to identify the "most important" characteristic in deciding which job to choose. To streamline the question and simplify the ranking process, we combined some similar job characteristics. Respondents had to consider all the descriptions and then were asked to select the one they consider most important. Here is the list:

- Having the training needed to do your job effectively.
- A good supervisor who gives you recognition for work well done.

- A healthy work environment free from harassment and discrimination.
- Senior management you can trust.
- Having the freedom to decide how to do your job, as well as a say in workplace decisions.
- Good job security and opportunities for career advancement.
- A flexible schedule that allows you a good balance between work and personal life.
- Good pay and benefits.
- Challenging work that gives you a sense of accomplishment.

Two job characteristics stand out as most important (see Figure 4.8). More than a quarter of respondents selected a challenging work experience that provides a sense of accomplishment as their first priority in choosing a job. Another one in four respondents looks most of all for good pay and benefits, which is understandable in today's uncertain economic environment. Flexibility and work-life balance are third-ranked, given top priority by another 17 per cent of respondents. Fourth-ranked is security and career opportunities, considered by just over 1 in 10 to be the most important selection criterion for a job. We asked the same question in Rethinking Work 2015 and got similar answers. So this is a stable set of job priorities in Canada's post-recession workforce.

At this juncture, let's return briefly to our previous discussion, in chapter 3, of work motivation. We asked the survey question about the most important characteristic of a job not knowing how Rethinking Work 2012 respondents would describe what makes them look forward to work. These two questions provide complementary definitions of a high-quality job. To underscore one point in this regard, challenging work providing a sense of accomplishment is a priority when job hunting as well as a motivator for engaged workers. The biggest motivator, workplace relationships, wasn't on the list of job selection criteria because it is more difficult for job applicants to glean accurate information about the actual work environment. However, leading employers such as those on the list of

Figure 4.8. Most important job characteristic

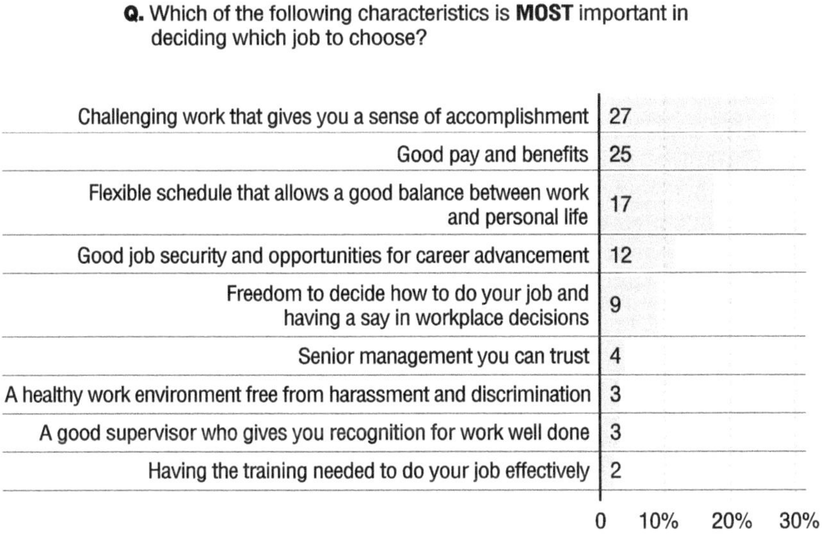

Q. Which of the following characteristics is **MOST** important in deciding which job to choose?

Challenging work that gives you a sense of accomplishment	27
Good pay and benefits	25
Flexible schedule that allows a good balance between work and personal life	17
Good job security and opportunities for career advancement	12
Freedom to decide how to do your job and having a say in workplace decisions	9
Senior management you can trust	4
A healthy work environment free from harassment and discrimination	3
A good supervisor who gives you recognition for work well done	3
Having the training needed to do your job effectively	2

0   10%   20%   30%

Employed Canadians, Rethinking Work 2012.

Best Workplaces in Canada emphasize their supportive and friendly culture to prospective recruits.

Figure 4.8 also has a few surprises. Certainly larger and more progressive employers have been addressing HR issues such as recognition, bullying and harassment, healthy workplaces, training, employee consultation, and trust. HR practitioners widely consider these essential ingredients of an attractive job. So we might expect more workers to highly value these job features. But they don't. Very few respondents (2 to 4 per cent) rank a healthy and inclusive work environment, management they can trust, job-related training, and recognition from their supervisor as the most important consideration if they were choosing a new job today.

Employers hiring new staff may find it useful to ask prospective recruits what is important for them in a job, using a list similar to that in Figure 4.8. And it's also important to examine whether the positions being filled actually provide meaningful work experiences as well as competitive pay and benefits. Because it's a safe bet that one in four of all potential job applicants are looking for these things in a job. Employers also should be careful not to read too much into the low rankings received for a healthy workplace, trust, recognition, and training. The absence of any of these can be demoralizing for any employee, leading to engagement and retention problems.

Who Considers Which Job Characteristics Most Important?

Which types of workers are most likely to select each of the four top-ranked job characteristics in Figure 4.8? Differentiating the workforce according to this values profile provides employers further insights about how specific job features appeal to different demographic groups. The profiles below also update labour market models based on general concepts like "precarious work" and "good jobs–bad jobs." As we will see, the profiles reveal how people's work values guide their job choices and career decisions.

Furthermore, the connection between satisfaction and values suggests that what people value in a job is calibrated to what individuals realistically can expect to achieve – at least within the constraints of today's job market. Fulfilled aspirations mean actualized values, which for the more privileged workers today equates to greater job satisfaction and engagement.

To create these profiles, we examined a wide range of demographic characteristics that could explain why some consider a certain job feature to be very important while others don't. We looked for variations in responses to the "most important job characteristic" question by the following demographic characteristics: education, age, income, gender, immigrant status, region, marital status, spousal employment, and dependent children or adults living in the household. We also looked at each respondent's employment situation (union or professional association membership, occupation, self-employed or employee, precarious work, workplace size, weekly work hours). Finally, we looked for variations in what's "most important" by respondents' level of job and life satisfaction. We carried out this analysis using data from both Rethinking Work 2012 and 2015 – with similar results.

Meaningful Work

Individuals who place highest priority on meaningful work – having a challenging job that gives a sense of accomplishment – are best positioned to obtain such jobs. These are the knowledge workers who have already found decent jobs. While they now account for over a quarter of the workforce, it's crucial to future prosperity to find ways to increase these numbers.

Most of the survey respondents in this group are university educated, in management or professional jobs, not union members, and earning at least $60,000 annually. They also are likely to be self-employed or contingent workers, rather than full- or part-time employees.

This profile suggests that these respondents already have found meaningful work, which reinforces the importance they place on it. In short, for these individuals meaningful work is a realistic aspiration because they have the education and job opportunities most likely to provide it. This point is reinforced by the fact that survey respondents 55 years and older, compared with younger workers, give highest priority to a job that is challenging and provides a sense of accomplishment – the things people are more likely to attain later in their career. So do individuals who are single and who do not have children at home.

It's clear that the quest for meaningful work may lead some people to opt for self-employment or contract work instead of being an employee. The fact that the self-employed and people in contract jobs are more likely than employees to highly value these characteristics suggests that a person's labour market status may be influenced by their work values.

Meaningful work contributes to a person's well-being. Workers who placed highest priority on meaningful work also reported high levels of job satisfaction and life satisfaction. And they look forward to going to work on a regular basis, which is consistent with the discussion in chapter 3 of how intrinsic job features are big motivators. Here, then, is further support for the conclusion that for this fortunate minority, what they want most in a job either has been largely achieved or is well within reach.

Pay and Benefits

Standing in stark contrast are those workers who consider good pay and benefits to be most important when deciding which job to choose. This group also is sizeable, accounting for about one-quarter of all workers. The group mainly includes individuals with less education who work in routine jobs. Respondents with an education level of high school or less or who work in sales, service, and manual jobs are significantly more likely to give top ranking to pay and benefits than other groups. An emphasis on good pay and benefits also is found among older workers (55 years and older), males, union members, and those who are full-time employees.

Clearly, this is a distinct workforce segment that wants and needs decent pay and benefits but whose current jobs are likely not providing these. This disconnect between values and job rewards helps explain why this is not a happy or engaged group of employees. Workers who rank pay and benefits as the highest priority in job selection tend to have relatively low job and life satisfaction and often don't look forward to work.

Workers adjust their values and aspirations to what is realistically attainable given the constraints of their education and occupation. Those whose jobs do not provide the intrinsic rewards so vital for overall satisfaction in work and life tend to focus, by default, on the economics of work. For them, intrinsic psychological rewards have been out of reach. And they likely will remain so, without concerted efforts by decision-makers to improve the quality of the jobs these people occupy.

Flexibility

The third-ranked "most important" job characteristic is "a flexible schedule that allows you a good balance between work and personal life." Given this family-friendly description, it is not surprising that women, respondents who are married or living with a partner, and those who have children under 18 living at home consider flexibility and work-life balance essential job features. People who prefer flexible employment also tend to be working in para-professional, technical, administrative, clerical, or sales and service jobs – most of which are female-dominated jobs.

This group also includes a lot of part-time and self-employed workers. It may be that the preference for family-friendly flexible work has led some people into jobs that are less demanding, both in terms of time requirements and work commitment. This involves a trade-off, with important implications for employers. The fact that this group is satisfied with their life as a whole suggests that a focus on meeting family responsibilities – juggling kids and work – reduces the enthusiasm one has for going into work on a daily basis. For these individuals, there's a lot more to life than their job.

Secure Career

There's one more group that also deserves the attention of employers. For about 1 in 10 workers, job security and career advancement opportunities are the top job priority. These people want to build a career with one employer, climbing the corporate ladder in sure and steady steps knowing that their commitment to the company is matched by the company's commitment to them. Many of them are full-time employees.

A secure career with one employer describes the stable employment relationships that many large private- and public-sector employers cultivated in the 1950s, 1960s, and 1970s. This employment model held out prospects of a slow but predictable climb up the corporate ladder in return for loyalty. These were the "good jobs" of the post–Second World War era – the foundation for an expanding middle class. Yet since the 1980s this model has been largely displaced by the rise of outsourcing, downsizing, contract work, and self-employment. The meaningful work group, described earlier, no doubt includes workers in this sort of work arrangement. Nonetheless, the fact that only 10 per cent of the workers we surveyed aspire to a stable career reflects an adjustment to these broader labour market trends.

Our profile of who most wants security and career advancement suggests these are cautiously aspiring individuals. These are workers who typically have some college or university courses but are short of completing a diploma or degree. They also are middle income, with reported earnings between $40,000 to $59,000. Immigrants also are more likely in this group than non-immigrants, as are males and workers under age 35. In terms of their employment situation, those putting a premium on security and advancement tend to be union members and work more than 40 hours per week. This is a group of workers who are striving to get ahead and have taken steps to make this happen, such as acquiring more education or working longer hours.

Are Work Values Fulfilled?

Now that we have provided a detailed description of work value patterns in the Canadian workforce, we can address the last question posed at the start of the chapter: Do people's jobs meet their expectations as defined by their work values? We believe that an important test of a person's quality of work life is whether or not their current job meets the expectations defined by their values. Knowing what these gaps are offers a new perspective on job quality. When a worker experiences a deficit in this regard, or what we call a "want-have gap," they are less satisfied and engaged. These not only undercut employers' HR goals, they also mean a reduced quality of work life for individual Canadians.

To begin on a positive note, between half and three-quarters of Rethinking Work 2012 respondents tell us that their current job provides what they consider most important "to a great extent" (Figure 4.9). Those workers who consider decision input and job autonomy, challenging work that provides a sense of accomplishment, and training to be most important experience the smallest deficits. More than 70 per cent say that their job provides these things. In contrast, the job features with the biggest deficits have to do with trustworthy senior managers, pay and benefits, and job security and career opportunities. Only about half of the workers who place the highest priority on these features of work report having them to a great extent in their current job.

We further examined these results looking for differences across demographic groups. There are no statistically significant differences based gender or immigrant status. However, the "want-have gap" closes steadily with age. While 59 per cent of workers under age 35 say they have what is most important to them in their current job, this increases to 75 per cent among workers age 65 or older. And there also is a clear education effect. Workers with a university degree are more likely than those who do not have this level of education to have what they consider most important (67 per cent compared with 59 per cent). This adds further support to our argument that knowledge workers, at least a good proportion of them, have access to jobs with overall higher quality in the twenty-first-century labour market.

Looking into the future, there are encouraging signs of what is possible as we contemplate how to redesign jobs. A majority of workers in the 2012 Rethinking Work study have jobs that meet their needs, based on what they value most. In addition, the ideals of knowledge work – challenging, meaningful, and autonomous – seem readily available for many who want these things. Similarly, employers' initiatives to improve training and flexibility seem to be paying off, at least based on the fact that many workers who want these features have them in their current job.

Figure 4.9. Gaps between workers' values and current job characteristics

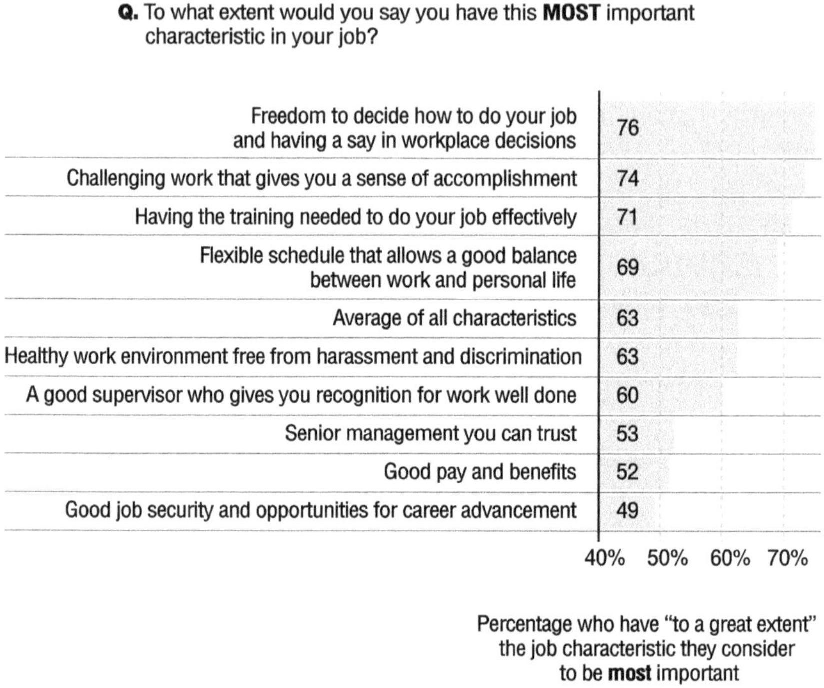

Q. To what extent would you say you have this **MOST** important characteristic in your job?

Freedom to decide how to do your job and having a say in workplace decisions	76
Challenging work that gives you a sense of accomplishment	74
Having the training needed to do your job effectively	71
Flexible schedule that allows a good balance between work and personal life	69
Average of all characteristics	63
Healthy work environment free from harassment and discrimination	63
A good supervisor who gives you recognition for work well done	60
Senior management you can trust	53
Good pay and benefits	52
Good job security and opportunities for career advancement	49

40%   50%   60%   70%

Percentage who have "to a great extent" the job characteristic they consider to be **most** important

Employed Canadians, Rethinking Work 2012.

But that's only part of the story. Of immediate concern to employers and policymakers is the fact that so few workers highly value what researchers tells us are critical for well-being and job performance – job features such as autonomy, trust, recognition, a healthy work environment, and training. In chapter 7 we return to this point in search of opportunities to design these features into future jobs.

Conclusion

This chapter has shown that people's work values matter. A values perspective on the workforce tells us more about Canadians' aspirations, expectations, and adaptations in uncertain and rapidly changing times. Acknowledging the role that values play in people's work life can, we hope, guide positive changes in people's work situations aimed at improving job quality.

Equally important, corporate and policy decision-makers will benefit from our discovery that some features of healthy, engaging, and productive work are not highly valued across the workforce. In particular, we have drawn attention to how little importance workers place on opportunities for a say in decisions, autonomy, training, and advancement. These specific values could stand in the way of positive change, to the extent that they are not high-priority changes sought by workers.

To wind up our discussion of work values, we'll leave readers with two questions for further reflection and action: First, should employers and policymakers strive to close the gaps on all or most of these job features so that Canadians are more likely in future to have jobs that align with their aspirations? And second, if we were able to close these gaps, what would be the benefits to workers, employers, and society as a whole?

Basically, how you answer these questions has implications for the design of future jobs and workplaces – a topic to which we return in chapter 7. As a prelude, we encourage an expanded discussion of "Canadian values" to include what individuals value in a job, with attention paid to how these values vary across groups in the workforce. We are quick to admit that the 16 work values we measured are far from being a definitive or exhaustive list of what matters to Canadians and would welcome other researchers adding to our evidence by measuring other work values.

A positive sign for the future is the high importance placed on having a workplace free from harassment and discrimination. Recent well-publicized allegations of toxic work environments in major institutions such as the RCMP, the Canadian Forces, and the CBC highlight the need for employers to have more proactive HR policies and practices. The ideal future workplace is welcoming for all workers, regardless of race or ethnicity, gender, age, and other personal characteristics. Inclusive workplaces are respectful and fair, qualities that contribute to a productive and ethical business. And as we have already suggested in chapter 2, they also are psychologically healthy and safe environments – meeting an increasingly important goal for both employees and employers.

Diversity is a dominant theme in our analysis of work values. We've seen this in terms of how different groups hold distinct views on what's important in a job. These value patterns mirror the increasingly heterogeneous composition of Canada's workforce, with more older and younger workers, immigrants and visible minorities, and women moving into previously male-dominated jobs. Corporate recruitment and retention strategies must recognize that not everyone wants the same thing in a job. Tailoring HR strategies to specific demographic groups could be more effective than a one-size-fits-all approach. This is especially true for well-educated knowledge workers, who put a premium on work with purpose and meaning.

We've also added a Canadian perspective to Daniel Pink's claims about purposeful work. Indeed, it's not Gen Y but the front edge of the baby boom generation who hold the most distinct work values. Workers age 65 and older are the most likely of any age group to seek out and find meaningful work. This is a relevant insight for those employers wanting to retain or hire older workers. Clearly, a good number of baby boomers eagerly anticipate the next phase of their work life. Chapter 5 will pursue this point, arguing that employers must tap this growing reserve of experienced talent in order to meet future labour demand and grow the economy.

5 Generations at Work

Demographers argue that demography explains two-thirds of everything.[1] A bold claim to be sure, yet there's no question that population aging presents huge challenges for employers, governments, and society. The dynamics of aging are altering Canada's social fabric in profound ways and will continue to do so well into the future. Economic growth, living standards, and the sustainability of social programs – from healthcare to pensions – could be threatened unless Canada quickly brings its institutions in line with the reality of fewer younger people and more seniors.

Indeed, population aging is a megatrend that indicates the broader social context in which the economic forces documented earlier in the book affect Canadians. In this respect there's a big difference between economic and demographic forces of change. Unlike the uncertainty swirling around the future of the economy, we can predict far more accurately the direction and impact of population trends.

So far, how Canadians are adapting to this demographic reality has focused on changes to retirement. Indeed, this is a prominent topic in the media, with headlines such as "Working in Retirement: The New Normal?"[2] However, responses to workforce aging must address the needs, values, and capabilities of the three generations in today's workforce: baby boomers, Gen X, and millennials or Gen Y.[3] Some workplaces may even have four generations, if there are employees born before 1946.

We argue that the aging of Canada's workforce has enormous implications for the future design of work. In this chapter, we examine these implications – both negative and positive. We outline what can be done to manage the demographic transformation of the workforce by employers, human resource professionals, policymakers, and others who are in a position to influence workplace practices. Using evidence from Rethinking Work surveys, we address the following questions:

- What will influence boomers to stay working or leave the workforce altogether?
- Want can enable Gen Xers to move into leadership roles vacated by boomers?
- How can millennials be provided better opportunities to launch their careers?
- How can generational transitions be managed effectively, fairly, and in ways that maximize the contributions of workers of all ages?

Answers to these questions can guide those in the work arena who may be able to moderate growing generational disparities. Generational equity is front and centre in the public mind. Given the flatline post-recession trajectory of the economy, most Canadians expect living standards to decline.

Add to this the long-standing complaints by Gen X and millennials that baby boomers have a lock on the good jobs and corporate decision-making. Some younger workers are bound to feel that their career advancement has been slowed, their middle-class aspirations are fading, and their potential contributions to the economy are being stifled because of the boomer bottleneck in the workplace. But at the same time, some boomers perceive a bias against older workers as they seek employment opportunities well into their 60s, or even their 70s.

We propose an inclusive and flexible approach to managing generational transitions in the workforce. This approach is consistent with Canadians' widely shared work values, as we outlined in chapter 4. Employers need to maximize the contributions of all age groups by giving three areas of action equal priority:

- Smoothing the ascent of Gen X and millennials into positions of responsibility now held by baby boomers – a slower process because older individuals are staying in the workforce longer.
- Tapping into the ideas, digital savvy, and creativity possessed by younger workers, because this is a huge potential source of business innovation.
- Using the experience and knowledge of baby boomers. However, this will be selective, presenting the challenge of retaining or recruiting those older workers who add the most value – which in some organizations will require more robust merit-based performance management systems.

It is entirely possible for future workplaces to support all workers to thrive, regardless of age or any other personal characteristic. That vision of the kind of job many Canadian workers want will contribute to reducing generational inequities by giving younger and older workers alike better access to rewarding jobs. Our evidence shows that conditions are right for employers, policymakers, and other workplace change advocates to make this happen.

Generational Equity

When Canadians look into the future, many see rising social inequality and declining living standards for the next generation.[4] Generational downward mobility is already underway. "Generation Squeeze" is the label some analysts have affixed to Canadian workers up to their mid-40s. These millennial and Gen X workers, better educated than the generations before them, earn less than they would have back in the 1970s and find the middle-class dream of home ownership more difficult to attain.[5]

The result is a growing sense of generational inequity, mostly directed at the institutions of work. If younger workers think the employment system is stacked against them, they will have less trust in labour market institutions and perceive them to be unfair. This creates a problem for employers, because fairness and trust are prerequisites for a motivated and productive workforce.

Baby boomers have more accumulated wealth – the houses they own and their Registered Retirement Savings Plans (RRSPs) and other savings – so they are visibly better off than millennials and Gen X. Millennials may inherit some of their parents' wealth, but baby boomers are healthier and will live longer, so this wealth transfer could be in the distant future. More immediately, as the baby boomers enter their 70s, strains will surely show on publicly funded healthcare and pension systems. And we know that any cost increases in these areas will be borne by Gen X and millennial workers.

Generational equity is not a new issue. Canadians have been debating since the 1990s how fairly different generations are treated, especially in terms of being able to access decent opportunities in the labour market.[6] This public concern about generational equity was initially sparked by fears that the Canada Pension Plan (CPP) would run out of money unless contributions were increased. Paul Martin, finance minister in the mid-1990s, increased employees' and employers' CPP contributions. As a result, Canada's public pension plan is solvent today. Contrast this with the United States and some European countries, where public pensions are running huge unfunded liabilities.[7]

Indeed, the inability of US politicians to find solutions to the ballooning federal debt and its symptoms, like the so-called fiscal cliff, has escalated the generational equity debate to a far more strident tone south of the border. *New York Times* columnist Paul Krugman criticizes deficit hawks for the alarmist view that not cutting the soaring US debt amounts to "cheating our children."[8] Another commentator, writing in the *Huffington Post*, argues that "the mother of all guilt trips" is being laid on citizens who are 50-plus by those who claim that America's current medical care and social security for the elderly will unduly penalize younger generations.[9]

Back in Canada, the solvency of the CPP is a glimmer in an otherwise gloomy outlook. Today's younger workers can expect it to become more difficult to support themselves in old age. According to calculations by CIBC, close to six million people – mostly Gen Y – may see their living standards decline by at least 20 per cent.[10]

Contributing to this bleak prognosis are changes to the pension system. The federal government recently increased the eligibility age for receiving old age security for future retirees. Employers have switched from defined benefit to less generous defined contribution pension plans. There is a slow but steady decline in employer pension plan coverage, down to about one-third of workers today. And younger workers who have the means to sock money away in RRSPs won't see the good financial returns that their parents did, given today's rock-bottom interest rates.

Actions taken by employers can unintentionally benefit one generation at the expense of another. For example, bureaucratic organizations move people up the career ladder into jobs with more pay and power, often using age as a main criterion – a system that rewards older workers. And some employers are preparing for the exodus of boomers by fast-tracking high-performing younger employees through a talent management strategy – without fully considering how to keep older workers employed longer. But as we will see, these trade-offs can be avoided. Finding ways to balance the interests of workers across the age spectrum has become one of the most pressing HR challenges today.

Declining Living Standards

Expanding on our discussion in chapter 1 of public concerns about widening inequality and falling living standards, we now consider longer-term trends in how Canadians assess the changes in their quality of life before and after the Great Recession.

According to EKOS polls, people believe that their quality of life has declined over the past 25 years. Furthermore, the same polls show that Canadians expect the next generation to be worse off 25 years in the future (see Figure 5.1). When EKOS polled adult Canadians in 2012, 37 per cent thought they were worse off than the

Figure 5.1. Perceived changes in quality of life over time

25 YEARS AGO	25 YEARS FROM NOW
Q. Thinking about your overall quality of life, would you say that **you are** better off, worse off, or about the same as the previous generation was **25 years ago**?	**Q.** Thinking about your overall quality of life do you think **the next generation will be** better off, worse off, or about the same as you are **25 years from now**?

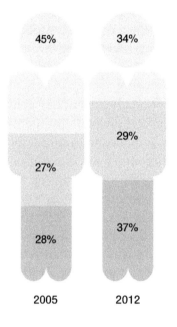

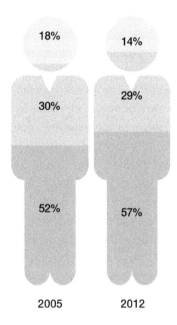

Better
About the Same
Worse Off

Canadian adults, 21–8 February 2012.

previous generation, while only 34 per cent believed they were actually better off. When the same question was asked in a 2005 poll by EKOS, the "better off" group outnumbered the "worse off" group.

This pessimism goes even deeper when Canadians are asked whether they think the next generation in 25 years will be better off, worse off, or have about the same quality of life as they do. Even in 2005, when the economy was growing and there were lots of jobs available, most poll respondents foresaw the next generation becoming worse off. This view became more widespread after the Great Recession, a reaction no doubt to the gloomy outlook for the global economy and reduced employment prospects at home.

Younger Canadians are not optimistic that governments will do anything about this problem. In 2012, EKOS asked Canadians the following question: "About half of Canada's population, younger Canada, is under the age of 42, while the other half, older Canada, is over 42. Do you think the Government of Canada focuses more on the values and interests of younger Canada or older Canada?" Responses to the question, presented in Figure 5.2, reveal sharply divided opinions on this point. "Younger Canada" thinks that government favours older people, while "older Canada" perceives more equal treatment of the different generations.

Societal concerns about generational equity play out within workplaces. The view among Gen X and millennials that employment systems are geared to the needs of older Canadians can have corrosive effects in workplaces. If employers' human resource policies and practices are seen as favouring older workers, it could undermine young workers' sense of fairness – or what is called "organizational justice" – and their trust in management (who often are baby boomers). That's why it is so important for employers to strive for age-inclusive work environments, based on the fair treatment of all generations.

There are concrete steps employers and governments can take to alleviate this generational inequity and, at the same time, reduce the potential for intergenerational tensions in workplaces. In particular, three actions can help:

Figure 5.2. Perceived treatment of older vs. younger Canadians

Q. About half of Canada's population, younger Canada, is under the age of 42, while the other half, older Canada, is over 42. *Do you think the Government of Canada focuses more on the values and interests of younger Canada or older Canada?*

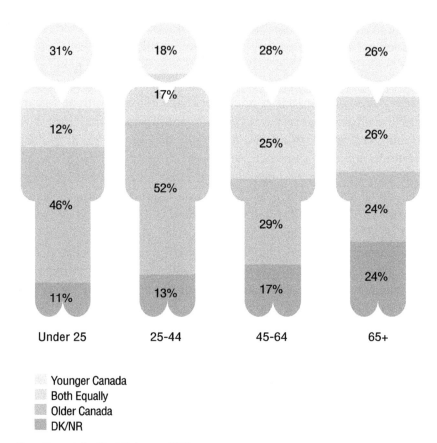

Younger Canada
Both Equally
Older Canada
DK/NR

Canadian adults, 21–8 February 2012.

- Employers must factor into long-range workforce planning the career goals and aspirations of each generation.
- Employers and governments can promote an inclusive approach to workforce management. This means not giving priority to the needs of one age group over another, but rather treating all ages in the workplace in a fair and even-handed manner.
- Employers can introduce flexible HR policies and programs to give employees more choice over benefits and work schedules that meet changing career and personal needs through their working life.

Why We Need to Work Longer

We can expect the future workforce to have many more people working into their 60s and 70s. This trend is visible today, pushed by a combination of demographic and economic changes that will affect all generations. Work is less physically wearing, each generation is healthier than the previous one, and with longer life expectancy and less generous pensions there will be financial pressures to continue earning income into our senior years. Furthermore, many individuals want to keep working for the satisfaction, meaning, and social connections it provides – important personal motivations we discussed in chapter 3. This is especially true for well-educated knowledge workers.

Consider these basic demographic facts. Life expectancy is rising; individuals who are 65 today will live an average of 20.2 more years. Statistics Canada's population projections show that by 2030, 25 per cent of Canadians will be age 65 or older, up from about 14 per cent today.[11]

An inevitable feature of the aging trend is that each year the average age of the workforce rises. It is this stark demographic reality that leads to predictions of labour shortages and faltering pension plans. Decades ago, when there were more than two younger workers for every older worker, the replacement of one generation by the next was fairly orderly. There were lots of younger workers ready to move into the jobs vacated by retiring workers. Now, there are fewer younger workers to replace departing baby boomers, to pay taxes, and to make the pension contributions needed to support the growing population drawing pensions.

One way to adapt to these societal shifts is to work longer. Canada could be facing a future of lower productivity and slower economic growth due to a smaller working-age population. The Conference Board of Canada's economic forecast predicts that baby boomer retirements will put a damper on the economy through 2030.[12] If productivity declines, so will living standards. As individuals, we can better maintain our living standards if we delay retirement. Based on current retirement patterns, half of middle-income baby boomers will experience a drop in living standards of 25 per cent or more in retirement.[13] That alone is a strong incentive to work a few more years.

Extending working life will address intergenerational equity within society as well – although it could add to inequities in workplaces if employers don't also find new ways to provide career opportunities to younger workers. Workforce aging will result in fewer workers and businesses paying the taxes needed to fund social programs necessary to support a much larger elderly population. If older workers stay in the labour force longer, earning income and paying taxes, this will help alleviate – at least for a few years – the fiscal burden baby boomers are going to place on the shoulders of younger workers to help care for them in old age. Governments are addressing this problem. For example, the 2013 federal budget changed CPP rules so that anyone claiming benefits between ages 60 and 65 while still employed must continue paying into the CPP.

Finally, a prolonged transition into retirement will reduce the risk of losing core knowledge possessed by experienced baby boomers when they do retire. Knowledge retention solutions must bridge a firm's knowledge management, talent development, and HR strategies.[14] Long-range workforce planning can guide organizations as they craft solutions, identifying knowledge critical for achieving future business success. New roles for experienced workers will give them time and support to be coaches and mentors to junior staff.

These kinds of solutions are welcomed by workers of all ages. That said, employers still must take steps to ensure that delayed retirement is not perceived by younger workers as further reducing their career opportunities. This poses two practical questions: First, how can employers retain those older workers who are most essential to achieving future business goals? Second, what adaptations in HR policies and practice will ensure that all older workers in the organization are as productive as possible? Finding answers to these questions clearly will be more difficult in organizations with seniority-based career systems. Moving to merit-based performance management systems could take years, while the need to resolve these workforce transition issues is immediate.

Redefining Retirement

Baby boomers already are redefining retirement. Mandatory retirement is a relic of the past; most Canadian jurisdictions have eliminated this barrier to older worker employment.[15] But will 70 become the new 60?

We are moving in this direction, albeit very slowly. Over a 10-year period, from 2004 to 2014, the median male retirement age increased from 61.8 to 64.1 years.[16] Among females, the median retirement age has also started to move up, from 60.8 to 62.3 over the same period. The financial turmoil of the recession added momentum to these trends.

However, these retirement ages only measure individuals who have exited the workforce. In recent years, there are signs of greater diversity in work-retirement transitions. Retirement no longer can be defined as a permanent exit from paid work. So just looking at changes in the median retirement age won't tell us how retirement behaviour is changing. Indeed, more people are retiring and then returning to the workforce or delaying retirement altogether. Statistics Canada's survey of older workers, conducted before the Great Recession, confirmed the emergence of these new work-retirement patterns.[17]

Until now, we've lacked reliable national data showing how the Great Recession affected retirement decisions and behaviour. To fill this gap, the Rethinking Work surveys offer a pre- and post-recession comparison of just how much Canadians' retirement plans are changing. And the survey findings leave little doubt that the Great Recession has accelerated the trend to delaying retirement.

Between 2004 and 2012, retirement plans shifted in the direction of working longer. While about half of the EKOS survey respondents had retirement plans in 2004, this number had declined to 30 per cent in 2012. Over half (56 per cent) of those in the workforce do not have retirement plans and another 13 per cent are undecided about whether or not they will retire. EKOS asked the same question in the Rethinking Work 2015 survey and got the same results as in 2012.

The dream of "Freedom 55" – a popular financial planning slogan in the 1990s – has been fading in the twenty-first century. In 2004, just under half of poll respondents (44 per cent) planned to retire before age 60, yet by 2012 early retirement was planned by just one in four of those polled. We also see more individuals planning to work beyond age 65. Indeed, younger and older workers alike expect to work longer. Young workers, in particular, have grasped this new reality. Only 22 per cent of those under age 35 expect to retire. In the workforce as a whole, the new planned retirement age is 67, and over 70 among workers who are 55 or older (see Figure 5.3).

Canada's workforce will be transformed if today's workers follow through on these plans. For employers, the good news is that many of the older workers who are planning to stay in the workforce are motivated and looking for new challenges. For policymakers, it is important to recognize the diverse needs and capabilities among older workers. And for a growing number of workers, a prolonged work life means continued opportunities to derive the financial, psychological, and social rewards that a job can provide.

Retirement decisions are influenced by one's health, education, and financial status.[18] Well-educated older workers with adequate retirement savings have the luxury of choice regarding continued employment. For them, the non-financial rewards of work are a priority and they also have needed human capital – two reasons why retention strategies must understand and respond to this group's needs.

Figure 5.3. Retirement plans by age group

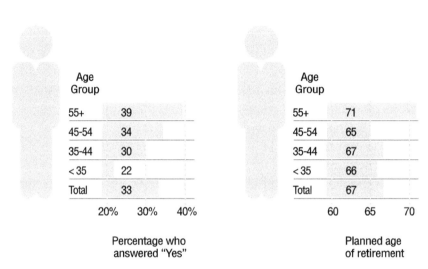

Q. Do/Did you plan to officially retire from your (last) employment or career?

Q. [IF YES] At what age do/did you plan to officially retire from your (last) employment or career?

Age Group	
55+	39
45-54	34
35-44	30
< 35	22
Total	33

20%   30%   40%

Percentage who answered "Yes"

Age Group	
55+	71
45-54	65
35-44	67
< 35	66
Total	67

60   65   70

Planned age of retirement

Employed Canadians, Rethinking Work 2012.
Age group differences in both graphs are statistically significant ($p < 0.001$).

The situation is starkly different for older workers with low incomes and the least education. While financially they need to keep working, poor health may be a limitation. If these individuals can find employment, they'll take as many hours as they can get. This group of less-advantaged workers raises public policy issues related to the future adequacy of old-age income support programs. That's why a beefed-up public pension system is on the agenda for the federal and Ontario governments.

Moving Up

The much larger issue for employers and the economy is being able to renew the workforce through orderly succession from older to younger workers. Workforce renewal requires two types of worker mobility. People can move into positions of greater responsibility as they gain experience, or they can switch careers or lines of work as a route to better work opportunities and rewards.

Canadian workers seem far more interested in making a career transition that involves taking on management responsibilities in their current organization, rather than switching to a new line of work or a new employer. About half of Rethinking Work 2012 respondents agreed with the statement "I would be interested in taking on management responsibilities (or taking on greater responsibilities if already a manager) in my organization" (see Figure 5.4). The recession clearly did not dampen workers' ambitions in this regard. When EKOS asked the same question in 2004, only 35 per cent of those polled expressed interest in becoming a manager in their organization.

What's more, aspirations to move up are found across all age groups. About 60 per cent of workers under age 45 would take on management responsibilities. Surely this tells employers that today's younger workforce provides a deep talent pool among Gen X and millennials, perhaps deeper than they thought.

The desire for an expanded role is not limited to younger workers. Indeed, close to half of the workers between 45 and 54 years of age also are willing to take on more responsibility. Moreover, one in three workers age 55 or older – the boomers that some employers, and younger co-workers, might assume want to coast into retirement – is actually interested in managerial responsibilities. According to Rethinking Work data, we may need to revise our image of older workers to account for the fact that a good number are seeking new and bigger challenges.

Moving On

Today, workers are less likely to consider switching careers than a decade or so ago. This signals another significant shift in Canadians' career plans.

Figure 5.4. Age group differences in career transition indicators

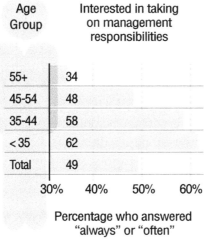

Age Group	Interested in taking on management responsibilities
55+	34
45-54	48
35-44	58
< 35	62
Total	49

30%   40%   50%   60%

Percentage who answered
"always" or "often"

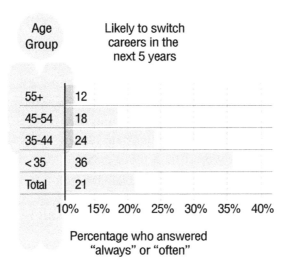

Age Group	Likely to switch careers in the next 5 years
55+	12
45-54	18
35-44	24
< 35	36
Total	21

10% 15% 20% 25% 30% 35% 40%

Percentage who answered
"always" or "often"

Employed Canadians, Rethinking Work 2012.
Age group differences for both indicators are statistically significant ($p < 0.01$).

In 2004, about 30 per cent of Rethinking Work respondents said it was very likely they would "switch careers or enter a new line of work" in the next five years. In 2012, just over 20 per cent expected a career change in the near future (see Figure 5.4). This is not restricted to young workers. Indeed, 12 per cent of workers 55 and older are considering a career change, which fits with the new retirement scenario we described earlier whereby some individuals plan to work into their 70s. Older workers with no set retirement age are more interested in having greater responsibility, so in this respect they also are open to new job opportunities.

The majority of workers want to stick with what they have rather than move into a new line of work. This amplifies our finding in chapter 1 that prospects of slow global economic growth will push many Canadians into a "hunker down" mentality. What we've been able to show here is a similar self-protective, risk-averse approach when it comes to considering career options.

What's more, the fact that only one in five workers are contemplating a career change deflates popular claims that we can expect to have "7 careers" in our lifetime.[19] Nobody seems to know where the prediction of seven careers came from, but let's take it as another way of saying "many." Both the 2004 and 2012 Rethinking Work surveys found that only 60 per cent of respondents had ever switched careers at all. This means 40 per cent had stayed with the same job or line of work. So rather than having many careers, "one or several" careers would be a more accurate description of how work life actually has been unfolding. This is an important issue to track into the future, especially because it offers a complementary perspective on the debates about increased labour market instability discussed in chapter 1.

In light of these findings, employers may want to take a fresh look at their approaches to performance appraisals and talent management. Most workers want to stay in their current jobs. But sizeable numbers of workers in all age groups also want more responsibility with their current employer. Companies' talent management strategies and succession plans therefore should consider workers of all ages when promoting or recruiting into management positions.

Achieving this will require more robust performance management systems so that actual job performance – merit – is the basis for moving up. Moving in this direction will inject a greater sense of fairness into workplaces.

Work Motivation

There's another reason for employers to be open-minded about hiring and promoting older workers. To emphasize, this must be part of a workforce strategy that is age-inclusive so that younger workers do not perceive unfairness.

Basically, older workers are more motivated in their jobs than younger workers (see Figure 5.5). Among the millennial cohort, 62 per cent look forward to going to work always or often – a good predictor of the level of an employee's engagement in her or his work. Compare this with the 81 per cent of baby boomers who are enthusiastic about going to work.

These age differences in levels of work motivation have three direct implications for employers:

- The lower motivation among younger employees needs attention. It may be partly a function of young people's entry-level jobs. Even so, optimal motivation levels among young workers surely should be higher. Understanding why young workers are less inspired by their jobs than older workers could be one of the keys to a more fully engaged workforce. One way to do this is to ensure that young workers don't get trapped in low-quality, precarious employment.
- Older workers' strong sense of work engagement could be infectious in a positive way. Imagine it being a source of positive energy in the workplace, especially if older workers' roles are designed to given them regular interaction with junior employees. One way to do this is by using older workers as mentors, trainers, or coaches. Younger workers who are new recruits, just promoted to a management position, or other team members could benefit.

Figure 5.5. Work motivation by age group

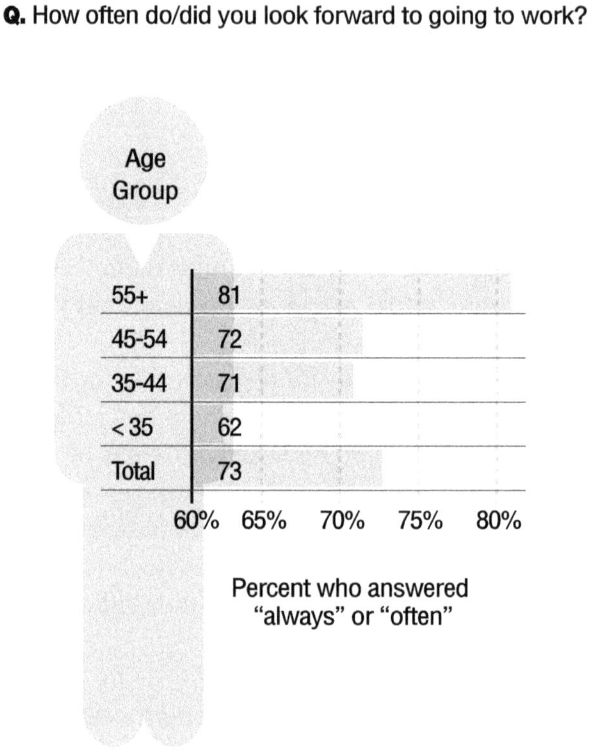

Q. How often do/did you look forward to going to work?

Age Group	
55+	81
45-54	72
35-44	71
< 35	62
Total	73

60%   65%   70%   75%   80%

Percent who answered
"always" or "often"

Employed Canadians, Rethinking Work 2012.
Age group differences are statistically significant ($p < 0.001$).

• If indeed the average older worker is more motivated, this should be reflected in their higher job performance. One way that employers can check this is to use their internal employee engagement survey results to determine how engagement levels vary by age group. This is a first step in identifying and removing any barriers that older workers – or workers of any age – may face to doing their job well.

Another way to bridge cross-generational work experiences is two-way mentoring, which values the unique perspectives and contributions of the different generations. The result would be greater intergenerational understanding, which surely is needed. According to US human resource experts, "Much of the difficulty that older workers have in getting hired and then functioning successfully in the workplace appears to centre on the relationship with younger supervisors."[20] Two-way mentoring could help to prepare younger managers to supervise older workers. Given delayed retirement plans, this will become a more common scenario in tomorrow's workplaces.

Meaningful Work

There is much talk in HR and management circles about clashing generations in the workplace. For example, the *Harvard Business Review (HBR)* identifies generational conflict in work teams around issues such as where and when to work, how to communicate, how to arrange meetings, and how to learn new things.[21] As the *HBR* recommends, employers need to dispel any negative stereotypes people may have of co-workers who are older, or younger, than themselves. An effective way to do this is by bringing the perspectives and experiences of different generations into the light so they can be understood by all.

In this regard, the potential for intergenerational misunderstanding can be reduced if we accept that our perspective on work changes as we go through life. We adapt to our changing circumstances, become more accepting of our limited opportunities, and recalibrate our expectations accordingly. Case in point: the quest for meaning in work increases with age. Indeed, it takes on a special urgency among baby boomers as they confront their unrealized dreams. As Daniel Pink argues in *Drive: The Surprising Truth about What Motivates Us*, "When the cold front of demographics meets the warm front of unrealized dreams, the result will be a thunderstorm of purpose the likes of which the world has never seen."[22] In other words, the quest for purpose in work will only increase as more baby boomers catch sight of the end of their careers.

Many baby boomers actually may be close to achieving these "unrealized dreams" because they are more likely than Gen X or millennial workers to think that their work already makes a useful contribution to society. Rethinking Work 2012 asked respondents if they agreed or disagreed with the statement, "The work I do in my job makes a useful contribution to society." Close to 80 per cent of workers 55 and older agreed, compared with only 62 per cent of those under age 35.

While younger workers are over-represented in lower-quality jobs, this alone does not explain the gap in perceived meaning. Minor improvements in entry-level jobs to expand opportunities for applying and developing skills will give younger employees greater psychological rewards from their work. Above all, for employees to feel that their job makes a difference to society they first must understand how their job contributes to the goals of the organization and, furthermore, see tangible results in this regard. A good manager is a people leader who enables these things to happen.

Convergent Work Values

Revisiting a point we made in chapter 4, the meaning of work evolves through a person's working life. This has more to do with the aging process and our movement through stages in life than it does with generationally specific work values. As we have argued, generational differences in work values are overstated.

Indeed, when it comes down to what really matters in a job, there is fundamental agreement between millennials and baby boomers. We discovered this when we asked Rethinking Work 2012 respondents to select the *most* important characteristic to them in deciding which job to choose (see Figure 5.6). The top three most sought-after job characteristics by millennials and boomers are identical:

- challenging work that gives a sense of accomplishment;
- good pay and benefits; and
- a flexible schedule that allows a good work-life balance.

What sets older and younger workers apart is their relative emphasis on these issues, measured as the percentage of each group rating a characteristic as most important. So when it comes to challenging work that gives a sense of accomplishment, 29 per cent of millennial respondents consider it to be most important, compared with 36 per cent of boomers. The generation gap is even greater when it comes to pay and benefits, with fewer older workers considering these features to be most important (18 per cent, compared with 28 per cent of workers under 35). When it comes to flexible schedules and work-life balance, the two generations are similar, with around 15 per cent selecting this as their priority job characteristic.

Rethinking Work 2012 also presented respondents with the same list of job characteristics and asked them to choose the one that for them is *least* important in deciding which job to choose (see Figure 5.6). Perhaps most telling, boomers are divided on the importance of having a flexible schedule that provides work-life balance. About the same percentages of respondents ranked this as the least and as the most important consideration in deciding what job to take. Given the boomers' life stage, it's no surprise that "job security and career advancement" is most frequently mentioned by this age group as least important.

One interesting finding is that for millennials and boomers alike, job-related training is one of the least important job features. This surprisingly low importance placed on training should raise a red flag for policymakers and employers alike, because it poses an attitudinal barrier to skill development strategies. For Canada to compete successfully in a global knowledge-driven economy – and for its public and not-for-profit sectors to thrive – employees and employers alike must embrace the principle of continuous skills enhancement. This principle is the centrepiece of the next chapter.

Finally, there's a paradox in what millennials consider the most and least important job features. On one hand, millennials want challenging work and a sense of accomplishment. On the other hand, 23 per cent of these young workers also consider decision-making autonomy

Figure 5.6. The three most and least important job characteristics
for younger and older workers

Q. Which of the following characteristics is **MOST / LEAST important**
in deciding which job to choose?

MOST Important

35 and Younger	55 and Older
1. Challenging work that gives you a sense of accomplishment. (29%)	1. Challenging work that gives you a sense of accomplishment. (36%)
2. Good pay and benefits. (28%)	2. Good pay and benefits. (18%)
3. A flexible schedule that allows you a good balance between work and personal life. (16%)	3. A flexible schedule that allows you a good balance between work and personal life. (15%)

LEAST Important

35 and Younger	55 and Older
1. Having the freedom to decide how to do your job, as well as a say in workplace decisions. (23%)	1. Good job security and opportunities for career advancement. (20%)
2. A healthy work environment free from harassment and discrimination. (15%)	2. Having the training needed to do your job effectively. (16%)
3. Having the training needed to do your job effectively. (12%)	3. A flexible schedule that allows you a good balance between work and personal life. (14%)

Employed Canadians, Rethinking Work 2012.

and having a say in decisions to be unimportant – despite these job features being at the core of a challenging and meaningful job. For employers, this paradox has implications for employee engagement strategies. Specifically, what changes are needed to make work more personally rewarding and productive for younger workers?

Designing Flexible Work

Flexible schedules are the third most important job feature sought by older and young workers alike. However, this refers to schedules, not other aspects of a job. We argue that when defined more broadly, flexibility is a versatile tool for making work improvements. There may be more immediate, and easier, opportunities to design flexibility into work than enriching jobs to make them more challenging or to improve pay and benefits.

Nonetheless, an aging workforce has been the "burning platform" prompting some companies to embark on more fundamental work redesign. A good example is BMW. The company recognized that an aging production workforce threatened its competitiveness.[23] Older workers were absent more and worked harder just to keep up, yet their experience and skills are essential for productivity. Project 2017 recruited a team of production workers age 50-plus (supported by engineers and health professionals) to help redesign assembly line work so there would be less physical strain and chance of error. Most suggested changes were simple and inexpensive, such as wood flooring, orthopaedic footwear, magnifying lenses, adjustable worktables, large-handled tools, larger fonts on computer screens, rest breaks, and ergonomically optimal job rotation. BMW built a new factory based on Project 2017, sending a powerful message to all employees that it cares about their well-being.

BMW also adopted a flexible retirement policy to support Project 2017 goals. Work-retirement transitions have been too rigid in the past. This is changing. To quote prominent US demographers, "In an ideal world, flexible retirement would allow employees to move in and out of the workplace seamlessly, without ever choosing a moment to retire."[24] Phased retirement is slowly emerging in Canada.[25] Typically, it is one option within a menu of flexible work arrangements available to all workers. Included here would be flexible daily work hours, compressed workweeks, job sharing, telecommuting (only relevant for certain types of jobs, of course), reduced work hours for full-time employees, temporary or project-based assignments in other areas, and unpaid short-term or long-term leaves.

Gradually, employers are responding to the needs of an increasingly diverse workforce by reconsidering the one-size-fits-all approach, not just to retirement but also to work schedules and locations, employment arrangements, and career paths. In coming years, information technology surely will make it easier for more work to be done outside the physical boundaries of an organization. This positive approach to flexibility responds to workers' changing needs and, at the same time, benefits employers.

Flexible work represents an HR strategy with the potential to address the needs of all age groups. As the Conference Board of Canada concludes, companies need to revamp their work-life approach to better engage and retain all employees. It recommends that employers move beyond flextime, adopting a holistic approach that reflects an employee's commitment to their community, family and personal life, and career.[26]

One interesting use of the flexibility principle comes from UK retail businesses. Some retailers who face annual sales peaks have set up permanent seasonal employment pools, consisting mainly of older individuals and young students but open to workers of all ages. Managers and colleagues of seasonal workers required training in order to ensure the program's success. These UK cases demonstrate the importance of educating other workers and managers and addressing their concerns about flexible work options to ensure there is a perception of fairness.

By contrast, the flexible "just-in-time" labour and outsourcing strategies that have led to precarious forms of work, discussed in chapter 1, are introduced by employers solely to reduce labour costs. What's now clear, however, is that some workers choose these less rigid work roles to exercise more control over their work lives – in other words, to achieve a better quality of work life.

Customized Employment Relationships

Organizational experts advocate greater use of individualized employment relationships to meet the needs of an increasingly diverse workforce.[27] Employers who give priority to cultivating their human capital recognize that an effective way to attract, retain, engage, and develop talent is through customized employment deals.

This concept is already being used by some Canadian employers to retain older workers, customizing the employment relationship based on what best meets the needs of the employee and the employer. However, it does raise two HR challenges. The first is how to discuss options with older workers in ways that are consistent with prohibitions against age discrimination in federal and provincial human rights legislation. The second is having in place a performance management system that can identify those older employees whose capabilities are crucial for the future success of the business.

Basically, these deals are negotiated one at a time, with fairness as a guiding principle. Managers and supervisors would have to be trained to have conversations with older staff to gain an understanding of their retirement plans and needs. The key to making this work is finding a "win-win" arrangement that meets both the employer's and the older worker's needs. So while access to this opportunity can be available to all older workers, the onus is on both parties to make it viable. One challenge is preserving a sense of fairness. On this point, it is interesting that a customized retention model has been negotiated into some collective agreements with unions.[28] This is a promising sign, showing that unions can be open to selectively applied HR practices – which they traditionally opposed – if their members stand to benefit.

A related trend is cultivating stronger relationships with retirees. Some of the award-winning companies for older employees have full-time coordinators of retiree relations. This practice is found among companies that have been on the AARP (American Association of Retired Persons) Best Employers for Workers Over 50 list.[29] A range of social and recreational programs is offered. Retirees and their families are included in corporate events. Sometimes company fitness and other facilities are open to them. Employers can achieve a number of goals in this way: maintaining active connections with retirees who, at some point, may return for short periods of employment; fostering a positive image of the organization in the community, especially among retirees' peers; and signalling to younger employees that it cares for workers even after they have retired.

A flexible employment policy must consider all of these needs and balance them with what is realistic for the business. Employees of all ages value flexibility in their jobs and work schedules. This principle must guide how organizations respond to the challenges of workforce renewal. Not only will flexibility be essential for managing the downside of workforce aging, but it also will have an upside, if employers take advantage of opportunities for more flexible approaches to work schedules, benefits packages, and careers.

Age-Inclusive Workplaces

Comprehensive employer strategies for older worker recruitment and retention can benefit individuals and organizations. For example, companies designated by AARP as a Best Employer for Workers Over 50 foster a culture that supports older workers to succeed. In fact, workplace culture is one of the assessment criteria for the AARP award. To be a "best employer" of older workers, an organization actively cultivates a work environment that is inclusive, supportive, and respectful. These workplace features provide all groups of workers ongoing opportunities for learning and development.

Employers who attract older workers tend to be equally welcoming to workers of all ages and backgrounds. That's because their HR practices, leadership, and culture aim to be inclusive – in short, they transcend demographics. Here are some examples of age-inclusive HR practices:

- Inclusive cultures support programs to meet the unique needs of specific groups. A hallmark of being inclusive is accommodating employees' differences, which could include functional ability to perform certain tasks. This principle applies to workplace and equipment adaptations for persons with disabilities. As we saw in the BMW example, employers are beginning to respond along the same lines to the needs of an older workforce.

- Employers need to assess their existing HR programs for built-in age biases. For example, older workers sometimes perceive a bias towards giving younger workers training and development opportunities.[30] However, workers of all ages who receive training are more likely to stay with the organization, which for older workers could result in delayed retirement.

- An inclusive approach to recruitment targets all underrepresented labour pools, as advocated by leading employer associations and sector councils.[31] Firms such as Home Depot strive to reflect within their workforce the diversity of the communities in which they operate. However, each group – from older workers to Aboriginals to persons with disabilities – faces unique barriers. Needed, then, is a comprehensive recruitment strategy with tactics tailored to each group.

- Health and family-support benefits can be adapted to the needs of a more diverse workforce. For example, some organizations offering phased retirement options (i.e., reduced work hours) maintain full benefits until the employee retires. This can be seen as unfair to younger workers in part-time positions. So a more inclusive approach would be to extend health benefits to all part-timers.

- Rather than creating a range of age-specific benefits, it is more cost-effective and equitable to design flexibility into an entire benefits plan, offering work-life support options that each employee can access according to her or his needs. This avoids the perception that the needs of one age group take priority. As a result, all employees will be better able to maximize their performance while maintaining a healthy work-life balance regardless of career stage or personal circumstances.

Policy Options for a Multigenerational Workforce

Population aging provides promising opportunities to update existing work-related policies, programs, and practices. Canada's public policy regime affecting work-retirement transitions recently has evolved in ways that support the retention of older workers. Yet as we've argued, even more concerted efforts by employers and governments are needed to meet the challenges of an aging workforce.

Discriminatory attitudes and stereotypes towards older workers can be addressed by government action. Human rights codes in Canada bar age discrimination, yet it persists. We can learn from other countries that have taken more vigorous steps to eliminate age discrimination and adapt policies to an aging workforce. The United Kingdom, some European countries, and Australia have adopted an "active aging" approach. Rather than viewing aging as a problem, it is reframed as an opportunity to tap into the capabilities and experience of older workers.[32] Consider these examples:

- The United Kingdom's Age Positive initiative provides guidance and case studies of good practices in an era of no fixed retirement age. These resources address how to manage the performance of older workers, flexible work arrangements, the health and safety of older workers, and research studies on aging and employment.[33]
- Nordic countries have promoted "active aging," which adapts public policies and institutions to an aging population.[34] As a result, Norway has one of the OECD's highest employment rates among workers aged 55 to 64.[35] Work is designed to encourage lifelong learning, offering ongoing opportunities for formal and informal training and development.
- Australia's workforce initiatives have been guided by research on the county's intergenerational challenges.[36] Rather than casting aging as a problem, it is presented as an opportunity to better harness the experience and human capital of older people. The policy goal is increased participation and productivity in an aging workforce. The emphasis on productivity goes beyond simply encouraging older workers to remain working.[37]

Two recent reports lay out specific policy options for Canada in this regard.[38] The OECD points out that Canada's spending on active labour market policies, such as the examples just given, as a share of the GDP is among the lowest in the OECD – something which could very well change under the new Liberal government in Ottawa. A high-priority active measure would be to reduce age discrimination. The OECD also recommends that Canada expand its employment services and supports for older workers seeking to re-enter the workforce or transition to post-retirement employment. The federal government's Expert Panel on Older Workers' 2008 report also recommended a government-led awareness campaign to reduce ageism and negative stereotypes about older workers.

There is some movement in these directions, but not at the federal level as of yet. For example, Alberta launched a provincial action plan, called *Engaging the Mature Worker*.[39] The action plan was part of a wider provincial labour force strategy designed to improve productivity, encourage economic growth, better utilize the experience and skills of older workers, and avert potential labour shortages. Measures include developing age-friendly work environments, introducing flexible work arrangements and phased retirement, supporting employers with tools for succession planning, providing mature workers employment and career services and post-secondary educational options, raising public awareness of changing expectations for older workers, and changing pension policies to facilitate the continued employment of mature workers.

While employers must consider the needs of older workers, equally crucial for managing generational transitions are a range of age-neutral human resource strategies. Above all, employers can better utilize older workers' talents by ensuring that age does not matter in the workplace. The overriding HR goal is to foster an inclusive, welcoming, and supportive culture for all workers, regardless of age.

Conclusions

Population aging is without exaggeration one of the most profound social changes we will experience in the coming decade and beyond.

Baby boomers are extending their working lives, which is good news for those employers who would otherwise face a labour squeeze or the loss of vital knowledge and experience. Governments and employers can facilitate by adopting flexible retirement and active aging policies. Many Gen X and millennial workers want to move up and contribute more; employers can do more to enable a smooth generational handover. An innovative and dynamic economy 10 years in the future will need to tap the potential of all generations in the workplace, starting now.

Employers must address the twin challenge of keeping productive older individuals in the workforce and at the same time expanding opportunities for younger workers to contribute more. As we have noted, achieving both goals may require updating how organizations approach performance and talent management. At a minimum both initiatives must happen in tandem, otherwise age differences in opportunities and rewards will only increase, fuelling an already growing sense of generational inequity. Fairness therefore must be a guiding principle for how employers, and policymakers, take action to address the diverse needs of a multigenerational workforce.

There are compelling social and economic reasons to extend our working lives. Canadians are planning to work longer, and a growing number do not have a specific retirement date in mind. Whether these plans are carried through depends, in large measure, on how well employers meet older workers' need for work that is challenging, interesting, and flexible and that offers decent economic rewards.

We dispelled any notion that older workers just want to coast into retirement. Older workers are highly motivated, even more so than younger workers. Indeed, it is notable that a sizeable minority would welcome taking on management responsibilities. Others are looking for a career change, which clearly does not fit the traditional image of retirement.

We also deflated the myth that millennial and baby boomers value very different things in a job. These age groups are more similar than many people think. Both groups would describe the ideal job as one that offers challenge and a feeling of accomplishment, pays well, provides benefits, and gives them the flexibility they need to balance work and personal or family responsibilities. Workers of all ages will benefit from more flexible and challenging jobs and age-inclusive workplaces. Through workplace innovations, generational diversity will become a business asset.

Other workplace reforms also are necessary if Canada is to achieve higher living standards and a higher quality of life. To highlight a prominent theme in this chapter, there are many ways in which employers can expand their use of the nation's already abundant human capital. Helping younger workers move up or older workers continue working are but two ways. This raises larger issues about the effectiveness of Canada's training and development systems and, more crucially, whether existing jobs let workers contribute to the best of their abilities. The next chapter focuses on these critical issues, exploring better ways to use and cultivate workers' capabilities.

6 Cultivating Workers' Capabilities

Canada's resource riches have shaped its history. For more than a century, we've tried to shed the "hewers of wood and drawers of water" mantle. True, Canada's new economy is more service-based, value-added, and knowledge-intensive. Yet the recent plunge in global prices for natural resources shows we're still on the roller-coaster ride of a resource economy. Given this dominant economic narrative, it is easy to lose sight of the nation's most abundant resource – our people.

With so many well-educated workers, Canada is punching below its weight internationally when it comes to competitiveness and innovation. This involves a basic paradox, which is our focus in this chapter. On one hand, business executives are concerned that their companies will fall behind in global competitiveness if they can't find the skilled workers they need. On the other hand, the view from the front lines of the workforce we've gleaned from Rethinking Work surveys shows that employers are not making adequate use of existing skills.

With such a capable workforce, Canada must do more to cultivate these valuable human resources. That's a sure route to more productive and innovative industries for the future – a route we lay out here. To this end, the chapter addresses three questions that lie at the core of redesigned work:

- How effectively are Canadian workers able to develop and apply their capabilities in their jobs?
- How can employers make better use of workers' skills, knowledge, and abilities in the future?
- What can be done to further develop the capabilities of Canadian workers?

We argue that tapping the workforce's capabilities more effectively will strengthen Canada's economic performance. Consider Canada's productivity gap with the United States, which is estimated to cost Canadians over $300 billion a year in lost income – about $10,000 per person. As Kevin Lynch, a BMO Financial Group executive and former head of the federal public service, puts it, the post-recession global economy provides opportunities "to make Canada more innovative in what we produce and more productive in how we produce it."[1] In our view, one of the most promising opportunities in this regard is work redesign. And as we show, unleashing workers' capabilities also will improve their well-being through a greater sense of pride, purpose, and satisfaction.

Is There a Skills Shortage?

One of the biggest myths about today's labour market claims that there's a skills and talent shortage which only will get worse. Yes, there are not enough workers entering some occupations to meet future demand – electrical utility operators and software code writers come to mind. And some organizations have been slow to groom their next-generation leaders to replace retiring baby boom executives. However, as we argue in this chapter, in general terms the country is not short of skills or talent.

This conclusion challenges a widely held view in the business community. Canadian employers want a labour supply tailored to their specific needs. For example, the "Employability Skills" initiative (later relabelled "essential skills") was launched in the late

1990s to lobby for educational changes that would equip graduates with work-ready skills, with the understanding that employers would build on these.[2] CIBC chief executive Victor Dodig recently claimed that "Canada's post-secondary institutions are not producing the types of skills that industries need."[3] The Canadian Chamber of Commerce and other employer lobby groups warn that a shortage of human resources is putting the brake on economic growth. The Chamber claims, "The skills shortage is becoming one of the great challenges facing Canada. We will all need to confront it."[4]

However, not all business experts agree about the nature and sources of this "talent gap" or "skills mismatch" that Canada faces. Employers definitely are not investing enough training. The Conference Board of Canada documents a 40 per cent reduction in employer spending on formal training since the mid-1990s.[5] And employers aren't keeping up their side of the employability skills bargain. A recent survey of 800 Canadian employers confirmed that successful businesses need essential skills, such as thinking and problem solving. However, only 39 per cent were willing to provide training in this area.[6]

These are not new concerns. Statistics Canada's Workplace and Employee Survey (WES) found that at the end of the twentieth century, only 36 per cent of employers considered it "crucial" or "very important" to increase the skills of their employees as part of their business strategy.[7] Cutbacks at Statistics Canada forced the cancellation of the WES, the only reliable source of national information on employers' human resource practices, but not before the WES was able to document that companies with successful HR-focused business strategies trained more and used high-involvement work practices to improve job performance – the type of work systems made famous by successful global corporations such as Toyota.

These human resource issues raised by the WES demand renewed attention as we search for ways to kick-start progress. If anything, the stakes are even higher because the workforce is now better educated.

Workforce 2020, a global survey of executives and employees in private- and public-sector organizations conducted by Oxford

Economics, offers a window on current HR practices.[8] Results for Canada show that over 80 per cent of employers rely increasingly on contract or temporary workers and provide less training than their employees think they need. Despite a growing need for technology skills, such as cloud-based software applications and data analytics, only 38 per cent of the organizations surveyed provide training in these areas. And just two in five employees surveyed believe that their company encourages continuing education and training. According to Oxford Economics, all of this adds up to a significant "talent gap" that could leave employers unprepared for the future.

The Case for Training and Development

The case for training and development should be self-evident in an era when knowledge is the driving force behind successful companies and economies. Some employers clearly understand the value of training investments and are finding new ways to promote workplace learning. The Institute for Performance and Learning, a not-for-profit organization, recognizes organizations that are training and development leaders through its annual Canadian Awards for Training Excellence.[9] For example, Home Depot provided sales associates with iPad Minis so they could learn more about store products and provide that information to customers on the spot – a good example of how mobile technology is both a learning and a performance-enhancing tool.

More companies are on a quest for innovation. The Global Innovation Barometer, a GE-sponsored survey of 3,100 executives in 25 countries, included 100 from Canada. Nine out of 10 Canadian business leaders identified innovation as a strategic priority for their company. Kim Warburton, a vice president at GE, explains what this means for companies: "Innovation is really a global phenomenon and it's tied to competitiveness and growth opportunities, so if you're not innovative, you're not going to be growing and you're not going to be fighting your competition."[10] Innovation requires a workplace culture that enables employees to use their skills, learn, and take initiative.

A study of US business competitiveness, conducted by the Harvard Business School (HBS), raises issues that should also resonate for Canadians. The critical message from this US study is the interconnection between firm competitiveness, living standards, and skilled jobs. This echoes the links between well-being and prosperity we have been exploring in this book.[11]

The HBS study reveals a growing divergence between large firms and knowledge workers, who are prospering in the post-recession environment, and small businesses and the average worker, who are struggling. The authors, Michael Porter and Jan Rivkin, ask a fundamental question: "How can we create a U.S. economy in which firms *both* thrive in global competition *and* lift the living standards of the average American?" Two of the study's conclusions are especially relevant for our discussion. First, managers' short-term focus leads to investing in more technology, contracting out work, or hiring part-timers – rather than investing in a skilled, full-time workforce. And second, employers are not forging needed partnerships with educational and training institutions to meet more immediate skills needs.

Two US examples of successful collaborations to achieve workforce development goals are relevant north of the border. Siemens, a German engineering and technology conglomerate, faced a shortage of advanced manufacturing workers at its North Carolina facility, so it partnered with a local community college to meet this workforce need, providing curriculum, equipment, apprenticeships, funding, and instructors. Electrical utilities face a fast-aging workforce, so companies got together to form the Center for Energy Workforce Development, a non-profit consortium that partners with educational institutions and unions, targeting low-income youth and military veterans.

Canada also has its own shining lights of how to grow a knowledge-based economy. Waterloo, Ontario, provides a model of how business, universities, and governments can partner to build a local tech start-up ecosystem.[12] The birthplace of BlackBerry, the Kitchener-Waterloo region has supported hundreds of other tech start-ups. The goal of building a high-tech hub is facilitated by Communitech, a unique government-industry collaboration that supports business development. Leveraging residents' knowledge and ingenuity is the key, especially that of University of Waterloo grads, thousands of whom have worked as co-op students in local tech firms.

An Inclusive Approach to Talent

An inclusive approach to learning and development is what's needed for innovation. Returning to the example of Waterloo's budding tech firms, it's "all hands on deck" – which translates into everyone contributing the most they can to build the business. Front-line employees often have more to contribute than managers realize. The solution to the talent problem is staring employers in the face: redesign jobs, management systems, and organizational supports in ways that enable all employees to make a full and meaningful contribution to corporate goals.

The inclusive approach we are advocating turns on its head the exclusive model of talent development that is common HR practice these days. Consultants at McKinsey coined the term "war for talent" in the late 1990s to make the point that a company's success depends on recruiting and grooming its "top talent." The underlying assumption is that these individuals are scarce and potentially can make a far greater contribution to growth and profits than the average-performing employee.

However, "talent" isn't just Siemens engineers or software coding whizzes from the University of Waterloo. It's everyone who works in these companies. As British academic Phillip Brown and his colleagues argue in their book *The Global Auction*, the "war for talent" has had some unintended consequences. It has increased global competition for knowledge workers, pushed companies to find ways to reduce the costs of knowledge work, and sharply polarized job rewards. An HR executive in London, England, interviewed by Brown and his team puts it this way: "We have segmented our employees brutally just in terms of talent. They've gone through quite a tough assessment process over many years now. So we have the group that is recognized as talent, and sadly, there is this group who are recognized as not talent. I don't know how to fix that."[13]

In contrast, here's what an inclusive approach to cultivating talent looks like. Take healthcare, where patient care requires a vast range of knowledge and skills, from surgeons and nurses to admission clerks and janitors. The best hospitals in the world, such as the famed Mayo Clinic, have cultures that value everyone's contribution and promote team-based patient care. And here's the key: teams are broadly defined to include all roles that impact patients. So a room cleaner who is well-trained in the risks of the latest superbugs can take pride that by doing their job well, they will reduce the risk of deadly *C. difficile* infection to near zero and improve the quality of patient care.

The concept of "talent" is widely used in management circles. We advocate a shift away from an exclusive focus on "top performers" and "future leaders." This leaves out the vast majority of workers. Building a prosperous economy requires us to leverage the capabilities of all workers. In this chapter, we use the term "capabilities" as shorthand for the skills, knowledge, ideas, abilities, and future potential of the entire workforce.

Workers as Active Learners

Leveraging workforce capabilities isn't something that employers (or governments, for that matter) can do on their own. The low level of workplace training in this country can't all be laid at the feet of employers. Training is a two-way street, requiring the active involvement of both employees and employers. Furthermore, educational institutions have a supportive role to play. In this regard, many university programs have emphasized higher-level skills (like problem solving, information analysis and synthesis, communication, and teamwork) in their curricula. These are general competencies that can be applied to any job, providing a foundation on which to build job-specific expertise.

We've already flagged employers' thinking about training as a barrier to people investments. It's just as important to recognize that workers' attitudes can also be a barrier to developing their capabilities. Indeed, some workers don't grasp the necessity of making lifelong learning a personal habit. Specifically, not all workers offered training by their employers take advantage of these opportunities.[14] Some 16 per cent of Canadian workers offered workplace training declined to participate. The reasons vary, including a perceived lack of benefits from the training, family responsibilities, inconvenient times for training, and heavy workloads.

For employees, keeping their knowledge and skills current is the best insurance against unemployment. Or more positively, lifelong learning can lead to a more personally meaningful career path. For decades, researchers focused on job dissatisfaction as the main impetus for finding another job. Now, explanations of turnover include workers' desire to acquire diverse career experiences. Employers' downsizing, subcontracting, and outsourcing in the past few decades have given rise to what former GE boss Jack Welch labelled the "boundary-less organization." The same market pressures have encouraged some skilled and educated workers to pursue "boundary-less careers."[15] These individuals choose to trade job security for a wider range of career experiences and competencies, which translates into continued employability and, they hope, a more satisfying work life.

Furthermore, there are promising signs that workers are making more use of online learning. The rise of MOOCs (massive open online courses) is reshaping university education for the digital age. Elite institutions like MIT and Stanford now offer open-access, free courses – but not for credit. Yet for virtual learning opportunities to be useful, workers must build it into their career plans. This assumes that a worker's supervisor has regular discussions with them to fashion such a plan and encourages follow-through – something that does not happen enough. And a lack of time may be the biggest barrier for self-employed and freelance workers, whose jobs often involve long hours or unpredictable schedules. Clearly, informal learning can't substitute for formal training. Still, the OECD makes a strong case for Canadian public policies and employer practices to do more to support lifelong and continuous learning.[16]

How Workers View Human Capital

How, then, do workers view learning and skills in an uncertain economic environment? Basically, skill development is not a prominent personal survival strategy for most workers. Rethinking Work 2015 determined that workers view mounting debt and growing inequality as the greatest threats to the global economy – things that the average citizen can't directly influence. A lack of innovation and productivity is barely on the radar screen of global economic threats, cited by just 1 in 17 EKOS poll respondents.

Readers will recall from chapter 1 that if faced with a prolonged economic downturn, a worker's most common response would be to "hunker down." This is a defensive response. In contrast, fewer than one in six would be proactive by improving their skills. In order for the nation's capabilities to develop, not only do employers need to invest in people, workers also need to invest in themselves. Given Canada's well-educated workforce, it does seem surprising that more wouldn't rely on skills development to get through tough times.

The key insight we can draw from these survey results is how little emphasis workers give to innovation or skills development. Anecdotally, our own experience supports these survey findings. Based on talks we have given to numerous audiences over the years, we know that people's eyes quickly glaze over at the first mention of "productivity," "innovation," or even "skills." Many Canadians are not aware of the importance of these issues to the future health of the economy, which could be a barrier to taking action.

Possessing up-to-date and marketable skills is vital for a sense of personal security in today's labour market. Perhaps there is a pervasive feeling of among Canada's well-educated workers that they already have enough education and training to meet their career goals. EKOS polls have tracked this sense of workers' confidence in their human capital – or capabilities – by asking respondents if they agree or disagree with the statement, "I am confident that I have the skills and knowledge necessary to move easily in today's labour market." Canadian workers generally feel confident in their ability to compete in the job market. Even though the Great Recession reduced this confidence to the lowest level in the past 10 years, still about three out of five respondents agreed with this statement (see Figure 6.1).

What does it mean if someone lacks confidence in their skills and knowledge? They may be very proficient at what they do, but technological advances have made their skill set obsolete. It also could mean that the frontiers of knowledge in their area have advanced in leaps and bounds, and they have not kept up because their employer did not support upgrading or they were not personally motivated to do so. Either way, these scenarios describe workers who are stuck in their current jobs and reluctant to venture outside their comfort zone to learn new things. As a result, these individuals' contributions to their employer and the economy fall short of what they could be.

Workers' confidence in their skills and knowledge has been eroded by a more competitive labour market and a less predictable economy. Bolstering this confidence by upgrading one's education is not as easy as it should be. This is not surprising, given confusing messages about the importance of learning. Governments and educators promote "lifelong learning." However, with no clearly defined roles and responsibilities for work-relevant learning, workers are left to sort through a thicket of options on their own. And that's unfortunate, because learning opportunities make jobs more challenging and meaningful – which we know from chapter 3 are sought-after job attributes.

Figure 6.1. Confidence in skills and knowledge

Q. Please rate the extent to which you agree or disagree with the following statement: *I am confident that I have the skills and knowledge necessary to move easily in today's labour market.*

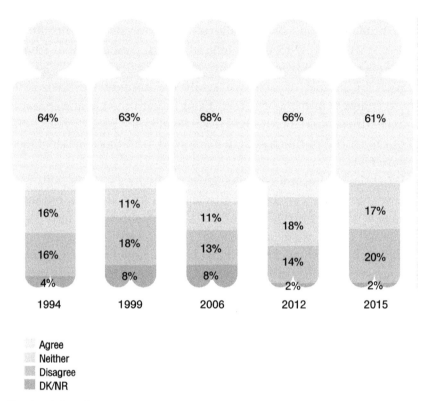

	1994	1999	2006	2012	2015
Agree	64%	63%	68%	66%	61%
Neither	16%	11%	11%	18%	17%
Disagree	16%	18%	13%	14%	20%
DK/NR	4%	8%	8%	2%	2%

Employed Canadians.

A Well-Educated Workforce

Rather than Canada facing looming skills shortages, we may face the opposite problem: well-educated people unable to find jobs that make use of their credentials. By international standards, Canadians are well educated. Over half the working-age population is a post-secondary graduate, more than in any other OECD country.[17] Over

22 per cent of men and 25 per cent of women in the workforce have a university degree, double the numbers 20 years ago. Labour market projections show most future jobs will require higher education and skill levels than today, a trend evident in post-recession job growth.[18] That sounds impressive, but it raises a crucial question that usually does not get asked in discussions about skill shortages: Do these jobs actually utilize the knowledge and skills they claim to require?

Richard Florida's image of a well-educated creative class only partly fits our Rethinking Work evidence. There are lots of university-educated professionals. However, just over half of all workers in para-professional, technical, and administrative and clerical jobs also have university degrees – and these are jobs that typically don't require a degree. Around 16 per cent of workers in skilled, semi-skilled, and unskilled manual jobs are university educated, which also seems high considering that at most these jobs require an apprenticeship. In short, there's an underemployment problem.

Despite this, investments in higher education continue to pay off. Among Rethinking Work 2015 respondents, the highly educated earn more than those with low levels of schooling. A look within income categories tells this story. Some 4 per cent of survey respondents earning $60,000 or more annually have high school diplomas or less, 19 per cent have a community college diploma or trade certificate, 12 per cent have some college or university courses, while 65 per cent have one or more university degrees. But what this income data can't tell us is the overall quality of these jobs and whether the values and expectations Canadian workers expressed in chapters 3 and 4 are being met.

This income–education link reflects the economic value created by knowledge workers. In theory, improving what economists call the "human capital" of the least educated – through support for either upgrading their educational credentials or acquiring job-related training – would help to reduce income disparities by raising the income floor. It also would improve the economy's overall performance. But this is not easy to achieve. Employers would have to make a strategic choice to upskill their businesses by offering high-er-value services or products, hiring better-qualified workers, and enabling them to fully contribute.

The global knowledge economy depends above all on a highly educated workforce that is able to apply their human capital to the most productive uses in their jobs. Education without application is squandered human resources. Canadians have for a long time valued university education above other types of credentials. So it is indeed interesting to discover that a university education has lost some of its lustre in the public mind. In 2004, over 80 per cent of Rethinking Work respondents agreed or strongly agreed with the statement, "The cost of a university education is a good, long-term investment for today's young people." Eight years later, in the wake of rising university tuition and a tougher job market for grads, agreement with this statement had dropped to 67 per cent. Signs point to growing disenchantment with the proposition that a university education pays off. One reason for this could be the lower quality of work life that results from doing a job for which you are overqualified.

Moreover, these views also speak to the growing divide between well-educated knowledge workers and the rest of the workforce. This point is underlined by the fact that 70 per cent or more of managers and professionals clearly see the value of a university education. In contrast, this positive assessment is shared by only half of workers in skilled and semi-skilled manual jobs. Some respondents, especially younger ones or those with lower incomes, may be reacting to the rising costs of university education – assuming they are even aware of this trend. But while university fees have gone up faster than the rate of inflation, the cost is far from onerous.[19] But there's another explanation, which has to do with how work is designed.

Our discussion of the inconsistencies in people's education levels and their job requirements suggests the problem is bigger than that the labour market does not efficiently match people with jobs. Particularly important in this regard are employers' work design decisions. To what extent are workers able to use their education, abilities, and experience in their job? To answer this question, we need to look inside the country's workplaces to determine whether workers' capabilities are being strengthened or squandered.

Making Better Use of Canadians' Capabilities

One reason, often overlooked, that Canada "punches below its weight" in the global economy is that we don't make full use of available capabilities. A clear indicator of unused capabilities is the 1.3 million unemployed Canadians.[20] Also relevant is the labour force participation rate – the percentage of adults gainfully employed or actively seeking work. The participation rate was around 68 per cent prior to the recession, falling to below 66 per cent after the recession.[21] The unemployment rate would be higher if people didn't give up looking for work and withdraw from the labour force because their prospects are limited. A strategy to make better use of available human capital requires an expansion of the workforce through more job opportunities, encouraging more people to seek and find work.

These are obvious signs that Canada has untapped human potential. Less obvious but much larger is underemployment, which results when people work fewer hours than they want or end up in a job that doesn't take advantage of their skills or education. While unemployment is tracked monthly by Statistics Canada as a key economic indicator, we know far less about the extent of underemployment. One global estimate suggests that there are at least twice as many youth who are underemployed than are unemployed.[22] The result is a huge productivity loss, not to mention the psychological, social, and economic impact on those young people affected.

There is some Canadian evidence that underemployment is common among recent graduates. Consider that university graduation has increased substantially between 1991 and 2011 among young Canadians. Despite there being many more degree-holders in both Gen X and Gen Y, throughout this 30-year period some two in

Figure 6.2. Key indicators of skill use and development

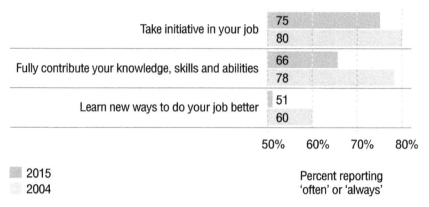

Take initiative in your job 75 / 80

Fully contribute your knowledge, skills and abilities 66 / 78

Learn new ways to do your job better 51 / 60

50%   60%   70%   80%

2015
2004

Percent reporting
'often' or 'always'

Employed Canadians. Rethinking Work 2004 and 2015.

five grads spent the early part of their careers working in jobs that didn't require a university degree.[23] So employers not only need to increase their training investments, they also need to redesign jobs to better utilize workers' existing capabilities. But the underemployment problem isn't limited to young people. We're about to see how underemployment affects workers of all ages in Canada.

The Underemployment Problem

Recognizing that in a global economy powered by the creative application of knowledge, Rethinking Work 2015 explored how effectively employers are tapping into the capabilities of all their workers. Specifically, we examine three key indicators of skill use and development (see Figure 6.2):

• Being able to take initiative in your job.
• Fully contributing your knowledge, skills, and abilities
   in your job.
• Learning new ways to do your job better.

Figure 6.3. Key indicators of skill use and development

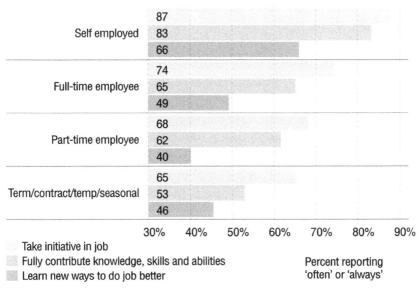

Employed Canadians. Rethinking Work 2015. Group differences statistically significant ($p < 0.001$).

Surely every employer in Canada would view these behaviours as signs of a highly engaged workforce. And for workers, their personal quest for intrinsically rewarding work involves all three.

Rethinking Work surveys provide a mixed picture of workforce skills. On the positive side, Figure 6.2 reveals that between half and three-quarters of Rethinking Work 2015 respondents learn, contribute, and take initiative in their jobs. On the negative side, however, all three indicators of skill use and development have declined since 2004, when between 60 and 80 per cent of workers reported these productivity-enhancing behaviours "often" or "always." While still at a fairly high level in 2015, the trend is moving in the wrong direction.

Being able to use one's capabilities is a pillar of high-quality work and essential in a thriving knowledge-based economy. Indeed, we find that our three measures of skill utilization add a further dimension to the labour market polarization we documented in earlier chapters (see Figure 6.3). Just as the self-employed are most satisfied and engaged in their jobs, they also are more likely than workers in other types of jobs to contribute and learn. Remarkably, close to 90 per cent of self-employed individuals responding to Rethinking Work 2015 frequently take initiative in their jobs – no doubt a basic survival tactic for people in business for themselves. About 75 per cent of full-time employees report frequently taking initiative, but this falls to around two-thirds among part-timers and contract workers. The clear message for employers is that the use of these contingent forms of labour may give a false sense of cost savings and efficiency, because the workers in these jobs contribute less than full-time employees.

The same overall pattern applies to being able to frequently contribute one's knowledge, skills, and abilities. Over 80 per cent of the self-employed do this, compared with just over 60 per cent of full- and part-time employees, and about half of contract workers. This latter finding underscores a significant hidden economic cost of precarious work: wasted human capital resulting from reduced skill contributions.

Despite much talk about lifelong learning and creating learning organizations, there is only one group in the labour market today that comes close to meeting these expectations: the self-employed. About two-thirds of these workers frequently learn new ways to do their job better, which again is probably a basic survival skill for these solo or small business operators. What should especially concern policymakers and employers is the fact that less than half of full-time, part-time, and contingent workers engage in regular on-the-job learning that could improve their performance.

Our evidence of underemployment also sheds light on a dark corner of Canada's knowledge economy. Some of the best-educated workers in the country are least likely to use their capabilities (see Figure 6.4). This points to one conclusion: that labour market institutions and employer HR practices have been slow to adapt to rising educational levels.

Figure 6.4. Key indicators of skills use and development
by highest level of education

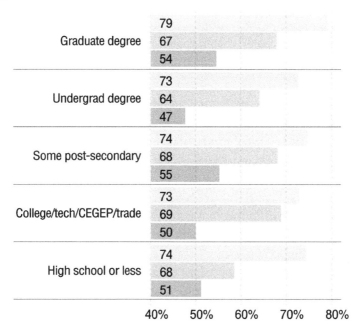

Percent reporting 'often' or 'always'

Take initiative in job
Fully contribute knowledge, skills and abilities
Learn new ways to do job better

Employed Canadians. Rethinking Work 2015. Group differences statistically significant
($p < 0.001$).

Rethinking Work 2015 respondents with graduate and professional degrees are most likely to take initiative, fully contribute their capabilities, and learn new ways to do their jobs. But if we look at the
much larger group of workers with undergraduate degrees, these
individuals are in jobs that use less of their capabilities than people
with a high school diploma or less. This underutilization is systemic
and pervasive, well beyond the media images of humanities grads

working as Starbucks baristas. Many of these people are in jobs that do require a university degree. The stark reality is that investments in post-secondary education are not benefiting individuals or the economy to the full extent that they could.

Capabilities, Engagement, and Job Quality

This finding spurred us to dig deeper into the Rethinking Work 2015 data in search of a more complete picture of underemployment. We used statistical modelling that combined a wide range of demographic, labour market, and job experience measures to find out which ones had the biggest net impact on each of the three skills indicators. While this analytic approach does not tell us what "causes" underemployment, it provides a more detailed and accurate description of which workers are most and least likely to use their capabilities.

Here's a summary of the more complete story of underemployment. Job location explains only a small part of how underemployment is distributed across the workforce, mainly through the positive effect of being self-employed. Having a university degree means you are somewhat less likely than less-educated workers to learn or take initiative on the job. More important influences on these performance-enhancing behaviours are being motivated and doing a job that meets one's expectations. As chapter 3 showed, better-quality jobs contribute to a more engaged workforce. Now we can say that the same job conditions also make better use of workers' capabilities.

Recall from chapter 3 that "looking forward to work" measured motivation, which is a prerequisite for being engaged at work. We also discussed the gaps between what workers rated as most important in a job and the extent to which their job actually provided this. These two measures have by far the biggest positive influence on underemployment (Figure 6.5). Workers who feel engaged and in a job that meets their expectations are best able to contribute, take initiative, and learn.

Figure 6.5. Key indicators of skills use and development by motivation and most important job characteristic

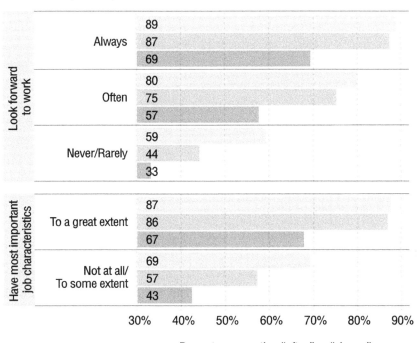

Percentage reporting "often" or "always"

- Take initiative in job
- Fully contribute knowledge, skills, and abilities
- Learn new ways to do job better

Employed Canadians. Rethinking Work 2015. Group differences statistically significant ($p < 0.001$).

We can't unravel the causal direction of these relationships. It is possible that looking forward to work also motivates people to contribute and further develop their capabilities. Conversely, it also is reasonable to argue that workers feel more engaged in their work when it provides them with ample opportunity to contribute and learn. Surely this is an important consideration for HR professionals and managers when planning corporate engagement strategies.

To view these Rethinking Work findings comparatively, according to a multinational employee survey conducted by HR staffing services firm Randstad, slightly more than 4 in 10 Canadian employees surveyed reported being overqualified for their job.[24] This is similar to the global average. The flip side of the person/job fit coin is being underqualified for your job, which was reported by 20 per cent of Canadians in the Randstad survey. In short, being overqualified for one's job is twice as common in Canada as being underqualified. However, in one important respect Canada has an advantage. Addressing underemployment will provide a pathway to improved productivity for Canada. That's because Canada has one of the world's best-educated workforces, so the quality of untapped capabilities is at a much higher level to start with than in other countries.

Barriers to and Enablers of Learning and Development

How ready are Canadian workers to contribute more to organizational success? And furthermore, what stands in the way of this happening?

Answering these questions takes us back to what people consider important in a job, the topic of chapter 4. Knowing these priority job features, and whether they are available to those who want them, helps to identify key enablers to and barriers of learning and development. Workers must want to learn, be supported to do this by their managers, have access to learning resources within their workplace, and be in jobs that are designed to take advantage of new skills and knowledge. Without these enabling conditions in place it will be difficult to unleash the full productive potential of Canada's workforce.

The Paradox of What Workers Want

Rethinking Work 2012 asked respondents to pick from a list of job characteristics and identify what is most important to them when choosing a job. Here we focus on just those characteristics that enable skill use, learning, and development. Challenging work providing a sense of accomplishment tops the list of most important criteria for selecting a job. More than one in four respondents ranked this as their most important job selection criteria. Of these, close to three in four said they experience this condition in their current job.

This finding adds a workers' perspective to arguments for making jobs more creative, innovative, and productive. But here's where we run into a paradox. Wouldn't we expect these meaningful jobs to have lots of autonomy and skill development opportunities? Rethinking Work 2012 results suggests otherwise. Less than 1 in 10 respondents to our 2012 survey selected "having the freedom to decide how to do your job, as well as a say in workplace decisions" as their top priority in choosing a job. Moreover, less than 2 per cent of respondents – which amounts to 1 in 50 workers – put access to training at the top of their list of most important job characteristics. Conversely, training is frequently viewed as the "least important" job selection characteristic.

Two implications for public policy and management practices flow from this evidence. First, there is a big disconnect in the minds of workers. While a good number of workers seek personally rewarding and meaningful work, they don't link this with having autonomy, decision input, and training. If employers and policymakers want to promote active on-the-job learning, enabling greater job autonomy and providing more opportunities for a meaningful say in decisions will help greatly. Workers will first need to be convinced of the benefits of these job enhancements, a tough sell if they are already disengaged, dissatisfied, or cynical.

Second, we can't assume that workers will leap at the chance to learn and contribute. Criticisms of employers for underinvesting in training need to account for the less-than-receptive audience for training. Perhaps workers have participated in training, considered it unhelpful and a waste of time, and so downplay its importance. People who feel underemployed in their job, especially if they have post-secondary education, also may not see the point of acquiring more knowledge. And as far as not wanting autonomy or a say in decisions, this could reflect the lowered aspirations of workers in dead-end jobs with low skill demands. In sum, if workers experience a sense of empowerment in their jobs and have positive learning experiences, they will desire more of this in future. The result is a positive upward spiral of learning, contribution, and engagement.

Who should take the initiative to institute these needed changes? We've argued that employers must lead the way. However, when it comes to training itself, workers don't agree about who is responsible. Rethinking Work 2012 asked, "Who do you think should be primarily responsible for the training and skills development of Canadian workers?" Responses were equally divided between employees and employers taking the lead in this regard (38 per cent each), with another one in four saying that training is the primary responsibility of the government.

Digital Literacy as a Learning Enabler

Information technology is a powerful driver of economic growth, productivity, and workforce development. We will now turn our attention to Canadian workers' abilities to use these new technologies. This "digital literacy" enables employers to make use of new technologies to meet business goals. And they also provide a valuable set of tools for workplace learning and training.

As millennials (Gen Y) enter the workplace, they'll bring with them the technology tools they've grown up with and which have become a part of their daily lives. Twitter, Facebook, LinkedIn, and numerous other social media are the fastest emerging forms of information technology, with potentially significant impacts on how we work and do business. Internet-based technologies are now commonly used in 9 out of 10 Canadian workplaces.[25]

Many jobs today require the ability to use an ever-expanding range of digital technologies, software, and applications ("apps"). Literacy (reading comprehension) and numeracy (math skills) are foundational skills required for success in work and life. Now we can add digital literacy to this list, referring to the "ability to effectively and critically navigate, evaluate and create information using a range of digital technologies."[26] Digitally literate workers can use information technology to accomplish work tasks and achieve organizational goals.

Employers are figuring out how social media can benefit their business. Few have mastered the use of social networking for business purposes.[27] Yet there are huge opportunities for social media to benefit employers through increased communication and collaboration among employees, customers, business partners, and community stakeholders.[28]

Capital One Financial Services Corporation is one company that has been recognized as an innovator in collaborative work by leveraging new technology. Capital One is a Fortune 500 company that provides a range of financial products directly to customers in the United States, Canada, and the United Kingdom.[29] The company's collaborative, values-based culture encourages employees to be innovative and independent and to take ownership of goals. Capital One's Future of Work (FOW) program uses laptops, smartphones, Internet phone calls, and reimbursed home Internet access to enable employees to choose how, when, and where to work so they can be most effective. Employees still come to Capital One locations, but these facilities were redesigned to reflect preferred work styles, work activities, and team interaction. The result is increased employee satisfaction and organizational performance, more cost-effective real estate use, and greater job flexibility.

Capital One's employees are young and well educated, which may explain the success of its FOW initiative. But the same approach works with a more diverse workforce. For example, Canada's TELUS Corporation encourages employees to work remotely from home or on the road. The company's Work Styles initiative features a new head office in Vancouver, with lots of shared workspaces. TELUS wants 70 per cent of its 43,000 staff nationally to work remotely. This required adjustments in how teams work and how performance is assessed. Already there's a big return on this work redesign investment: savings of over a million square feet of office space across the country and a reduced carbon footprint.[30] We should expect significant quality of work life pay-offs for the workforce too.

Revisiting the aging workforce theme that was our focus in chapter 5, it's important to consider the possibility of a "digital divide" in Canada, with the use of digital tools influenced by demographic characteristics, particularly age. Are there signs of this divide in the Canadian workforce now, given the rapid spread of these technologies in the last few years? The TELUS example suggests that age isn't a barrier to technology-based workplace innovations. But that's not surprising because this company is in the business of selling these new technologies to Canadians.

Let's start with age differences. Among respondents to Rethinking Work 2012, email use daily or several times a week is ubiquitous regardless of an employee's age (Figure 6.6). The same goes for regular use of the Internet to find information – a basic indicator of digital literacy. The only age group where this activity is not well above 90 per cent is those 55 and older. These older workers are most likely to be managers who can rely on others to do their Google searches for them.

Younger people are the early adopters of social media. Here we find expected age differences, with three in four employees under age 35 using Facebook, LinkedIn, and other social media very regularly, compared with 40 per cent or less among baby boomers. While the rate of regular social media use among boomers is about half that of Gen X, there are enough boomers using these tools to deflate any stereotypes of older workers being resistant to these new forms of communication. YouTube is somewhat less common across all age groups. This technology has limited workplace applications, although streamed video can be a useful communication and training tool. Finally, the use of Skype and other Internet phone services hover just above 10 per cent for the workforce.

We also checked for email, Internet, and social media use patterns based on gender, education, occupation, and immigration status.[31] We found a few differences but none that would amount to a "digital divide." Better-educated and higher-earning workers are somewhat

Figure 6.6. Information technology use several times a week to daily by age group

	Total %	< 35 %	Age group 35-44 %	45-54 %	55+ %
Type of IT					
Email	96	96	97	95	96
Internet to find information	94	98	95	94	88
Social Media (e.g., Facebook, LinkedIn)	50	76	64	40	32
YouTube	35	60	41	30	20
Internet to make phone calls (e.g., Skype)	11	14	11	10	11

Employed Canadians. Rethinking Work 2012. With the exception of email, age group differences are statistically significant ($p < 0.001$).

more likely to be frequent Internet and email users. Across occupations, skilled and unskilled manual jobs stand out for having low rates of frequent use of all three digital tools, which is understandable given the nature of these jobs. Even today, most workers on construction sites don't need laptop computers or smartphones to get their work done.

Canada's digital landscape has several additional interesting features. The use of email, Internet, or social media does not depend on where you were born (immigrants and Canadian-born have same rates of frequent use). Women (compared with men) are more regular users of email and social media, but not the Internet. And in a reversal of the digital divide scenario, social media use actually decreases as income rises. This no doubt is age-related, because millennials are the biggest users.

Three key points summarize this discussion of digital literacy. First, this form of literacy will only become an even more essential capability in the future. So encouragingly, the pervasive use of email and the Internet describes a workforce that is able to adapt to the digital age. Second, there are no major indications of a digital divide in terms of who possess these skills. And third, there is good potential for employers to tap these digital skills, especially among younger employees, for business purposes. This includes online and app-based training and development.

Seeking More Responsibility

Looking beyond the digital revolution, another workplace trend with important implications for workforce capabilities is the reduced numbers of managers. Management is one of the few occupations requiring post-secondary education to have shrunk in recent years.[32] Relatively speaking, there were fewer managers in 2010 than in 1999, as businesses and governments eliminated layers of managers to cut costs. The recession resulted in a 10 per cent reduction in management ranks during a period that saw a slight increase in overall employment.[33]

This thinning out of management has big implications. First, the remaining managers have more to manage and greater workloads. As discussed in chapter 2, these conditions lead to increased stress and work-life conflict. Second, managers will have less time for mentoring their staff, conducting regular performance appraisals, or providing communication and feedback. These have been basic ingredients of a supportive and productive work environment, at least in the past. Third, individual workers and teams have to take more responsibility for managing themselves. In both cases, new or different skill sets will be required.

The decline of management is a global trend. Take Unilever for example. This multinational consumer goods maker based in Britain has reduced its layers of management from 36 to 6 since the turn of the twenty-first century. Unilever and other firms busy de-layering are heeding the advice of experts such as Lynda Gratton, a professor at London Business School. Gratton argues that the position of general manager is obsolete.[34] That's because so many organizations use teams of peers who self-monitor performance and provide each other feedback, essentially taking over two traditional management roles.

Other business observers are not so quick to relegate managers to the corporate scrap heap. Research shows that an employee's relationship with their immediate supervisor impacts engagement and performance.[35] Less contact with that supervisor then becomes a problem. Still, thinning out management will be effective provided the organization implements an alternative model for decision-making. A few companies are known for having flattened the hierarchy and having taken steps that enable employees to self-supervise. Teams also can collectively handle management functions, as is the case in Valve Corporation, which makes video games, or W.L. Gore, known for its Gore-Tex waterproof materials.[36] For these companies, being able to work together respectfully and efficiently in team settings is an essential skill and the key to success.

Let's revisit our finding in chapter 5 that about half of Rethinking Work 2012 respondents would consider moving into management, up from 36 per cent in 2004. However, given the declining trend in management jobs, this may not be a realistic goal. Or is it? Even with this relative decline in management, still a good number of retiring baby boom managers will need to be replaced. Furthermore, what our respondents are expressing most of all is a desire for more responsibility in their work, which is the very sort of job enrichment that less-hierarchical organizations are able to provide.

Conclusion

The theme of this chapter is cultivating workers' capabilities in ways that benefit individuals, employers, and the economy. We have documented that Canada has abundant talent but too few opportunities for workers to use and develop it. To summarize the various threads of our analysis, here are the key points that employers, policymakers, and education and training providers should keep in mind as they rethink their approaches to human capital development and use:

- Canada has a well-educated but underutilized workforce. There is considerable opportunity for employers to help employees contribute their skills and knowledge, learn better ways to do their jobs, and take initiative.

- Despite Canada's high levels of education compared to other countries, the perceived value of a university education has declined this decade and fewer workers have confidence today that their knowledge and skills are competitive.
- There is no real sense of urgency among Canadian workers about the need to improve innovation or productivity. Skill development and training are not high priorities for Canadian workers.
- We can't assume workers will embrace the vision of a skill-rich and learning-intensive workplace. A barrier that must be overcome is the lack of importance placed on autonomy and decision-making – which are indispensable for continual workplace learning and innovation.
- Any digital divide that may have existed in the past is rapidly closing, given high rates of Internet and email use by most demographic groups.
- The decline in management positions, coupled with the readiness of many Canadian workers to assume greater responsibility, has positive implications for empowering front-line workers and teams to become more self-managing.

Above all, whether employees can apply their capabilities comes down to how managers decide to design work systems. As MIT researcher Zeynep Ton argues in her book *The Good Jobs Strategy*, successful retailers like Trader Joe's and QuikTrip in the United States make extensive use of cross-training with their front-line staff so that each worker is able to perform multiple tasks and has a much better understanding of how the business operates.[37] Workers' days are more varied and satisfying; the company has a workforce that is able to be consistently productive; and customers benefit by receiving better service from motivated workers. Ton uses the example of start-up businesses, where a small team builds a new company by everyone doing everything – and feels a sense of ownership and excitement as a result.

Better management practices also can close the gap between potential and actual job performance. In "high-performance" workplaces, business strategies revolve around developing and deploying workforce skills.[38] A recent study of 6,000 firms in 17 countries, including Canada, rated each firm on 18 basic aspects of good management practice.[39] Management scores largely determined each country's productivity ranking, with the United States first, followed by Germany, Sweden, Japan, then Canada. Inside countries, skills-based management strategies accounted for variations in firm performance. High-performing firms evaluated senior managers and held them accountable for attracting, retaining, and developing employees throughout the organization. The future challenge will be adapting these effective people practices to flatter organizations with fewer managers.

Peter Drucker, one of the greatest management thinkers of the twentieth century, recognized that the biggest economic challenge of modern society is "the productivity of knowledge work and the knowledge worker."[40] Writing in the 1990s before the Internet and globalization transformed businesses, Drucker was troubled by the growing divide between knowledge workers and the rest of the workforce, which performed routine service and manual jobs. It is timely to reinterpret Drucker in light of Canada's circumstances in the twenty-first century. In the next decade, concerted efforts will be required to make more jobs knowledge-based and turn more employees into motivated innovators.

Unleashing the nation's capabilities requires individual workers, employers, governments, and educational and training institutions to do things differently. We're not talking about a talent revolution – more like tweaks and small improvements that, when added together, can result in significantly better development, use, and application of people's actual and potential abilities. Our twenty-first-century revision of Drucker's thinking holds that the productivity of all workers matters. So whether you're a lawyer, a nurse, a call centre worker, or a retail sales clerk, it is how you acquire and apply knowledge in your job that results in better products or services. "Better" can mean higher quality, new ways of meeting customers' or clients' needs, more profitable, cost-effective, or market-leading. And as we'll see in the next chapter, better also means a stronger economy and improved quality of work life.

7   A Blueprint for Redesigning Work

Canadians face arrested progress with the real possibility that their quality of life will slowly slide backward. The effects won't be felt immediately but could reduce the prospects for today's millennials and Gen Xers. And the longer this decline takes root, the more difficult it will be to reverse. In this chapter, we counter this bleak scenario, presenting a blueprint for constructing a more optimistic future by redesigning work.

Pulling together the views and experiences of Canadian workers, we construct a vision for the future of work. This vision describes what a great job looks like through the eyes of Canadian workers. By mobilizing around this vision, employers, workers, governments, and a wide range of other groups able to influence the future of work can craft durable solutions to the current malaise in workplaces. We integrate the EKOS survey evidence presented throughout this book to identify promising opportunities to strengthen the "quality triangle" – overall quality of life, quality of work experiences, and quality of working conditions. Reviving prosperity depends, we believe, on improving these three dimensions of well-being – starting with people's jobs and work environments.

We don't claim to have a grand scheme to boost well-being and prosperity. That would need coordinated changes addressing technological innovation, governments' fiscal policies, immigration, climate change, community infrastructure renewal, and other issues beyond the scope of this book. Rather, we target the day-to-day work Canadians do, which has received scant attention as a source for solutions to Canada's current social and economic challenges. And we offer a unique perspective in this regard, tapping workers' insights about what future jobs and workplaces can and should look like.

Our blueprint for redesigned work is one route to a better future. We aren't alone in considering this a priority. Each year, the world's business and political leaders gather at the World Economic Forum (WEF) in Davos, Switzerland, with a host of invited academics and other experts. Its elitism aside, the WEF is good at thinking big. The future of work is squarely on its agenda. A WEF report by MIT scholar Andrew McAfee argues, "We definitely need to rethink the social contract that our societies offer to workers, but trying to protect existing jobs at this pace of innovation is a deeply flawed idea."[1]

Rethinking the deal for workers requires breaking out of the status quo. As we will outline, through work redesign we can make a decent quality of life available to more citizens. This calls for rebalancing working relationships to achieve greater fairness and wider societal benefits. Far from being utopian, this must be a basic goal for all advanced industrial societies. The OECD (a rich-country think tank of which Canada is a member) advocates inclusive growth, focusing on how the benefits of growth are distributed. The OECD's research shows that "there does not have to be a trade-off between growth and equality. On the contrary, the opening up of opportunity can spur stronger economic performance and improve living standards across the board."[2] In this chapter, we explain how work redesign can address two challenges posed by the OECD: breaking down barriers to prosperity and finding new frontiers for taking action to reach this goal. We offer a blueprint to help guide work redesign, based on what Canadian workers have told us matters most to them in their work. The concluding chapter gives practical suggestions for using the blueprint to achieve better jobs and workplaces.

Envisioning the Future of Work

We now will distil the views of thousands of Canadians into a compelling vision of work. Earlier chapters described what motivates workers, changes that could further energize them, what they value in a job, and their most and least important criteria for choosing a new job. When these complementary perspectives are combined, we have a vision of a great job.

Indeed, our evidence from Rethinking Work confirms that Canadians aspire to more than "decent" or "good" jobs. Borrowing the "good to great" business metaphor, this is what needs to happen on the job front.[3] We think the future of work can be better than "good," so we talk about "great jobs." This reflects the fact that many workers already have good jobs, placing the features of a great job within reach. The vision of a great job raises the bar for job quality all across the workforce. Doing so will provide an important counterbalance to existing sources of inequity in the labour market.

Blending the Best from All Jobs

We've argued that the "good jobs–bad jobs" distinction from the 1990s is too black-and-white to capture the varied and sometimes contradictory work experiences in today's labour market. We're not suggesting that the full-time permanent job become the norm again, as it was decades ago. Some temps and part-timers prefer these work arrangements and are reasonably happy; some full-timers on corporate career paths are miserable and disenchanted; and many self-employed have a high quality of work and life.

So the challenge, then, is making the most desirable features of contract and part-time work and self-employment more widely available, without requiring significant trade-offs in other aspects of job quality. This requires building into HR strategies more flexible options and setting higher goals for job satisfaction and autonomy, or self-direction. Such changes should not be a stretch for those employers who already measure and set improvement targets for employee engagement. In the public policy arena, actions to set higher minimum wages and expand protection under employment standards legislation to include workers in precarious jobs would also be required.

Well-educated knowledge workers have fared the best in the post-recession economy. The good news is that Canada's workforce has lots of these workers: some 40 per cent of the total. However, there are some red flags when it comes to job quality. Employers do not take full advantage of this abundant talent. Furthermore, even for knowledge workers in full-time employment, job stress and work-life conflicts can reduce their overall well-being and job performance.

Work pressures have increased since the early years of the twenty-first century, so any effort to improve working conditions won't get very far without taking aim at reducing stress and better integrating work with other aspects of a person's life. Work has become more demanding for a growing number of full-time workers. This is particularly evident among those working long hours, especially if the extra hours are unpaid. This important finding puts the issue of fairness on the well-being agenda.

What Makes a Great Job?

Canadian workers have told us what constitutes a great job. The social and psychological rewards of work stand out as big motivators. The most frequently mentioned reason our respondents gave for looking forward to work is their co-workers. Next in importance is having work that is both challenging and interesting, followed by being able to help customers, clients, and society. Together, these three intrinsic features of work account for close to half of all the reasons people feel motivated by their job. Pay comes after these factors, mentioned by just 1 in 10 respondents.

What changes could encourage people to be more motivated? Here's where economic considerations come into play. To be sure, close to one in four workers would feel more engaged if their pay or job security was better. Next comes better hours and schedules, then better bosses and business leaders.

Work values are central to how workers define a great job. Values express their personal vision of a great job and what they aspire to achieve in their work. Work values tend to be fairly stable over time, although there were a few noteworthy changes after the Great Recession. There's slightly less emphasis now on what the Mental Health Commission of Canada calls a psychologically safe workplace (i.e., free of harassment and discrimination). There is also less importance placed on having a healthy and safe workplace, work-life balance, receiving training, pay, and trustworthy managers. Even so, these factors were considered "very important" by about half or more of the workers we surveyed. And a few job features are more valued now, particularly flexible hours and schedules, input on decisions, and autonomy – all features of higher-quality work.

We've seen that demographics explain some work values variations. Age differences in values mirror the career and life stages of younger and older workers. Generally speaking, workers of all ages want the same things, with a slightly different emphasis placed on their relative importance. Women place more value than men on a harassment- and discrimination-free workplace, security, a healthy and safe environment, work-life balance, trust in management, and relations with one's supervisor. Well-educated workers seek autonomy and challenges. Less-educated workers want basic things their jobs probably don't offer, namely good pay and benefits, a healthy and safe workplace, and training.

The lesson for employers: get to know the values of your workforce. For example, prominent values in a software firm with lots of young, university-educated male IT professionals will be different than in an extended-care facility with a mostly female workforce performing low- or semi-skilled helping roles. With minor adjustments, employee surveys can provide values profiles as well as helping to assess whether existing working conditions meet workers' needs and expectations.

When we then asked respondents about their top-ranked job selection criterion, we discovered that both intrinsic and economic characteristics matter. Most frequently mentioned were a sense of accomplishment, good pay and benefits, a flexible schedule that allows work-life balance, job security and opportunities for career advancement, and having autonomy and input into decisions – in that order. Again, workers are describing a great job.

Now let's integrate this worker feedback into a vision for the future. Figure 7.1 summarizes nine characteristics that matter most to Canadian workers, have relevance for all demographic groups, and would address major deficiencies in precarious or low-skilled jobs. We group these nine characteristics into four broad areas:

- **Relationships:** with co-workers, supervisors, senior management, and customers or clients
- **Tasks:** challenging and interesting and a source of pride and accomplishment
- **Environment:** safe, healthy, flexible, and enabling work-life balance
- **Economics:** pay, benefits, security, and advancement opportunities

Missing from this vision are three job features that, according to many studies, promote well-being and performance: decision input, autonomy, and training. These are required for a capable and healthy workforce, which is just what's needed in a thriving knowledge-based economy.

However, some components of the "great job" vision can easily incorporate these features. Psychologically healthy and safe work environments provide workers a higher degree of control over what they do and more say in decisions than most would have today. Ongoing learning and training is a way to provide new challenges. That half of the workers we surveyed are willing to take on greater management responsibilities surely is a call for career development. At the same time, we acknowledge that the relatively low

Figure 7.1. Canadian workers' vision of a great job

importance accorded to these job characteristics could be a barrier to improvements – a point we revisit later.

A Blueprint for Well-Being and Prosperity

The great job vision is common ground for action. The vision is backed by solid evidence that the job features in Figure 7.1 are essential for workers' well-being. Over time, these improvements in individuals' working lives enable organizations to be more productive, innovative, and effective. Strengthening this link between well-being and performance is what leads to a more prosperous society. That's how we can address the pervasive sense documented in EKOS polls that post-recession stagnation is turning into decline.

A Multi-stakeholder Project

Canadians are ready to consider bold actions to improve well-being and prosperity. An EKOS poll conducted in 2014 asked respondents whether they agreed or disagreed that "Canada needs a clear plan or blueprint to restore a growing and optimistic middle class." A huge majority (83 per cent) agreed. This group of respondents was then asked who they thought should lead an initiative to create such a blueprint for the middle class. Figure 7.2 documents who the public thinks should play a lead role in creating this blueprint (response options were lead role, senior partner, junior partner, or no role).

Most Canadians favour the involvement of a number of groups in this initiative. The public wants to see governments, experts, citizens, and private-sector groups collaborate on a blueprint for restoring prosperity. We've heard extensively from citizens in this book and have frequently drawn on experts' research and advice. Now it is time to suggest ways for governments and the private sector to play a constructive role. Even though most respondents did not see a major role for non-profits or unions, we believe it is important to include these organizations because of their influence in the labour market and workplaces. For citizens to play a constructive role, they will need the avenues for collective input that non-profits (which we define to include professional associations and unions) can provide.

Change Barriers

A successful blueprint must be able to overcome barriers to change. As we hinted earlier, the existing gaps in the economics of work – pay, benefits, security, and career advancement opportunities – could stand in the way of workplace changes if they are not addressed first. Psychologists have long recognized that people's basic needs must be

Figure 7.2. Public views on creating a new blueprint

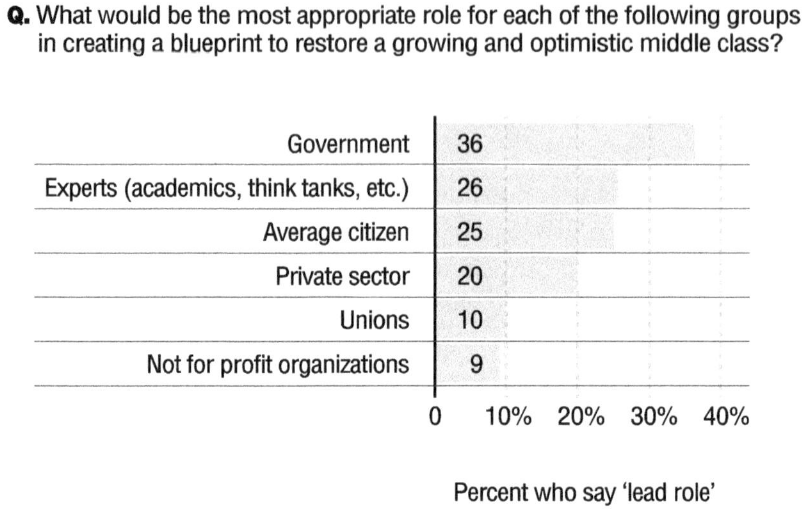

Q. What would be the most appropriate role for each of the following groups in creating a blueprint to restore a growing and optimistic middle class?

Government	36
Experts (academics, think tanks, etc.)	26
Average citizen	25
Private sector	20
Unions	10
Not for profit organizations	9

0   10%   20%   30%   40%

Percent who say 'lead role'

Canadians who agree that "Canada needs a clear plan or blueprint to restore a growing and optimistic middle class." 22–7 January 2014.

met before they feel able to focus on higher psychological and social needs. Workers in precarious jobs, most of all, are at risk of being overwhelmed with simply getting by, never mind getting ahead.

We also can't expect a blueprint to win immediate support without considerable effort to raise awareness about the need for specific changes. This especially is true for improving certain job characteristics that workers have told us are less important to them. Included in this list would be flexibility, being able to learn and use their skills, being creative, having a great boss, receiving recognition for their contributions, and having a high degree of autonomy over their work. And training is not a high priority for workers, even though Canadian workers are less confident now than at any time in the past two decades that they have the skills and knowledge to compete in the labour market. Ironically, these are the very changes that can help to alleviate problems like stress and work-life imbalance or to make jobs more personally rewarding.

A convincing case for work redesign also must help people see the broader social and economic benefits. Canadians don't see population aging or a lack of innovation and productivity as big threats to the economy, despite much expert evidence to the contrary. There's no sense of public urgency to improve productivity as a route to better living standards. Education and skills development also don't have the public's attention to the extent we might expect. Despite Canada's highly educated workforce, the perceived value of a university education is declining. Fewer now agree that a university education is a good long-term investment than in the early years of this century. In short, people need to be able to see the connections between micro change within jobs and these bigger trends affecting the country.

Many Canadians have told us that if faced with continued economic stagnation they would "hunker down," which means retreating from change and becoming more risk-averse. That's why it is important to tap into the resilience the workforce has displayed since the global financial crisis struck and the onset of the Great Recession. This resilience is the unsung story of what helped the Canadian economy survive the Great Recession better than most nations. It comes down to the often small ways that employees, managers, and the self-employed coped with economic uncertainties. Examples include early retirees becoming self-employed, employers cutting workforce hours rather than eliminating positions, workers upgrading their education, and until recently, workers in many trades migrating to Alberta. These examples display an openness to breaking out of the status quo in search of solutions.

Actions for Well-Being and Prosperity

This section lays out change options that can form the basis for a detailed "well-being and prosperity" blueprint. The changes we focus on are intended to make people's jobs and workplaces better. As we emphasized in chapter 1, the better future that Canadians want will require changing how we work. We give examples of what the lead actors in the change process can do, and what some are already doing. We also address barriers that must be overcome before progress can happen, notably low trust in governments and employers.

What Governments Can Do

Canadians want governments to play a central role in restoring prosperity. And when presented with broadly framed policy choices, the public opts for social and economic investments – just what a blueprint for prosperity would call for. That's what respondents have said in recent EKOS polls. Although these polls convey the public attitudes that led to the federal election of the Trudeau Liberals, they are also a starting point for exploring how governments at all levels can positively shape the future of work.[4]

Canadians are open to governments taking a fairly activist role, as long as actions are consistent with their shared values. An EKOS poll asked Canadians how they would address the major challenges facing the country if they were in leadership positions. The foremost goals and values would be freedom, integrity and ethics, and a healthy population. Also very important are human rights and a clean environment. Given the concerns about declining living standards and social equality that we documented earlier, it is interesting that these issues come next in importance (supported by between two-thirds and three-quarters of respondents). Least important is the small-c conservative approach to governing, with its emphasis on security and safety, respect for authority, traditional family values, and minimal government intrusion.

So while in the larger scheme of policy issues, addressing inequality and declining living standards does not top the list, government actions that target these problems have widespread support. A 2014 EKOS poll found strong support for initiatives that would benefit the middle class and the least well-off. A majority of respondents believed that placing limits on CEOs' salaries and raising the minimum wage would be effective initiatives in this regard.

Fairness is a prominent theme running through the policies and programs EKOS asked about in its 2014 poll. Based on majority support for these actions, Canadians appear to want a greater degree of fairness in taxation and compensation – plus support with caring for the young and the elderly. One action – limiting the salary of CEOs – falls outside the realm of public policy in Canada, although government certainly can set limits on executive pay in publicly funded organizations.

The public would like to see greater fairness as well in terms of the pension options available to all workers. A 2014 EKOS poll found little support for the argument advanced by the right-wing Fraser Institute that public-sector pensions are too generous and therefore underserved. EKOS asked a sample of Canadians the following:

> Some people say that public sector pension plans are far too generous and that they need to be seriously rolled back. Others say that while some changes should be made to public sector pension plans, the more urgent priority is to improve pensions for the majority of Canadians who have little or no pension coverage. Which of the following statements comes closest to your own point of view?

A majority (62 per cent) agreed that everyone else's pensions should be strengthened instead of focusing on public-sector pensions. Only 30 per cent agreed that public-sector pension plans are too generous and should be rolled back (8 per cent didn't know or did not respond).

Raising the minimum wage is a widely advocated and hotly debated policy response to labour market inequities.[5] Protests by fast-food workers led by groups like Fast Food Forward and Fight for 15 in the United States and dozens of other countries have advocated better working conditions and a living wage of $15 an hour. These grass-roots actions are having some effect: a growing number of US cities and states have legislated higher minimum wages.

In Canada the minimum wage hasn't budged since 1975, averaging $10.13 an hour after accounting for inflation. Minimum wage laws affect under 7 per cent of Canada's workforce (less than 2 per cent in Alberta) – about one million people. A number of governments are raising the minimum wage and more governments are tying future increases to inflation. According to the Caledon Institute of Social Policy, a think tank, these increases reflect the adoption of broader poverty-reduction strategies by governments.[6] Only one city, New Westminster in BC, has passed a law requiring businesses contracted to do work for the city to pay workers performing these jobs a living wage (about double the provincial minimum).

However, critics argue that legislated minimum wage hikes can backfire, leading businesses to cut jobs, hours, and training for low-wage workers. All kinds of experts, from Nobel Prize–winning economists to health professionals, advocate a decent wage as a way to raise living standards and improve quality of life. Legislation sends a strong message about fairness and the value society places on decent work. For wages to rise, however, this message needs to get through to more employers, especially large corporations, which employ far more low-wage workers than small businesses.

Governments also must modernize employment standards and occupational health and safety legislation. These frameworks were created for an earlier era, when full-time employment with one employer was the norm. Today they leave large numbers of precarious workers vulnerable. Ontario's 2014 Stronger Workplaces for a Stronger Economy Act closes this gap by extending protection to temporary foreign workers, co-op students, and interns and by holding employment agencies and their clients accountable for employment standards violations affecting temps.[7] An emerging issue for US policymakers, which can be added to this list of reforms in Canada, is fairer scheduling practices in retail and other sectors so that workers have adequate notice of shift changes.[8]

To be effective, however, standards must be monitored and enforced. Currently governments don't have sufficient staff in place to inspect workplaces for violations. In the absence of these checks built into the system, the onus falls on employees to complain – a difficult step for a worker who already feels disempowered and fears reprisal.[9]

Another headline-grabbing example is the growing practice of companies and governments using interns – an invisible free workforce not counted in official labour force statistics. Intended to give recent graduates work experience that could lead to paid employment, internships quickly became exploitative. After a Vancouver tech firm was accused of violating BC's labour code for its intern practices, *Canadian Business* labelled internships "a morally and economically indefensible practice" that should be banned.[10] One recent University of Toronto grad revealed that "there are a couple of marketing companies that are absolutely notorious – they have marketing graduates working 50-hour weeks and overtime without pay, and if you refuse to work the OT you don't get a reference."[11] Interns, for their part, have organized to lobby for legislation that would extend the same protections to them that paid workers get and to publicly shame employers into adopting fair practices.[12]

Governments need an integrated approach to workforce development, starting with raising public awareness and creating a sense of urgency for action on three issues: the social and economic implications of an aging population; the need for a culture of learning and development in order to meet the challenges of a fast-paced global knowledge economy; and the promotion of the fact that investments in higher education continue to have good pay-offs despite the more difficult job market for young people. It helps that there's solid evidence for government action in these three areas. And it also helps that some governments are already taking action by updating existing policies on minimum wages, employment standards, and occupational health and safety.

What Employers Can Do

Well-crafted public policies require employers to meet minimum standards for working conditions and also nudge them to voluntarily exceed these standards. Legislation alone can't lead to the sorts of jobs described in the great jobs vision given here. Employers must take responsibility for going further. Some progressive employers are improving job quality because it makes good business sense and demonstrates corporate values.

Take for example Mark Bertolini, the CEO of American insurance giant Aetna, who announced in 2015 that the company would give its lowest-paid workers a pay raise from $12 to $16 per hour.[13] It's easy to be cynical about such moves, particularly considering that Bertolini earned $8 million in 2013. But the result is a tangible step towards decent working conditions, as well as showing leadership that others just might follow – or already are following. The rationale was more ethical than economic, basically a move to restore the norm of fairness that was a pillar of the US labour market in the 1970s.

Different motives will move employers down this path. McDonald's and Walmart bowed to public and media pressure to raise the wages of their US workers.[14] McDonald's has been the target of global protests over its pay practices; its response to this public outcry was to agree to pay 90,000 workers in its corporate-owned outlets $1 above the minimum wage by 2016, but this leaves out the 90 per cent of its workforce employed by its franchise operators. Walmart is spending more than US$1 billion to boost pay for 500,000 of its US workers. This change in HR practices did not please investors, and Walmart's share price fell, sending a clear message to other publicly traded companies.

Despite this, other companies have responded to concerns about job inequities by adopting what can be considered fair labour practices. In Silicon Valley, high-tech firms rely on a huge workforce provided by third-party contractors, composed mostly of blacks, Latinos, and immigrants. After public-interest groups lobbied for fairer labour practices, Google decided to place security guards on its payroll with all the benefits other Google employees receive.[15] Stock markets didn't react, and no doubt other high-tech corporations are watching how this evolves.

Raising wages for low-paid workers costs corporations. A 10 per cent increase in overall wage costs cuts about 8 per cent from the profits of a large multinational.[16] But this isn't a zero-sum game. As

MIT scholar Zeynep Ton argues, providing good pay and working conditions can be part of a comprehensive operational strategy. The expectation is that "those well-paid, well-trained, well-motivated employees will generate even more than they cost."[17] And with case studies from low-cost retail industries, Ton shows how the success of companies such as Costco, Trader Joe's, and QuikTrip depend on the good jobs strategy.

Institutional change is gradual, so it is encouraging that a growing number of corporations have committed to being not just the best *in* the world but the best *for* the world. Close to 1,500 companies are now certified B Corporations. Similar to the LEED certification for green buildings or the Fair Trade standard for coffee, the non-profit organization behind the B Corporations certification explains that "B Corps create higher quality jobs and improve the quality of life in our communities."[18] In short, they are motivated by a higher social purpose than profit, striving to be good for society and operating "as if people and place matter." Many Canadian companies of all sizes have become B Corps, seeking a "return on values" in addition to returns on their investments.

Vancity is Canada's largest community credit union with an outstanding reputation for using a triple-bottom-line approach to business (i.e., people, planet, profits). Although Vancity is not a certified B Corp, it uses the B Impact Assessment in its investment decisions and to educate its business clients about how to improve their social and environmental impact. Vancity is a member of the Global Alliance for Banking on Values (similar to a B Corp), a network of banks that share a commitment to socially responsible and environmentally sustainable banking practices.[19]

Vancity has adopted a living wage policy as a way of enhancing the long-term well-being of the communities it serves. The impact on its own workforce was small, affecting a few dozen casual workers. The big beneficiaries were employees of Vancity's 1,500 suppliers, who now have living wage clauses in their contracts with the bank. The policy defines a living wage as what two adult earners must make to support a family of four, which in high-cost Vancouver is double the provincial minimum wage, or over $20 per hour (including benefits).[20] Vancity has developed a Living Wage Roadmap for large employers, sharing what the credit union has learned as a way of encouraging other employers to follow suit.

Experts argue that paying a living wage is the first and most obvious policy solution to poor-quality work and economic inequality. What really matters is a worker's take-home pay, which is affected by more than just a firm's pay practices. That's why coordinated action with governments is the best way to improve living standards for those on the bottom rungs of the labour market. Only governments can rebalance tax rates and rebates, invest in public services such as transportation, and, in the United States, address the high cost of healthcare and education. For their part, businesses could shift some of their lobbying effort to encourage faster and more effective action by governments to promote workforce well-being.

Employers also need to do more than give raises to their lowest-paid workers if they want to improve workforce productivity and well-being. A paradox of today's digital economy is that some employees don't have enough work and others have too much, a problem that reflects how management goes about allocating workloads. Despite the potential for mobile technologies to make work easier and flexible, that's not happening. This reflects employer resistance to telework and flexible work arrangements. Yet even minor tweaks in job design can give workers more latitude and relieve job stress. As chapter 2 outlined, directly engaging workers in initiatives to make their workplaces healthier and safer is a step in this direction. Indeed, the continuous improvement processes used in business operations and customer services can be applied to workplaces.

Employers don't have to go it alone. There are many public resources and industry-sponsored initiatives that can help achieve the great jobs vision. More are needed. The following examples show what is possible:

• The new National Standard of Canada for Psychological Health and Safety in the Workplace is a model for how experts, non-profits, employers, and governments can cooperate to stimulate change at a national level. The federal Mental Health Commission of Canada enlisted the help of many experts to develop the Standard, with financial contributions and resources from major corporations such as Great West Life and Bell, with the administration of the Standard taken on by the non-profit Canadian Standards Association.

- Industry associations also can be positive forces for change. The Ontario Hospital Association, representing over 150 hospitals in the province, launched the annual Quality Healthcare Workplace Awards (QHWA) in partnership with the provincial government.[21] The QHWA recognizes improvements in healthcare workplaces that benefit workers, physicians, and patients. Over 60 organizations participated in the 2014 awards, leaving little doubt that overall workplace standards and the quality of patient care have been raised.

- The BC-based non-profit safety association for the manufacturing and food processing industries – FIOSA-MIOSA – helps more than 2,000 businesses make their workplaces safer and healthier.[22] Its BC Safety Charter promotes healthy and safe workplace cultures as a basis for long-term success by having CEOs and other business leaders commit to actively promote this goal.[23] The Occupational Safety Standard of Excellence (OSSE) provides manufacturers with the tools needed to implement a comprehensive health and safety management system by adopting proven "best practices."

These partnerships among employers, non-profits, and governments demonstrate how collaboration can have widespread benefits. They generate momentum for change by sharing lessons about how other employers have overcome obstacles to make real progress. This shows the potential for designing safer, healthier, and higher-performing workplaces. Furthermore, the examples just offered highlight the importance of trust-based relationships. Trust is a precondition for collaborating on workplace issues – and for employees to believe that employer- or industry-led initiatives are going to benefit them.

Restoring Trust in Leaders

Canadians' lack of trust in political and corporate leaders makes it more difficult to develop a national plan to improve work. Restoring public trust in leaders and institutions is not an insurmountable obstacle to change. Indeed, the goal of improving work could be a rallying point that brings together leaders, citizens, and the organizations representing various groups of workers. Pursuing a shared agenda for change is itself trust-building.

Canadians would like to see their governments take leadership to address the nation's pressing economic and social challenges. However, government-led initiatives could be met with scepticism. That's because Canadians don't trust politicians. According to EKOS's annual polling, trust in politicians hovered just below 20 per cent positive from 2000 to 2008, when it started to decline, dropping to 9 per cent in 2014. This sentiment surely figured in the defeat of incumbent governments in elections at the provincial and federal levels during 2015, but it's too early to predict if trust is on the upswing.

In contrast, trust in public servants has remained higher, at above 40 per cent positive. So here's a basic paradox that has to be addressed in any blueprint: On one hand, Canadians want governments to take action to restore prosperity. On the other hand, they harbour a generalized distrust of politicians and only slightly less so of public servants. Government needs to make decisive moves resulting in real change to rebuild this trust and overcome public cynicism.

Employees also want to be able to trust senior management in their organization, as we saw in chapter 4. Recall that among those workers who consider trustworthy leaders the most important selection criterion for choosing a job, half actually felt they could trust the senior managers in their current organization. Indeed, lack of trust is the biggest gap between what workers want most in a job and what they actually have. This is a problem for developing a change blueprint because without trust, management-led change will stall or derail. Management can address this problem by acknowledging it first of all. Subsequent steps to rebuild trust must provide tangible workplace improvements, however small.

Employees have become less trusting of employers over the past decade. Rethinking Work asked respondents to what extent they trust the senior managers in their organization to "Take employees' interests into account when planning changes." This question gets at a fundamental expression of trust. Without it, planned change is certain to fall short of its intended goals. Between 2004 and 2015 the percentage of workers who had no trust at all in managers jumped from 31 to 44 per cent, no doubt in reaction to corporate downsizing and hiring cutbacks (see Figure 7.3).

Trust is influenced by a worker's location in the labour market (see Figure 7.4). The unemployed are the most obvious casualties of job market upheavals and have much lower trust than anyone with a job. In contrast, the self-employed are the most trusting because they observe the impact of employers' decisions at a safe distance. Full-time continuing employees are slightly more trusting than contingent workers. What's most interesting in this regard is the uniformly low level of trust in management across full-time, part-time, and contract workers.

Two other considerations: First, when workers are satisfied in their jobs – basically feel they have been treated decently – they are more trusting of management. Second, workers between the ages of 45 and 54 have the lowest trust of any age group. Given that this is the very group from which the next cadre of corporate leaders will be recruited, their lack of confidence in today's senior managers raises questions about what they would do differently to rebuild trust.

Low trust is symptomatic of weak employment relationships. This we diagnosed as a potential problem for employers, workers, and society in the *What's a Good Job?* study.[24] When relationships between employers, employees, and contract or temporary workers are not trust-based, organizations will lack the loyalty and commitment required to thrive. The weaker the bonds of trust, the more self-interested workers become and the less personally connected

Figure 7.3. Trust in employers 2004–15

Q. To what extent do you trust the senior managers in your organization to...
Take employees' interests into account when planning changes?

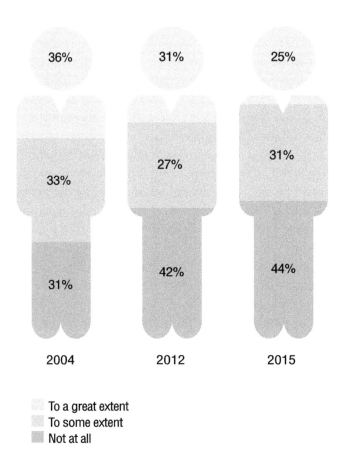

To a great extent
To some extent
Not at all

Canadians in the labour force. Rethinking Work 2004, 2012, 2015.

Figure 7.4. Trust in employers by selected worker characteristics

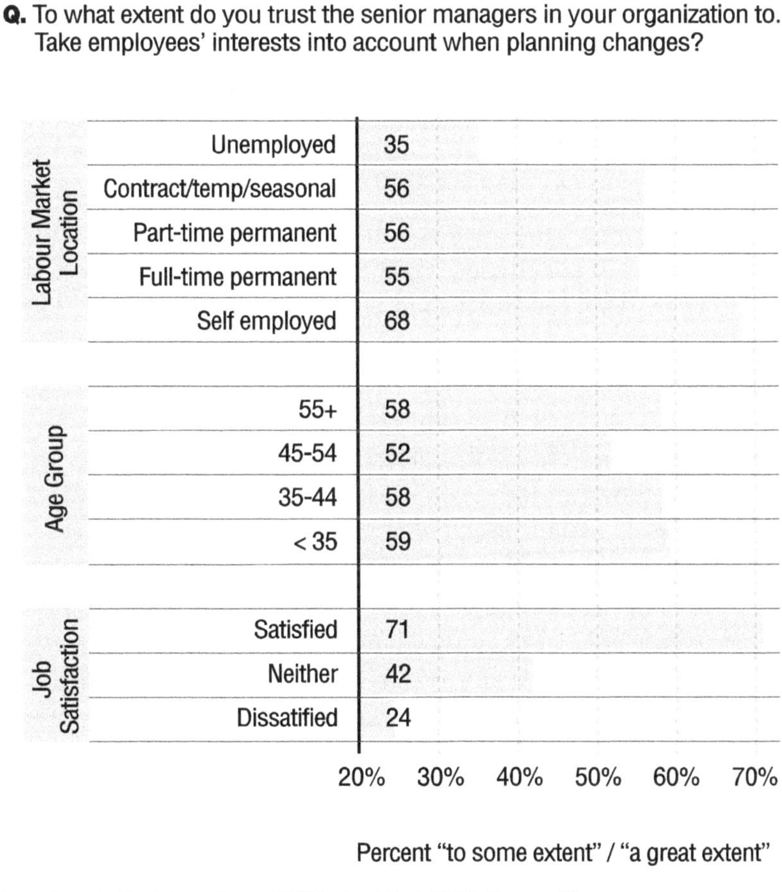

Q. To what extent do you trust the senior managers in your organization to... Take employees' interests into account when planning changes?

Labour Market Location	Unemployed	35
	Contract/temp/seasonal	56
	Part-time permanent	56
	Full-time permanent	55
	Self employed	68
Age Group	55+	58
	45-54	52
	35-44	58
	< 35	59
Job Satisfaction	Satisfied	71
	Neither	42
	Dissatified	24

20%   30%   40%   50%   60%   70%

Percent "to some extent" / "a great extent"

Canadians in the labour force. Rethinking Work 2015. Group differences statistically significant ($p < 0.001$).

they will be to the mission of the organization – even if they ultimately would enjoy the sense of pride and purpose this may provide. Building trust comes down to daily actions and interactions demonstrating that workers' interests are being considered. For this to happen, leaders need open channels of communication with workers and must actively listen to their ideas, suggestions, and concerns about change.

What Workers Can Do Individually

Workers can try to improve their working conditions on their own. Or they can pursue one of the many collective paths to change, for example through unions, professional associations, and advocacy networks, or by using the fast-emerging digital tools of social media or crowdsourcing.

We'll turn first to individual actions, which are a starting point for mobilizing workplace change. We are quick to admit, however, that individual workers can push change only so far given their limited power. One thing people can do is quit their job if they're dissatisfied, or switch careers to achieve their personal goals. We learned from Rethinking Work 2015 that just over one in five workers are likely or very likely to switch careers in the next five years. While fewer will follow through with these plans, those who do stand a good chance of expanding their career opportunities, increasing their economic contributions, and improving their living standards.

These are big "ifs" fraught with personal risks, so changing careers may not be a viable work improvement strategy for most. Quitting a job improves one's quality of life only if there is a better job to be had. Workers in high-turnover industries such as retail, tourism, restaurants, and hotels shop around for higher-quality jobs, but the choices are limited where low-quality jobs are the norm.

How can workers improve their existing jobs? One interesting tactic is "job crafting." This is when a worker purposefully redesigns tasks or working relationships to make work more personally rewarding. This is an informal way for people to reimagine and then reshape their jobs in more meaningful ways. For example, an experienced call centre worker voluntarily mentors a new hire during brief conversations throughout the day. Aspiring actors who wait tables to pay the bills can script their customer interactions to hone their acting skills. Hospital cleaners can make their tasks more meaningful by thinking about the benefits of a sanitized hospital room for patients.[25]

We can see that employees quickly run into the limits of their personal redesign solutions unless they are enabled by the leaders and culture of their organization. Job crafting is only viable if it contributes to organizational goals, not just employees' needs. In small ways, employee job redesign initiatives can be empowering. However, job crafting becomes a more effective work redesign tool when managers recognize its performance benefits and actively encourage it. This way, job crafting can morph into something far more powerful, especially if it becomes embedded in a company's continuous improvement processes and a culture that expects employees to find their own creative solutions.

These examples raise a bigger issue: How can workers gain more say in organizational decisions? There's been a lot written recently about employee "voice."[26] Organizational behaviour experts take an individual view of voice, encouraging employee feedback and suggestions as important inputs for management decisions. Voice also can take the form of speaking out on ethical grounds, or whistle-blowing. Or it can involve voicing concerns about workplace hazards, which is at the core of a "safety culture." Employees can choose to be "good citizens" in their workplace, by stepping forward to help a co-worker or to volunteer to do something that benefits others, such as organize staff fitness events or make a video of an annual employee awards night. As we will see shortly, collective voice is exercised through various organizations that represent employees' joint interests.

What Workers Can Do Collectively

How do workers find a collective voice? There are three main ways: unions, professional associations, and interest groups, which increasingly use the Internet and social media to mobilize around specific improvement goals.

Critics view unions as relics of a bygone industrial age. True, the rise of craft unions in the nineteenth century, industrial unions in the interwar period of the twentieth century, and public-sector unions in the 1960s and 1970s were responses to poor working conditions, unfairness, and all-powerful employers. Unions contributed to the rise of Canada's post–Second World War middle class.

However, unions' future prospects will be dim unless they adapt to the challenges we have documented in the post-recession environment. Just like employers, unions must be more attuned to what's on the minds of Canadian workers, updating their agendas to meet workers' current needs and future aspirations, and to avoid being perceived as too self-interested in the process. And as critics point out, unions' basic business model is under enormous pressure.[27] The costs of recruiting new members are high, the union wage advantage has shrunk, and a tough labour market encourages greater individualism among young workers as a survival tactic.

In early 2015, there were about 4.7 million union members in Canada, accounting for a quarter of the entire workforce.[28] That leaves over 10 million employees with no union representation. Union membership growth since the 1960s has been concentrated mostly in the public sector. That's why public-sector pensions are better than in the private sector and why low-level employees earn more than in the private sector, whereas the opposite is true for senior managers and executives. For example, none of the highest-paid public-sector executives in Ontario earned more than $1.7 million in 2013, compared to between $17 million and $49 million for top private-sector executives.[29] Eye-popping salaries to be sure, but the point is that top earners in the private sector have upwards of a 10-to-1 wage premium over their public-sector counterparts.

Canadians have told us they want to restore middle-class progress and reduce income inequality. Unions can help attain these goals. Critics will argue that collective agreements tie pay increases and career advancement to seniority, not merit, reducing the performance of public organizations. However, this assumes that the private sector has figured out how to evaluate and reward employees who perform their jobs really well. But as some HR professionals admit, performance management is difficult to do well. Relying on annual performance reviews is not enough. Might it be possible for unions and management to find common cause here, agreeing on fairer and more effective methods for providing the feedback, coaching, and recognition that employees need to do a better job? Some public-sector unions in healthcare and other areas have already responded to this need.

Rethinking Work surveys showed stable union membership between 2004 and 2015. In contrast, professional association membership increased to 22 per cent of the workforce – a sure sign of the rise of a knowledge-based economy. A smaller group of workers (6 per cent) are represented by staff associations, which are basically in-house and management-friendly versions of a union. Added up, just over half of all workers have some form of collective representation to address job and workplace issues.

Compared to Americans, for whom union membership has plummeted, Canadians have been more accepting of unions and collective bargaining as a means of improving working conditions. When EKOS asked Canadian workers in 2015 if they agree or disagree that "All in all, unions are a positive force in society," close to half agreed (see Figure 7.5).

Indeed, collective bargaining is a fundamental right entrenched within Canada's Constitution. This point was made by the Supreme Court in recent landmark decisions affirming RCMP officers' right to form a union and the right of Saskatchewan public-sector employees to strike.[30] These rulings illustrate the importance of aligning labour relations laws with rights. For example, under the Harper Conservatives, the federal government moved in the opposite direction by making it more difficult for workers to form unions in workplaces in the transportation, telecommunications, and banking industries and easier to decertify existing unions (changes which could be reversed by the newly elected Liberal government).[31]

Unions will not be surprised to learn that support for them is highest among contract and temporary workers – the most difficult group to organize under existing labour legislation. That's because these laws reflect traditional employee-employer relationships and

Figure 7.5. Support for unions by selected worker characteristics

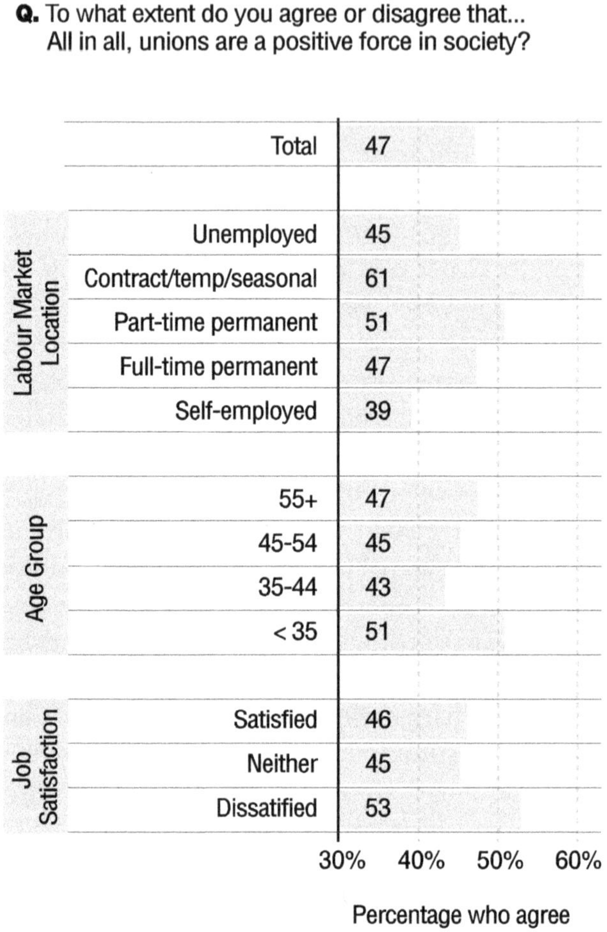

Q. To what extent do you agree or disagree that...
All in all, unions are a positive force in society?

	Total	47
Labour Market Location	Unemployed	45
	Contract/temp/seasonal	61
	Part-time permanent	51
	Full-time permanent	47
	Self-employed	39
Age Group	55+	47
	45-54	45
	35-44	43
	< 35	51
Job Satisfaction	Satisfied	46
	Neither	45
	Dissatified	53

                          30%   40%   50%   60%

                          Percentage who agree

Canadians in the labour force. Rethinking Work 2015. Group differences statistically significant ($p < 0.001$).

clearly are in need of updating. What's more, the fact that younger workers see unions as a positive social force is a direct challenge for unions to find more effective ways to reach out to Generation Y.

Happier workers also will be more difficult to organize. Employers should reflect on their HR practices in light of the finding that workers view unions less favourably when they experience job satisfaction. This raises a classic dilemma for unions. Many unions join with other groups to advocate for higher minimum wages, expanded rights for precarious workers, and generally more decent working conditions. Still, unions need to keep contributing to these "public good" initiatives to maintain their relevance, even though success may reduce their appeal among individual workers.

The number of professional, technical, and other well-educated knowledge workers will continue to grow. Whether nurses and environmental scientists, engineers and accountants, occupational health and safety specialists and computer programmers, professions organize to advance the collective interests of their members. Self-regulating professions (such as law and medicine) have a legal responsibility to ensure that members live up to ethical standards and codes of conduct. Career development and working conditions are priorities.

Generally speaking, professional bodies are well-positioned to influence government policies and employers' HR practices. For example, nursing associations have addressed issues ranging from nurses' safety and workloads to what's called "scope of practice" – ensuring that nurses' work settings support them to deliver the best-quality patient care. Associations can survey their members to document their quality of work life, as medical associations have done over the past decade. They also benchmark salaries and benefits, as professional engineers' associations do, which sets basic standards of employment across the profession.

Human resource professionals and psychologists address work issues in their professional roles, so they are especially well-positioned to be catalysts for change. Provincial HR associations in Canada have done much in the past decade to establish HR on a solid professional footing, providing learning and development opportunities and professional certification for members. Most of all, HR associations are clearing houses for effective people practices, benchmarking pay and benefits, and monitoring changes in employment relationships. As the HR profession achieves its goal of being a "strategic partner," with a chief human resource officer or HR vice president at the executive table, it is more likely that a wider range of employee issues will inform corporate decisions.

Psychologists also are influencers, more often as independent experts or through corporate employee assistance programs. And professional psychologists have actively promoted mentally healthy workplaces. Initiatives include the annual Psychologically Healthy Workplace Awards, sponsored by the American Psychological Association and offered in 52 US states and Canadian provinces, as well as making important contributions to the Mental Health Commission of Canada and the National Standard of Canada for Psychological Health and Safety in the Workplace. Promoting healthy workplace practices through public education and the development of easily accessible resources contribute to a better working future.

Conclusion

This chapter laid out a blueprint for achieving better jobs and workplaces. At its centre is a vision of a great job, which we created thanks to the insights provided by thousands of Canadian workers. We've argued that a convergence of forces makes the timing right for a national project to improve work. An anaemic economic recovery, heightened concern about inequality and declining living standards, public support for a significant multisector initiative to improve well-being – these all provide an impetus for change.

History holds out many lessons for how breakthroughs have been made in the promotion of safer, healthier, and fairer workplaces. Governments, employers, NGOs, unions, and professional groups have succeeded in reducing workplace injuries and fatalities, improving human rights, preventing bullying and harassment, and reducing barriers to the advancement of women and minorities. If our reading of the public mood is correct, then Canada may have the enabling conditions in place for another breakthrough.

Canadians' outlook on the economy and society mixes optimism and pessimism. Our reading of the extensive feedback we have received from workers is that optimism can trump pessimism, providing a path into the future. But the pessimism can't be ignored, for its here that we find potential barriers to creating better jobs. These are the standard ones that have slowed or prevented improvements in people's jobs and workplaces in the past. These include corporate leaders who don't see the strategic value of improved workforce well-being, a lack of political will to update regulatory frameworks for the labour market, and the low priority some workers place on the kinds of improvements we argue are urgently needed.

To guide the way forward, we tapped into the experiences and perspectives of workers. Using many EKOS surveys, we have been able to see the ideal future job and workplace through the eyes of workers. Canadians have been very articulate about what they value in a job, what they would look for in a new job, what motivates them, and what could motivate them more. We distilled this input into a vision for a great job – which essentially describes work that contributes to the well-being of the workforce and the success of organizations. With this vision, we sketched out a blueprint for the future of work, outlining how all key labour market actors have a vital role to play. In the final chapter, we suggest actions that employers, workers and their organizations, governments, and a host of other interested groups can take to lead Canada towards a more prosperous future.

8 Actions to Improve Well-Being and Prosperity

In this final chapter, we consolidate our suggestions for improving jobs and workplaces. We use the blueprint for redesigning work in chapter 7 as a guide to creating higher-quality jobs and workplaces. It's a guide for individually and collectively shaping a more promising future, one in which the goals of well-being and prosperity are mutually reinforced through people's daily work experiences.

The blueprint we have sketched is an invitation to readers to join in a constructive discussion about how to craft the future of work. A national dialogue like this happens all too infrequently. We can think of a few occasions when Canadian workers and their representative organizations, managers, executives, policymakers, and experts have come together in search of common ground to make improvements in workplaces and people's work lives.

Sometimes it happens at conferences. For example, the Conference Board of Canada's annual Better Workplace conference has addressed future-of-work issues. The October 2015 conference theme was "working together to build a better workplace," and one of us (Lowe) had an opportunity to raise the issues laid out in this book.[1]

Also in 2015, each of us participated in conferences which, in their own distinct ways, were about the future of work. The Future of Work and Workers of the Future, held in Rome, reflected European concerns about high youth unemployment and better pathways for the millennial generation into gainful employment. In stark contrast, the other conference was South by Southwest (SXSW) in Austin, Texas. It's a hub where thousands of young "digital creatives" from America and around the world share ideas, find funders and partners for start-up ventures, and cultivate the networks that will grow businesses in technology, media, or marketing. They didn't talk as much about "the future of work" because these millennials were too busy making that future. Two very different futures indeed.

But the European youth at the centre of the Rome conference are the marginalized and alienated, so they are certainly not part of any discussion about the future. And the tech entrepreneurs at SXSW are mostly in it for themselves, although a growing number are motivated by doing good. This raises a bigger question: How can people collectively craft a better working future? A promising opportunity for a wide range of interested organizations and individuals was the 2014 Good Jobs Summit held at the former Maple Leaf Gardens arena in Toronto.[2]

The summit was sponsored by Unifor (the country's largest private-sector union), the Canadian Federation of Students, Ryerson University, and the Canadian Centre for Policy Alternatives (CCPA). The focus was on how to reverse the decline of good jobs. Unifor, for its part, encouraged workers to cooperate with employers to find solutions. Interestingly, speakers at the summit included Ontario premier Kathleen Wynne and the CEOs of General Electric Canada and J.D. Irving Corporation – so it can't be easily dismissed as a left-wing confab. This collaborative dialogue sought to define the role of workers and their organizations, employers, and governments in creating better-quality jobs. Regional Good Jobs Summits are being held in other communities, including Thunder Bay, Vancouver, Kingston, and Oshawa.

The priority actions identified by summit participants included strengthening employment standards by extending protections and rights to all workers and establishing a threshold living wage. Such proposals are bound to spark an ideological debate. The right-wing Fraser Institute advocates exactly the opposite: less labour market regulation and no increase in the minimum wage.[3] As one of the institute's researchers asked, based on a comparison of public- and private-sector compensation in British Columbia, "is it fair that a private-sector worker working a similar job as a public-sector worker is getting paid less in terms of total compensation?"[4] The institute's answer is no, with the logical outcome being an erosion of living standards for public-sector workers. Other labour market stakeholders, notably the Canadian Federation of Independent Business (CFIB), likely would come down on the side of the Fraser Institute on these issues. The public-sector jobs the Fraser Institute considers to be overgenerous are the sort of "good jobs" that the Unifor Summit wants more of.

We don't expect that a broad coalition spanning the ideological spectrum, bringing together the likes of the CCPA and the Fraser Institute for example, is a realistic way to craft a pathway to "great jobs." But *Redesigning Work* has staked out some new common ground.

Individual Canadians' work experiences, aspirations, and behaviour can provide a fresh starting point for discussions about the work ideals for the future. This is evidence-based, non-ideological, and defined by workers who are in all sorts of jobs. For example, some of the self-employed are among the happiest and most productive workers in the country. Interestingly, this group includes the small business owners and entrepreneurs championed by the Fraser Institute and represented by the CFIB. Nobody would dare claim that it's unfair for these individuals to attain decent work and high levels of well-being. Nor is it reasonable to conclude that therefore more employees need to become self-employed. Perhaps, then, our unique ground-level view of challenges and opportunities in the working lives of Canadians can provide a basis for crafting a broadly based, collaborative change agenda.

We've suggested that employers have a lead role to play in creating healthy, fulfilling, and more productive work. Some already are. As we've seen, Canadian corporations such as Bell and Great West Life have made significant contributions to promoting mental

health in the workplace. Outside Canada, there are also good examples of this happening. Paul Polman, the CEO of consumer products
multinational Unilever, has pushed the company to the forefront
of ethical and sustainable business practices by committing to improving the health and well-being of its customers and employees.[5]
Billionaire Carlos Slim, who owns much of Mexico's telecommunications sector, has come out advocating a three-day workweek as a
way to encourage older workers to stay employed – and followed
through by introducing this option for employees at his phone company Telmex.[6]

Some larger organizations have added a new executive position
of "chief culture officer," responsible for keeping the workforce focused on living the corporate values, which often embrace respect,
teamwork, innovation, trust, and more. A people-focused culture
sets the tone for more effective HR policies and practices, which
are a prerequisite for improving the quality of jobs. And we can expect these executive roles to evolve. *Fast Company*'s recent portrayal
of the workplace in 2030 highlights the future need for a "chief of
work."[7] This individual would do more than support the organization's culture; they also would ensure that people have a productive and healthy work environment and the right technologies to do
their jobs well.

So as readers can see, there are lots of ideas already on the table for
consideration. Here, then, are some suggestions for how to achieve
Canadian workers' vision of a great job. Readers should take this as
an open invitation for further discussions in the public sphere and
inside organizations about the kind of jobs and workplaces Canada
needs to have to restore prosperity and improve the overall quality
of work life.

Connect the Quality Dots

As we think about what actions will improve well-being and prosperity, it's helpful to keep in mind the "quality triangle": quality of

life (or what we called "happiness" in chapter 2), quality of work experiences, and quality of working conditions. Quality of life can't be separated from three key aspects of work experience: job satisfaction, work-life balance, and engagement. These quality-of-life dimensions form a larger picture of well-being, which encourages a holistic and integrated approach to change. Concerted action to improve these work experiences are on the HR work plans of a good number of organizations. Not only will making progress on these three issues improve organizational performance, but the overall well-being of the workforce also will be enhanced.

The polarized distribution of well-being in the workforce reveals that educated knowledge workers, notably professionals and managers, have the highest life satisfaction while low-wage, less-educated workers are least satisfied. Feeling optimistic about one's personal finances and the direction of the economy also contributes to being more satisfied with life. However, the Canadian dream of achieving a middle-class lifestyle is slowly slipping from the grasp of most workers, and there are heightened worries about society becoming more divided into haves and have-nots. Thus it is critical that changes targeting jobs and workplaces are understood in the public mind as part of the solution to these challenges. Communicating these links must be a public policy priority. This basic dot-connecting will require far-sighted policy analysts and communication experts to put these dots together for the public. Some governments across the country – notably the new Liberal government in Ottawa – may be in a position to articulate the links between people's daily work experiences and society's well-being as a basis for action.

Adopt a Multidimensional Approach to Well-Being

Canadian workers' satisfaction with work and life in general has declined in the past decade. All signs point to the economic trauma inflicted by the Great Recession as the main culprit, but these are symptoms of a broader malaise that we have called "arrested progress." Reversing this decline in well-being should be a public policy priority, because it directly impacts public health, healthcare costs, and economic performance. Governments therefore must find ways to connect health and economic policies, enabling an integrated approach.

A minority of workers are still reeling from the shocks of the Great Recession. They are worried about the prospects of lower living standards, years of slow economic growth ahead, increased social inequality, and their own financial struggles. This group exemplifies the besieged middle class. Their fate is now a defining political issue, as confirmed by numerous EKOS polls leading up to the 2015 federal election. What this book clearly documents is that these middle-class concerns about bigger economic and social forces make individuals less engaged in their work, less satisfied with life and work, and in all likelihood resistant to change – even if that change would benefit them. The lived experiences and current state of mind of these workers has to be addressed in any initiative to improve workforce well-being.

One interpretation of Canadians' response to the Great Recession, in comparison with the previous recession in the early 1990s, is that today's workforce may be more resilient. This psychological capacity to bounce back in the face of adversity will only become more important. If we are correct in this interpretation, then this is a workforce trait that employers can foster as a way of developing well-being and preparing for the next economic shock wave. Actions in this direction have potential partners, notably organizations such as the Mental Health Commission of Canada and the Canadian Mental Health Association, as well as companies that provide employee assistance plans for employers.

Discussions about how to improve job quality must expand beyond pay and job type (whether it is full-time or part-time employment, contract work, or self-employment) to include a range of social and psychological features of work, because these have a direct impact on workers' well-being and job performance.

Begin with the Great Job Vision

Workers' vision of a great job provides a useful starting point for key stakeholders to take the next steps required to achieve this vision. For employers, this involves an assessment of how their company or organization measures up against the four pillars of a great job: relationships, tasks, the work environment, and economic features. Knowing where the gaps are, and also knowing what your workforce most needs and values, can then help you to recalibrate and integrate existing HR, training and development, diversity, workplace wellness, and other strategies.

The first question policymakers must ask is whether their government's departments and agencies measure up as employers, just as we have encouraged other employers to do. The second crucial question is which dimensions of a great job can (and should) be supported by public policy. The most obvious would be promoting a healthy, safe, discrimination- and harassment-free work environment – ensuring that employment standards and basic rights are extended to all workers, with adequate monitoring and enforcement. And third, governments should pay careful attention to the wide support among Canadians for a more equitable tax system, more help with caring for children and the elderly, and a higher minimum wage. These issues reflect immediate needs and concerns. They also reflect broadly shared social values of fairness, equity, and quality of life for all.

The great jobs vision complements the criteria used for awards such as the Best Workplaces in Canada, Canada's Best Employers, the Ontario Hospital Association's Quality Healthcare Workplace Awards, Canada's Safest Employers Awards (which now include psychological safety), similar local and regional awards, and various forms of recognition for diversity, gender equity, ethical business practices, workplace safety, and psychologically healthy workplaces. All of these document progress, provide practical lessons that other employers can adapt, and generate momentum towards the vision of great jobs.

Link Engagement to Worker Well-Being and Organizational Performance

The Canadian workforce is less satisfied and engaged now than at the start of the twenty-first century. The Great Recession accentuated trends already under way, particularly the steady intensification of work and the weakening of employment relationships. Regardless of the causes, we've made a strong case for why employers need to reverse these trends. As a start, they can take the pulse of their own workforce and identify what changes in working conditions will turn things around.

We know that many larger employers have well-developed engagement strategies, so these findings are encouragement to redouble those efforts. In doing so, employers can expand those strategies to include health and wellness, which we have shown to be directly connected to engagement and job satisfaction. Engaged employees contribute more to organizational success in terms of skills, ideas, and initiative. So we offer a comprehensive approach to engagement: happy, healthy employees are motivated and involved in their work and contribute their capabilities – all essential for achieving an organization's goals.

By asking workers to describe what motivates them to look forward to work, and what changes would make them even more motivated, we have gained important practical insights about the preconditions for workforce engagement. For workers, what stands out is positive and supportive co-workers, working with clients and customers, and having meaningful work to do. Better pay would be a further incentive for people to look forward to their jobs. Again, employers will need to find the right combination of social, psychological, and economic work rewards that respond to the needs and aspirations of their workforce.

Also relevant for employers, as priority changes that would increase motivation, workers identify more pay, more flexibility, and better "bosses" – three improvements that employers should consider carefully. But as our analysis shows, raising pay alone won't go that far, because in the larger picture the psychological and social features of a job trump economic features.

To kick-start collaboration, why not rally around the goal of a more engaged workforce as the centrepiece for a national innovation strategy? So far, engagement strategies have been employer-specific, although there has been some effort at information sharing in the public sector in this regard. And while HR conferences routinely address engagement issues, there have been few if any attempts to approach higher levels of workforce engagement as a "public good" – in other words, a goal that stands to benefit individual workers, employers, society, and the economy.

Take a Participatory and Collaborative Approach to Crafting the Future

Canadians are less concerned about job security and high unemployment in the wake of the Great Recession, their overall quality of work life has eroded in this decade, and they harbour a bleak view of our economic prospects. But rather than feeling besieged and demoralized, most of the workers EKOS has surveyed would welcome cross-sector collaboration to create a better economy and society for the future. And they want to play an active role in shaping that future.

Workers themselves must actively participate in redesigning work to achieve well-being and prosperity goals. Just as we have given them a voice through a vision for great jobs – and through the extensive survey evidence based on their input – we encourage any government- or employer-led initiatives to build in meaningful roles for front-line workers and their organizations, which means in some industries and occupations unions and professional associations.

Backed by academic research and the input we received from thousands of Canadian workers, the best route to a satisfied, happy, and productive workforce is to empower front-line workers to actively create healthy and productive work environments. Doing so gives employees a greater sense of ownership over their work (like the satisfied self-employed), instils pride and meaning into their daily work, fosters camaraderie, and encourages them to contribute their ideas for improving the organization. This is a sure win-win scenario, benefiting employees and employers.

Standing at the intersections of employers, governments, and leaders are a range of industry and professional associations, unions, university researchers, and NGOs. An issues-based focus for collaboration may be an easier way to find common ground for action than taking on expansive topics like "the future of work." We've given examples of how this has happened (psychologically healthy and safe workplaces spring to mind, but there are others too).

Understand and Overcome Change Barriers

As partnerships are forged around a well-being and prosperity agenda, or as specific organizations take on these issues as their own goals, it will be important for leaders to identify and reduce barriers to progress.

We highlighted in this regard the low importance workers place on specific job and workplace features – such as training, autonomy, and input – which research tells us are essential for healthy, knowledge-intensive, and productive workplaces. Also standing in the way of change is the tendency for many workers to "hunker down" when confronted with bleak longer-term economic prospects. Yet these personal reactions can be countered with the public's more enthusiastic collective endorsement of a positive role for government in restoring prosperity.

A bigger problem is the low levels of trust in governments and corporations. This is an argument for starting with a more focused agenda and limited short-term goals that are easily attainable. On the policy front, an example is 2015 Ontario legislation that makes it illegal for employers to keep workers' tips – which shows basic fairness. Initiatives like this that achieve tangible change will help restore trust by showing that large institutions are genuinely committed to improving jobs and workplaces and have the integrity to follow through.

Within workplaces, the barrier that looms largest is the increased strains and demands faced by the very knowledge workers who are in positions to influence decisions and launch changes. With relatively fewer managers now than a decade ago, there are fewer mid-level influencers in large organizations. That point alone speaks to the importance of internal change agents – who may be front-line workers – collaborating with like-minded colleagues, as well as external partners in the non-profit and public sectors.

Update Labour Market Models to Fit New Realities

The "good jobs–bad jobs" model of the labour market has dominated experts' thinking since the late twentieth century. This dichotomous view of the employment system has evolved into a narrative about a growing underclass of individuals who are stuck in precarious jobs.

However, our evidence reveals more nuanced patterns of job quality, which reflect the tumultuous economic changes of the twenty-first century. When non-economic features of work are taken into account, the labour market looks more varied and complex than a simple dichotomous model suggests. Some workers in permanent full-time jobs have long hours, stressful working conditions, and considerable work-life conflict. So their overall quality of life could be higher.

Many self-employed and some contingent workers who move from contract to contract or take temporary assignments find their jobs very fulfilling and rewarding. The fact that growing numbers of these contingent workers are age 55 and older highlights the importance of flexible employment arrangements for keeping older workers productive for longer than they were in the past.

The overriding goal must be to replicate the best features of these different types of work arrangements. For example, employers should look at what adjustments are required in job descriptions and expectations so that employees feel greater "ownership" of their work – just as the self-employed do. The fact that the most stressed-out workers are full-time employees puts the onus squarely on employers to redesign jobs so workers have the autonomy, input, flexibility, manageable workloads, and resources needed to be psychologically healthy.

Labour market analysts will note that a person's labour market location has some bearing on their work values. This doubtless reflects the job and career choices people have made. Self-employed and contract workers place a higher value on flexibility than do employees, the self-employed highly value autonomy, and contingent workers seem less concerned about job security, benefits, and career advancement. Some of this may be adaptation to limited opportunities, but in a knowledge-based economy, increasingly these values signal what people ideally seek in a job.

Introduce Age-Inclusive Workplaces and Active Aging Policies

Canadians are concerned about generational inequities. This is a promising sign, not only because these are bound to increase if left unchecked, but also because it shows a readiness for solutions.

Most people believe that the young generation will not achieve the same standard of living as those today. This is a macro trend driven by large economic and demographic forces, over which individuals have almost no control. However, when it comes to workplaces, there are ample opportunities to address the needs and wants of multiple generations. This won't reverse the decline in the next generation's living standards, but it could go some way to improving their career changes and quality of life in the short term.

Canadian governments can learn from successes in other countries that have adopted active aging policies and taken steps to minimize age discrimination in workplaces. While age discrimination is prohibited under human rights legislation in Canada, its systemic nature, often based on negative stereotypes about the abilities and attitudes of older persons, still needs to be brought out into the open so such discrimination can be prevented.

These sorts of initiatives are ideally suited to collaboration between the public and private sectors. For example, federally funded sector councils – especially those representing industries that foresee labour and skill shortages – could be among the leaders in this area. One step forward would be to pilot active aging programs for interested employers, using evaluation findings to roll out such programs across an entire sector.

Thinking more long term, actions taken now by governments to manage the demographic transition in the workforce have the potential to reduce future generational inequities. For one thing, the longer older workers remain gainfully employed, the more taxes they pay – an important consideration for funding healthcare and public pensions.

Make Digital Technologies Tools for Well-Being and Productivity

Also important is monitoring the impact of new digital technologies to ensure that they enhance, not reduce, the well-being and productivity of workers. Our examples of crowdsourced labour and a global cadre of "micro-gigging" freelancers raise the spectre of digital exploitation – the twenty-first-century version of a nineteenth-century industrial proletariat.

For their part, governments can modernize and expand existing employment standards and occupational health and safety policy frameworks. Doing so will help to ensure that contract and temporary workers have the same rights as employees in corporate settings.

For employers, the challenge is to monitor the use of new technologies to ensure that their positives – such as efficiency and flexibility – outweigh their negatives, notably intensified work demands. Employee surveys and other forms of direct consultation are tools for finding out if this balance is the right one.

Balance Goals for Improving Economic and Non-economic Job Features

Expert and media attention to income polarization and low-wage jobs has overshadowed an equally troubling trend: the polarized distribution of non-economic work rewards and, more generally, well-being. The quality of a person's work life tells us a lot about their overall well-being, so work and life are organically connected. Improving the quality of jobs, therefore, will improve the quality of life in society.

Setting higher minimum wages and instituting "living wage" policies are important steps to achieving economic security. But they are longer-term projects. No government so far has moved rapidly in this direction, opting instead for a slower, phased approach to give employers time to adjust. There are, however, immediate opportunities to improve the quality of life within workplaces, making changes that cost little and involve fairly simple job redesign initiatives.

Design Jobs with Well-Being and Performance Goals in Mind

The strongest argument for employers to initiate solutions to workplace stress and work-life conflict is the cost of inaction, measured by rising health benefit costs, absenteeism, turnover, and reduced satisfaction and engagement. Stated positively, the key point for employees is that happy, healthy employees are more engaged in their work and able to contribute more to business success.

Backed by academic research, and the input we received from thousands of Canadian workers, the best route to a satisfied, happy, and productive workforce is to empower front-line workers to actively create healthy and productive work environments. Doing so gives employees a greater sense of ownership over their work (like the satisfied self-employed), instils pride and meaning into their daily work, fosters camaraderie, and encourages them to contribute their ideas for improving the organization. This is a sure win-win scenario, benefiting both employee and employers.

The intensification of work is particularly problematic for some full-time workers, pushed by rising performance expectations, job demands, longer hours, and time pressures. This is unhealthy, stressful, and ultimately counterproductive. Tracking work pressures should be a priority in employee surveys conducted by organizations. And the pervasive reporting of unpaid overtime by the workers we surveyed raises concerns about employment standards violations because of HR practices that are not only unfair but illegal. It also contributes to job stress and work-life conflict.

We know from decades of research that solutions to quality of work life problems require giving workers more control over their work so they can manage demands. And as we've also documented, doing so will encourage more initiative and innovation – exactly what powers a strong twenty-first-century knowledge economy.

Use Work Values as Guides to Improving Jobs

Values are workers' personal yardstick for measuring whether their job meets their expectations. Employers therefore could benefit from a clear understanding of their employees' work values and how these vary by demographic characteristics – especially gender, education, and age.

Adding questions about work values to employee surveys is the easiest way to do this. Such an approach will provide firm-specific evidence that, most likely, will temper assertions that Gen Yers bring distinctly different values into the workplace. As we emphasized, it's helpful for HR planning to know how values evolve over an employees' life course. This can be gleaned by comparing values held by different age groups (e.g., 10-year cohorts) in an organization.

Also relevant from an HR perspective are the subtle shifts in values since the early years of this century, resulting in somewhat more importance placed in the post-recession era on job security, decision input, autonomy, and flexibility. There is less importance now placed on a healthy and safe workplace, training, and a respectful climate. So despite the resources some employers have invested in these latter areas, clearly more needs to be done to get worker buy-in. Better communicating the personal benefits of a healthy, safe, and learning-intensive work environment would be an easy first step – as would advising how to access available resources in these areas.

Despite these values shifts in this decade and the last, a healthy workplace and a meaningful job continue to stand out as very important to Canadians. Whereas job security is among the top three most important job features, pay and benefits are somewhat less important. For some workers, a bigger issue than their hourly wage level is the predictability and security of their monthly income to cover expenses. This latter issue deserves the same attention from policymakers as the minimum wage.

Make Healthy, Meaningful, Flexible, and Fairly Compensated Jobs a Priority Goal

The high value workers place on having a respectful and inclusive workplace – one free from harassment and discrimination – seems like an essential Canadian value. It confirms the efforts many employers, and some governments, have made in recent years to address workplace diversity, bullying, and harassment. It also underscores the importance of taking further actions to make workplace relations respectful. Respectful workplaces are fair. And they cultivate positive working relationships, which we know from our evidence are a big motivator in day-to-day work. These work environment features are hallmarks of ethical and productive organizations – so there are bigger goals that these values underpin.

The value workers place on having challenging work that provides a sense of accomplishment is good news for policymakers and employers who want to strengthen Canada's knowledge-based economy. These are skilled jobs that enable workers to make significant contributions to business goals. We need more of them.

Decent pay and benefits are a priority too, so the ideal job combines both economic and psychological rewards. There also is a pent-up desire for more flexibility to allow people to achieve better work-life balance. As we've emphasized, flexibility is a basic job redesign concept.

There are significant gaps in the important job features listed here, with from 25 to 50 per cent of workers evaluating their current jobs as lacking in these respects. This has direct implications for HR – and for an organization's overall strategy. Knowing what these gaps are in an organization may go some distance towards addressing recruitment, retention, engagement, and performance improvement goals.

Better Utilize and Develop Workers' Capabilities

The use and further development of workers' skills and knowledge are not only critical for organizations to succeed. They also lead to better job quality and, through this, happier and healthier workers. By making workforce capabilities the linchpin connecting economic performance and individual well-being, we've advanced an even more compelling case for public and private investments in work-relevant training and learning.

Generally speaking, there is no shortage of skills or talent in Canada. On the contrary, Canada has much untapped capability in its workforce. Yes, it is important for organizations, sectors, and regions to have long-range workforce plans, coordinated with post-secondary institutions and immigration policies, to ensure a future supply of workers with the right education and skills in the right locations. Equally critical for industry and policy leaders to recognize, and then act upon, is the immediate potential for higher-performing businesses and a more dynamic, knowledge-driven economy.

The underemployment of well-educated workers deserves to be a top policy concern because it means squandered private and public resources. This problem reflects more than worker-job mismatches resulting from an inefficient labour market. Underemployment commonly stems from employers' human resource and management practices. Simply put, the main cause of this problem is the limited opportunity people have in their jobs to use and further cultivate their skills and knowledge. This is a future challenge that requires collaborative solutions devised by governments, industry, and workers themselves.

Canadian employers have for decades underinvested in training. This is short-sighted considering the performance pay-offs when firms develop their human capital. But there is no point in ramping up training without at the same time focusing on how to ensure that existing capabilities in an organization's workforce are being fully used. Part of this assessment should include documenting the benefits, which range from higher engagement and satisfaction levels to more collaboration, innovation, and quality products and services – all key components of a dynamic business or a high-performing public or non-profit organization.

Produce and Disseminate Better Labour Market Information

A significant gap that must be filled is the lack of reliable and relevant labour market information. Ideally a national agency with adequate government funding should take responsibility for providing the missing pieces. Prospects for this improved with the election of the Trudeau government; certainly its quick reinstatement of the long-form census shows a commitment to evidence-based decision-making. But government doesn't have to do this alone. We see a timely opportunity for a coalition of public, private, not-for-profit, and labour groups to partner on a project that would create a useful public resource.

The goal must be "knowledge for action." Annual indicators and trends would inform a range of decisions and initiatives specific to a labour market, sector, or firm. It would be especially valuable to survey workers and employers – as Statistics Canada's now-defunct WES used to do. This is not to suggest that the WES be resurrected. Rather, new Internet-based survey technologies make it easier to do this sort of research now in ways that produce timely and relevant results.

Examples of issues that could be examined in such future surveys further explore points we raised in earlier chapters:

- If predictions about skill shortages are consistent with workers' job and labour market experiences.
- How self-employed and contingent workers acquire additional knowledge and skills.
- Retirement plans and incentives for older workers to remain in the workforce.
- The availability of flexible work arrangements, difficulties accessing these, and whether they meet the needs of workers.
- How digital technologies contribute to positive and negative changes in work.
- How workers in different age groups acquire more responsibility in their jobs.
- Organizational enablers of challenging and meaningful work.
- To what extent employers' workforce development strategies are inclusive.
- What employers are doing to promote psychologically healthy workplaces.
- Individual and organizational sources of workforce resilience.
- Employers' experiences with contingent workers and future plans in this regard.

Create an Annual Well-Being and Prosperity Report Card

It's important to measure and report Canada's quality of life, as some organizations have been doing. However, these initiatives could be even more useful if they were expanded to include the quality of work life and its links to organizational performance.

Canada needs a comprehensive, annual report card that monitors progress on well-being and prosperity. Many of the key indicators we have examined in this book belong in such a report card. We would include here job satisfaction, engagement, job stress, work-life balance, job security, and the development and use of capabilities. Tracking income distribution and living standards, along with how people perceive these trends, will document how Canadians are affected by the big economic trends that so concern them.

Obtaining these data can be achieved through annual surveys, as we have illustrated by sharing details of EKOS Rethinking Work surveys and ongoing EKOS polling. And any such report card must build upon, and ideally collaborate with, existing well-being and job quality indices.

A well-being and prosperity report card would raise awareness among decision-makers, and the general public, of many of the trends and issues we have documented in this book. It also would contribute to evidence-informed strategies for prosperity.

To wrap up, we'll revisit two big themes in the book. One is how Canadians' outlook on the economy mixes pessimistic with optimistic scenarios. The other is that despite declining quality of work life and engagement, sizeable groups in the workforce – not all of whom are knowledge workers or full-time permanent employees – thoroughly enjoy their jobs, believe they are making a useful contribution to society, and have a decent living standard. These themes speak to an optimistic scenario. Just imagine that by 2025, there are more great jobs, a larger number of workers experiencing the fulfilment that comes from making a useful contribution, and improved living standards for the many. For us, that's what a prosperous Canada looks like.

Notes

Introduction

1 Parkinson, D., Blackwell, R., & Marlow, I. (14 January 2015). The seven-year slump. *Globe and Mail*, B1.
2 Hall, C. (16 November 2015). Justin Trudeau keeps focus on economy as G20 shifts attention to security. CBC News. http://www.cbc.ca/news/politics/g20-summit-justin-trudeau-speech-1.3319700
3 Betcherman, G., & Lowe, G. (1997). *The Future of Work in Canada: A Synthesis Report*. Ottawa: Canadian Policy Research Networks. http://www.cprn.org/doc.cfm?doc=454&l=en
4 Serino, M. (2010). *Making Human Capital the Creative Core of Strategy Execution*. Cornell University ILR School, p. 1. https://www.ilr.cornell.edu/sites/ilr.cornell.edu/files/hcd-white-paper.pdf
5 Gratton, L. (2011). *The Shift: The Future of Work Is Already Here*. London: Collins, p. 16.
6 Sorensen, C. (13 January 2014). How safe is your job? *Canadian Business*, p. 18.
7 McMahon, T. (15 January 2015). Missing the mark: Five reasons why Target failed in Canada. *Globe and Mail*.
8 Rodriguez, J. (16 January 2015). Retail retreat: Target isn't the only chain closing up shop in Canada. *Globe and Mail*. http://www.theglobeandmail.com/report-on-business/retail-retreat-target-isnt-the-only-chain-closing-up-shop-in-canada/article22487550/

9 Toneguzzi, M. (31 August 2015). 35,000 jobs lost already in Alberta's oilpatch, says industry group. *Calgary Herald*. http://calgaryherald .com/business/energy/35000-jobs-lost-already-in-albertas-oil-patch-capp

10 Statistics Canada, CANSIM database, Table 282-0002. http://www5 .statcan.gc.ca/cansim/a26?lang=eng&id=2820002#customizeTab

11 Foot, D.K., Ambachtsheer, K., Drummond, D., & Thériault, L. (13 November 2015). The boomer shift: Four experts on where an aging Canada is headed. *Globe and Mail*. http://www.theglobeandmail.com/globe-investor/retirement/four-experts-offer-solutions-for-an-aging-canada/article27259129/

12 Grossman, N., & Woyke, E. (2015). *Serving Workers in the Gig Economy*. Sebastopol, CA: O'Reilly Media. E-book: http://www.oreilly.com/iot/free/serving-workers-gig-economy.csp

13 Standing, G. (13 June 2015). A new class: Canada neglects the precariat at its peril. *Globe and Mail*. http://www.theglobeandmail.com/report-on-business/rob-commentary/a-new-class-canada-neglects-the-precariat-at-its-peril/article24944758/

1 How Economic Change Affects Canadians

1 International Labour Organization. (2015). *World Employment and Social Outlook: The Changing Nature of Jobs*. Geneva: ILO.

2 Standing, G. (2011). *The Precariat: The New Dangerous Class*. London: Bloomsbury.

3 Ross, A. (2009). *Nice Work if You Can Get It: Life and Labor in Precarious Times*. New York: New York University Press.

4 Kalleberg, A.L. (2013). *Good Jobs, Bad Jobs: The Rise of Polarized and Precarious Employment Systems in the United States, 1970s–2000s*. New York: Russell Sage Foundation.

5 Osterman, P., & Shulman, B. (2011). *Good Jobs America: Making Work Better for Everyone*. New York: Russell Sage Foundation, p. 8.

6 Krueger, A. (9 October 2015). The minimum wage: How much is too much? *New York Times*. http://www.nytimes.com/2015/10/11/opinion/sunday/the-minimum-wage-how-much-is-too-much .html?smid=tw-share&_r=0

7 Autor, D. (2010). *The Polarization of Job Opportunities in the U.S. Labor Market: Implications for Employment and Earnings*. Washington, DC: The Center for American Progress and the Hamilton Project.

8 Burleton, D. (26 February 2013). Are medium-skilled jobs in Canada experiencing a hollowing out, U.S.-style? *TD Economics*, Special Report.

9 Banting., K., & Myles, J. (2015). *Framing the New Inequality: The Politics of Income Redistribution in Canada*. Montreal: Institute for Research on Public Policy. http://irpp.org/research-studies/aots5-banting-myles/

10 Tariq, B. (20 March 2015). Video: Turking for a living. *New Yorker*. http://www.newyorker.com/culture/culture-desk/video-turking-for-respect. See also Zawacki, K. (3 December 2014). Amazon's turkers kick off the first crowdsourced labor guild. *Daily Beast*.

11 See, for example, Shorenstein Center on Media, Politics and Public Policy. (19 October 2015). Uber, Airbnb and consequences of the sharing economy: Research roundup. *Journalist's Resource*. http://journalistsresource.org/studies/economics/business/airbnb-lyft-uber-bike-share-sharing-economy-research-roundup

12 Malone, T., Laubacher, R.J., & Johns, T. (July–August 2011). The age of hyperspecialization. *Harvard Business Review*, p. 59.

13 *Economist*. (3 January 2015). The future of work: There's an app for that; Tiku, N. (30 January 2015). Before Uber revolutionizes labor, it's going to have to explain these embarrassing emails. *The Verge*; Griswold, A. (2 February 2015). Uber wants to replace its drivers with robots: So much for that "new economy" it was building. *Slate*.

14 Rifkin, J. (1995). *The End of Work: The Decline of the Global Labor Force and the Dawn of the Post-Market Era*. New York: Putnam, p. xv.

15 Bridges, W. (1994). *JobShift: How to Prosper in a Workplace without Jobs*. Don Mills, ON: Addison-Wesley, p. viii.

16 Edwards, J. (13 November 2015). The Bank of England has a chart that shows whether a robot will take your job. *Business Insider UK*. http://uk.businessinsider.com/bank-of-england-chart-on-robots-taking-jobs-2015-11

17 Cowen, T. (2013). *Average Is Over: Powering America Beyond the Age of the Great Stagnation*. New York: Dutton.

18 Lowe, G., & Schellenberg, G. (2001). *What's a Good Job: The Importance of Employment Relationships*. Ottawa: Canadian Policy Research Networks.

19 Statistics Canada, CANSIM database, Table 282-0002. http://www5 .statcan.gc.ca/cansim/a26?lang=eng&id=2820002#customizeTab

20 Data are from Statistics Canada, CANSIM database, Table 282-0014.

21 Krahn, H. (1991). Non-standard Work Arrangements. *Perspectives on Labour and Income* (Statistics Canada, Catalogue 75–001-XPE) (Winter): 35–45.

22 Saunders, R. (2003). *Defining Vulnerability in the Labour Market*. Ottawa: Canadian Policy Research Networks; Law Commission of Ontario. (2012). *Vulnerable Workers and Precarious Work*. Final Report.

23 Grant, T. (5 May 2003). Canada's shift to a nation of temporary workers. *Globe and Mail*. http://www.theglobeandmail.com/report-on-business/ economy/jobs/canadas-shift-to-a-nation-of-temporary-workers/ article11721139/

24 Krahn, H., Hughes, K., & Lowe, G. (2015). *Work, Industry and Canadian Society*, 7th ed. Toronto: Nelson, pp. 104–5.

25 Galarneau, D. (January 2005). Earnings of temporary versus permanent employees. *Perspectives on Labour and Income*. http://www.statcan.gc.ca/ pub/75-001-x/10105/4096650-eng.htm; Galarneau, D. (November 2010). Temporary employment in the downturn. *Perspectives on Labour and Income*. http://www.statcan.gc.ca/pub/75-001-x/2010111/article/ 11371-eng.htm

26 Statistics Canada, CANSIM database, Table 282-0080. http://www5 .statcan.gc.ca/cansim/a26

27 Statistics Canada, Labour Force Survey, 2014 annual average. CANSIM database, Tables 282-0012 and 282-0080. Calculations of the workforce exclude the unemployed.

28 Statistics Canada, Labour Force Survey, 2014 annual average. CANSIM database, Tables 282-0012. Calculations of the workforce exclude the unemployed.

29 Buttonwood. (15 July 2013). Go freelance and work harder. *Economist*. http://www.economist.com/blogs/buttonwood/2013/07/work-and-growth

30 Statistics Canada. (4 April 2013). Study: Employment changes across industries during the downturn and recovery. *The Daily*.

31 Tal, B. (5 March 2015). Employment quality – trending down. Canadian Employment Quality Index. CIBC World Markets.

32 Cross, P. (10 March 2015). Why CIBC's so-called job-quality index just doesn't measure up. *Financial Post*.

33 Lewchuk, W., Clarke, M., & de Wolff, A. (2011). *Working without Commitments: The Health Effects of Precarious Employment*. Montreal and Kingston: McGill-Queen's University Press.

34 Quoted in Schachter, H. (22 September 2011). How corporate anorexia is hurting our work force. *Globe and Mail*.

35 Frenette, M., Morissette, R., & Chan, W. (2011). Workers laid-off during the last three recessions: Who were they, and how did they fare? Analytical Studies Research Paper Series #337. Ottawa: Statistics Canada (11F0019M2011337).

36 Picketty, T. (2014). *Capital in the Twenty-First Century*. Cambridge, MA: Belknap Press.

37 Poll of 2,620 Canadian adults, conducted July 2014. Just 17 per cent disagreed with the statement.

38 Statistics Canada. (20 September 2011). Study: Layoffs during the last three recessions. *The Daily*.

39 Working poor are wage earners living independently in low-income households and who are not students. Stapleton, J., Murphy, B., & Xing, Y. (2012). *The "Working Poor" in the Toronto Region: Who They Are, Where They Live, and How Trends Are Changing*. Toronto: Metcalf Foundation.

40 OECD. (2015). *In It Together: Why Less Inequality Benefits All*. Key country findings – Canada. http://www.oecd.org/social/in-it-together-why-less-inequality-benefits-all-9789264235120-en.htm

41 Freeland, C. (2012). *Plutocrats: The Rise of the New Global Super-rich and the Fall of Everyone Else*. Toronto: Doubleday Canada.

42 Pew Research Center. (9 October 2014). Emerging and developing economies much more optimistic than rich countries about the future. http://www.pewglobal.org/2014/10/09/emerging-and-developing-economies-much-more-optimistic-than-rich-countries-about-the-future/

43 In 2015, EKOS found that 70 per cent of workers polled who agreed that society was becoming more divided also expected a lower living

standard for young Canadians in the future. Among those who do not agree society is becoming more divided, only 29 per cent think young Canadians will experience lower living standards than their parents. The relationship between these attitudes is statistically significant ($p < 0.001$; $n = 6,727$).

44 Regression analysis using each of the five statements as dependent variables, with the following predictors: gender, age, province, marital status, immigrant status, education, and income. Very little (between 2 and 6 per cent) of the variation in perceptions was explained by these predictors.

2 Happy, Healthy, and Productive Workers

1 http://www.weforum.org/reports/well-being-and-global-success
2 Helliwell, J.F., Layard, R., & Sachs, J., eds. (2015). *World Happiness Report 2015*. New York: Sustainable Development Solutions Network. http://worldhappiness.report/ed/2015/
3 Kekic, L. (2013). The lottery of life. *Economist: The World in 2013*, p. 91.
4 Organisation for Economic Co-operation and Development, Better Life Index. http://www.oecdbetterlifeindex.org/countries/canada/
5 Fox, J. (January–February 2012). The economics of wellbeing. *Harvard Business Review*, pp. 78–83.
6 Spreitzer, G., & Porath, C. (January–February 2012). Creating sustainable performance. *Harvard Business Review*, pp. 93–9.
7 Ton, Z. (January–February 2012). Some companies are investing in their workers and reaping healthy profits. *Harvard Business Review*, pp. 125–31.
8 Hsieh, T. (2010). *Delivering Happiness. A Path to Profits, Passion, and Purpose*. New York: Business Plus.
9 See http://www.plasticitylabs.com/.
10 Oswald, A.J., Proto, E., & Sgroi, D. (2013). *Happiness and Productivity*. Department of Economics, University of Warwick, p. 14. http://www2 .warwick.ac.uk/fac/soc/economics/staff/eproto/workingpapers/ happinessproductivity.pdf
11 Robison, J. (27 November 2012). Wellbeing is contagious (for better or worse). *Gallup Business Journal*. http://businessjournal.gallup.com/ content/158732/wellbeing-contagious-better-worse.aspx

12 The Canadian Index of Wellbeing, University of Waterloo. https://uwaterloo.ca/canadian-index-wellbeing/wellbeing-canada

13 Blanchflower, D.G., & Oswald, A.J. (2011). International happiness: A new view on the measure of performance. *Academy of Management Perspectives* 25 (1): 13.

14 We used linear regression, with the 10-point life satisfaction scale as the dependent variable and all the demographic and attitudinal variables discussed in the chapter as predictors. Survey questions with negative scales were reverse-coded. The adjusted R-squared is 0.30. The only demographic factor having a significant "net" influence (i.e., taking all other factors into consideration) on life satisfaction is living in the province of Quebec, but this had the least explanatory power of any of the predictor variables. Removing the Quebec resident variable from the model does not change overall results.

15 Towers Watson Global Talent Management and Rewards Study. (December 2010). https://www.towerswatson.com/en-CA/Insights/IC-Types/Survey-Research-Results/2010/12/Creating-a-Sustainable-Rewards-and-Talent-Management-Model

16 Sauvé, R. (2012). *The Current State of Canadian Family Finances, 2011–2012.* Ontario: Vanier Institute of the Family.

17 For information on these class actions see http://www.unpaidovertime.ca/.

18 Statistics Canada, CANSIM database, Table 282-0084. Labour force survey estimates (LFS), employees working overtime (weekly) by North American Industry Classification System (NAICS), sex and age group. http://www5.statcan.gc.ca/cansim/a26?lang=eng&id=2820084

19 Wilson, J. (1980). Sociology of leisure. *Annual Review of Sociology* 6: 21.

20 Sun Life Wellness Institute. (2011). *2011 Buffett National Wellness Survey.* http://www.sunlife.ca/Canada/smallbusiness/Focus+news/Past+issues/2011/2011+Buffett+National+Wellness+Survey+results+now+available?vgnLocale=en_CA

21 White, J. (16 November 2009). Stress cited as top global health risk. *Benefits Canada.* http://www.benefitscanada.com/benefits/health-benefits/stress-cited-as-top-global-health-risk-8276

22 Karasek, R., & Theorell, T. (1990). *Healthy Work: Stress, Productivity, and the Reconstruction of Working Life.* New York: Basic Books; Siegrist, J. (1996). Adverse health effects of high-effort/low-reward conditions.

Journal of Occupational Health Psychology 1: 27–41; Maslach, C., Schaufeli, W.B., & Leiter, M.P. (2001). Job burnout. *Annual Review of Psychology* 52: 397–422.

23 See, for example, Vahtera, J., Kivimaki, M., Pentti, J., & Theorell, T. (2000). Effect of change in the psychosocial work environment on sickness absence: A seven year follow up of initially healthy employees. *Journal of Epidemiology and Community Health* 54: 484–93. Ferrie, J.E., et al. (2004). *Work, Stress and Health: The Whitehall II Study*. London: Civil Service Unions & UK Cabinet Office; Mustard, C.A., Lavis, J., & Ostry, A. (2006). New evidence and enhanced understandings: Labour market experiences and health. In *Creating Healthier Societies: From Analysis to Action*, Heymann, J., Hertzman, C., Barer, M., & Evans, R. (Eds.). New York: Oxford University Press, pp. 421–95.

24 Canivet, C., Choi, B., Karasek, R., Moghaddassi, M., et al. (2013). Can high psychological job demands, low decision latitude, and high job strain predict disability pensions? A 12-year follow-up of middle-aged Swedish workers. *International Archives of Occupational and Environmental Health* 86: 307–19.

25 Kraatz, S., Lang, J., Kraus, T., Munster, E., & Ochsmann, E. (2013). The incremental effect of psychosocial workplace factors on the development of neck and shoulder disorders: A systematic review of longitudinal studies. *International Archives of Occupational and Environmental Health* 86: 375–95.

26 Babu, G.R., Jotheeswaran, A., Mahapatra, T., et al. (2013). Is hypertension associated with job strain? A meta-analysis of observational studies. *Occupational and Environmental Medicine* Published online first. doi:10.1136/oemed-2013101396

27 Nakata, A. (2012). Psychosocial job stress and immunity: A systematic review. *Methods in Molecular Biology* 934: 39–75.

28 Fransson, E.I., Heikkilä, K., Nyberg, S.T., et al. (2012). Job strain as a risk factor for leisure-time physical inactivity: An individual-participant meta-analysis of up to 170,000 men and women. *American Journal of Epidemiology* 176 (12): 1078–89.

29 Gilboa, S., Shirom, A., Fried, Y., & Cooper, C. (2008). A meta-analysis of work demand stressors and job performance: Examining main and moderating effects. *Personnel Psychology* 61: 227–71.

30 Bellavia, G.M., & Frone, M.R. (2005). Work-family conflict. In *Handbook of Work Stress*, Barling, J., Kelloway, E.K., & Frone, M.R. (Eds.). Thousand Oaks, CA: Sage, pp. 113–47.

31 Pelletier, K.R. (2011). A review and analysis of the clinical and cost-effectiveness studies of comprehensive health promotion and disease management programs at the worksite: Update VIII 2008 to 2010. *Journal of Occupational and Environmental Medicine* 53 (11): 1310–31.

32 *Benefits Canada*. (15 April 2013). Employee absence costs rise. http://www.benefitscanada.com/news/employee-absence-costs-rise-38121?print

33 Dewa, C.S., Thompson, A.H., & Jacobs, P. (2011). The association of treatment of depressive episodes and work productivity. *Canadian Journal of Psychiatry* 56 (12): 743–50.

34 Sanofi-Aventis Canada Inc. (2012). *The Sanofi Canada Healthcare Survey 2012*, p. 17. http://www.sanofi.ca/l/ca/en/layout.jsp?cnt=65B67ABD-BEF6-487B-8FC1-5D06FF8568ED

35 Stewart, N. (2010). *Creating a Culture of Health and Wellness in Canadian Organizations*. Ottawa: Conference Board of Canada.

36 Kaspin, L.C., Gorman, K.M., & Miller, R.M. (2013). Systematic review of employer-sponsored wellness strategies and their economic and health-related outcomes. *Population Health Management* 16 (1): 14–21.

37 Robroek, S.J., van Lenthe, F.J., van Empelen, P., & Burdorf, A. (2009). Determinants of participation in worksite health promotion programmes: A systematic review. *International Journal of Behavioral Nutrition and Physical Activity* 6: 26.

38 Felter, E.M., Nolan, B.A., Colombi, A., Albert, S.M., & Pringle, J.L. (2013). We're working hard, but is it hardly working? Why process is critical in the delivery of worksite health promotion programs. *Journal of Occupational & Environmental Medicine* 55: 586–92.

39 Canadian Standards Association. (2013). *National Standard of Canada for Psychological Health and Safety in the Workplace*. http://shop.csa.ca/en/

canada/occupational-health-and-safety-management/cancsa-z1003-
13bnq-9700-8032013/invt/z10032013?utm_source=redirect&utm_
medium=vanity&utm_content=folder&utm_campaign=z1003

40 Goetzel, R.Z., Ozminkowski, R.J., Bowen, J., & Tabrizi, M.J. (2008).
   Employer integration of health promotion and health protection pro-
   grams. *International Journal of Workplace Health Management* 1: 109–22.
41 Guarding Minds @ Work. (2012). *A Workplace Guide to Psychological
   Health and Safety.* http://www.guardingmindsatwork.ca/info; Mental
   Health Commission of Canada. (2012). *Psychological Health & Safety:
   An Action Guide for Employers.* http://www.mentalhealthcommission
   .ca/English/node/505
42 Email from Mary Ann Baynton, program director at the Great West
   Life Centre for Mental Health in the Workplace, to Graham Lowe,
   21 January 2014.
43 See WorkSafe BC: http://www2.worksafebc.com/Topics/workplace-
   mentalhealth/introduction.asp?reportID=36882
44 Rashid, T. (9 April 2014). Swedish city embarks on 6-hour workday
   experiment. *The Telegraph.* http://www.telegraph.co.uk/news/
   worldnews/europe/sweden/10754656/Swedish-city-embarks-on-
   6-hour-workday-experiment.html
45 New Economics Foundation: http://www.neweconomics.org/
   publications/entry/21-hours
46 Lowe, G.S. (2012). *Creating Healthy Organizations: How Vibrant
   Workplaces Inspire Employees to Achieve Sustainable Success.* Toronto:
   Rotman-UTP Publishing.

3 Engaged Workers

 1 Gibbons, J., & Schutt, R. (2010). *A Global Barometer for Measuring Employee
   Engagement.* Research Working Group Report 1460-09-RR. New York:
   Conference Board; Macey, W.H., & Schneider, B. (2008). The meaning
   of employee engagement. *Industrial and Organizational Psychology* 1:
   3–30. Also see Ludwig, T.D., & Frazier, C.B. (2012). Employee engagement and organizational behavior management. *Journal of Organizational Behavior Management* 32 (1): 75–82; Shuck, B. (2011). Integrative

literature review: Four emerging perspectives of employee engagement. *Human Resource Development Review* 10 (3): 304–28; Attridge, M. (2009). Measuring and managing employee work engagement: A review of the research and business literature. *Journal of Workplace Behavioral Health* 24 (4): 383–98; Dalal, R., Brummel, B.J., Wee, S., & Thomas, L.L. (2008). Defining employee engagement for productive research and practice. *Industrial and Organizational Psychology* 1 (1): 52–5.

2 Saks, A.M. (2006). Antecedents and consequences of employee engagement. *Journal of Managerial Psychology* 21 (7): 602.

3 Bakker, A.B. (2011). An evidence-based model of work engagement. *Current Directions in Psychological Science* 20 (4): 265.

4 Schaufeli, W.B., Taris, T.W., & van Rhenen, W. (2007). Workaholism, burnout, and work engagement: Three of a kind or three different kinds of employee well-being? *Applied Psychology: An International Review* 57 (2): 173–203.

5 Bakker, A.B. (2011). An evidence-based model of work engagement. *Current Directions in Psychological Science* 20 (4): 268.

6 Gagné, M., & Deci, E.L. (2005). Self-determination theory and work motivation. *Journal of Organizational Behavior* 26: 331–62.

7 Bock, L. (2015). *Work Rules! Insights from Inside Google That Will Transform How You Live and Lead*. New York: Twelve.

8 Great Place to Work Institute Canada (2015), http://www.greatplace towork.ca/great-workplaces/best-workplaces-in-canada-large-and-multinational

9 Silliker, A. (25 March 2013). Google all about creativity, innovation. *Canadian HR Reporter*, p. 8.

10 See http://www.protegra.com/; Atchison, C. (March 2011). Secrets of Canada's best bosses. *Profit Magazine*, p. 23.

11 Carney, B.M., & Getz, I. (2009). *Freedom Inc.: Free Your Employees and Let Them Lead Your Business to Higher Productivity, Profits, and Growth*. New York: Crown Business.

12 Herzberg, F. (1959). *The Motivation to Work*. New York: Wiley. See the Special Topic Forum, The future of work motivation theory, in the 2004 *Academy of Management Review* 29 (3), Steers, R.M., Mowday, R.T., & Shapiro, D.L. (Eds.).

13 Judge, T.A., & Klinger, R. (2008). Job satisfaction: Subjective well-being at work. In *The Science of Subjective Well-Being*, Eid, M., & Larsen, R.J. (Eds.). New York: Guilford Press, p. 404.

14 Gibbons, J., & Schutt, R. (2010). *A Global Barometer for Measuring Employee Engagement*. Research Working Group Report 1460-09-RR. New York: Conference Board. Also see Macey, W.H., & Schneider, B. (2008). The meaning of employee engagement. *Industrial and Organizational Psychology* 1: 3–30; Harter, J.K., Hayes, T.L., & Schmidt, F.L. (2002). Business-unit-level relationship between employee satisfaction, employee engagement, and business outcomes: A meta-analysis. *Journal of Applied Psychology* 87: 268–79.

15 Kahn, W.A. (1990). Psychological conditions of personal engagement and disengagement at work. *Academy of Management Journal* 33: 692–724.

16 Faragher, E.B., Cass, M., & Cooper, C.L. (2005). The relationship between job satisfaction and health: A meta-analysis. *Occupational and Environmental Medicine* 62: 105–12.

17 Rethinking Work 2015 did not include these two open-ended questions. Based on similar responses to the motivation and satisfaction questions in the 2012 and 2015 surveys, we are confident that the answers to these open-ended questions would not have been different if they had been asked in the 2015 survey.

18 This methodology is used by social scientists to analyse qualitative data obtained from surveys. The questions tried to elicit a single factor that either contributed to looking forward to going to work or would make the respondent look forward to going to work more often. The majority of respondents gave one factor, but some included two related factors in a single sentence. These were coded using the first-mentioned factor. A smaller number of respondents to both questions provided two distinct points, so these were coded separately. That's why the response *n* is higher than the number of respondents. The percentages in Figures 3.2 and 3.3 are based on response *n*s.

19 Lowe, G. (2010). *Creating Healthy Organizations: How Vibrant Workplaces Inspire Employees to Achieve Sustainable Success*. Toronto: Rotman-UTP Publishing.

4 What Canadians Value in a Job

1 Brenna Atnikov, quoted on the Meaningful Work Project website, http://www.meaningfulworkproject.ca/2012/09/brennaatnikov/
2 Ibid.
3 Rethinking Work 2015 did not ask about work values.
4 For fuller discussion, see Krahn, H., Hughes, K., & Lowe, G. (2015). *Work, Industry and Canadian Society*, 7th ed. Toronto: Nelson, ch. 13.
5 De Botton, A. (2009). *The Pleasures and Sorrows of Work*. Toronto: McClelland & Stewart, p. 78.
6 Ulrich, D., & Ulrich, W. (2010). *The Why of Work: How Great Leaders Build Abundant Organizations that Win*. New York: McGraw Hill.
7 Ibid., p. 4.
8 Florida, R. (2002). *The Rise of the Creative Class: And How It's Transforming Work, Leisure, Community and Everyday Life*. New York: Basic Books, pp. 77–80, 87–8.
9 Pink, D.H. (2009). *Drive: The Surprising Truth about What Motivates Us*. New York: Riverhead Books, p. 10.
10 Ibid., p. 136.
11 Pink, D.H. (2009). *Drive: The Surprising Truth about What Motivates Us*. New York: Riverhead Books.
12 Foot, D.K., & Stoffman, D. (2001). *Boom, Bust & Echo: Profiting from the Demographic Shift in the New Millennium*. Toronto: Stoddard. Also see Statistics Canada. (2001). Shifts in the population size of various age groups. www12.statcan.ca/english/census01/Products/Analytic/companion/age/population.cfm
13 Owram, D. (1996) *Born at the Right Time: A History of the Baby Boom Generation*. Toronto: University of Toronto Press, p. 281.
14 Tapscott, D. (22 December 2008). The net generation takes the lead. *BusinessWeek Online*; Tyler, K. (2007). The tethered generation. *HRMagazine*, pp. 52, 40–6.
15 Cited in *Economist*. (3 January 2009). Generation Y goes to work, pp. 47–8.
16 Ibid.

17 Krahn, H.J., & Galambos, N.L. (2014). Work values and beliefs of "Generation X" and "Generation Y." *Journal of Youth Studies* 17: 92–112.

18 Based on differences in the percentage who "strongly agree" with a value statement across five age groups: under 35, 35–44, 45–54, 55–64, and 65 and older ($p < 0.01$).

19 Based on male-female differences in the percentage who "strongly agree" with a value statement ($p < 0.01$).

20 See Inglehart, R., & Norris, P. (2000). The developmental theory of the gender gap: Women's and men's voting behavior in global perspective. *International Political Science Review* 21 (4): 441–63; Soroka, S., Cutler, F., Stolle, D., & Fournier, P. (June–July 2011). Capturing change (and stability) in the 2011 campaign. *Policy Options*, pp. 70–7.

21 Based on a poll of 3,005 adults, February 2015.

22 Gray, J. (2004). *Men Are from Mars, Women Are from Venus*. New York: HarperCollins.

23 Education level differences reported in Figure 4.6 are statistically significant ($p < 0.01$).

24 See, for example, Sabattini, L., Warren, A., Dinolfo, S., Falk, E., & Castro, M. (2010). *Beyond Generational Differences: Bridging Gender and Generational Diversity at Work*. New York: Catalyst.

25 Statistics Canada. (9 March 2010). Study: Projections of the diversity of the Canadian population. *The Daily*. http://www.statcan.gc.ca/daily-quotidien/100309/dq100309a-eng.htm

5 Generations at Work

1 Foot, D.K., & Stoffman, D. (1996). *Boom, Bust & Echo: How to Profit from the Coming Demographic Shift*. Toronto: Macfarlane Walter & Ross.

2 *Benefits Canada*. (20 August 2012). Working in retirement: The new normal?

3 Baby boomers are individuals born 1946–65, Generation X are those born 1966–79, and Generation Y (which we also refer to as millennials) are born 1980–95. For more technical background, see http://www12.statcan.gc.ca/census-recensement/2011/as-sa/98-311-x/98-311-x2011003_2-eng.cfm

4 Graves, F. (21 March 2013). *Left – Right? Forward – Backward? Examining Longer Term Shifts in Values, Social Class, and Societal Outlook*. Presentation to the School of Public Policy and Governance, University of Toronto.

5 Kershaw, P. (2015). *Population Aging, Generational Equity and the Middle Class*. Vancouver: Generation Squeeze.

6 Foot, D.K., & Venne, R.A. (2005). Awakening to the intergenerational equity debate in Canada. *Journal of Canadian Studies* 39 (1): 5–21.

7 On the US old age security unfunded liability, see http://cnsnews .com/news/article/social-security-faces-unfunded-liability-86t-or-7316783-household

8 Krugman, P. (28 March 2013). Cheating our children. *New York Times*. http://www.nytimes.com/2013/03/29/opinion/krugman-cheating-our-children.html?src=rec&recp=13&_r=1&&pagewanted=print

9 Green, B. (21 May 2012). Intergenerational equity: The mother of all guilt trips. *Huffington Post*. http://www.huffingtonpost.com/brent-green/intergenerational-equity-_b_1534118.html

10 Tal, B., & Shenfeld, A. (20 February 2013). Canadians' retirement future: Mind the gap. *In Focus*, CIBC Economics.

11 Canadian trends are from Statistics Canada. (2007). Portrait of the Canadian population in 2006, by age and sex. *2006 Census*; Marshall, K., & Ferrao, V. (2007). Participation of older workers. *Perspectives on Labour and Income* 8: 5–11; Statistics Canada. (2008). Canada's changing labour force. *2006 Census*. Ottawa: Statistics Canada, Catalogue 97-559-X; Statistics Canada. (17 September 2014). Population projections: Canada, the provinces and territories, 2013 to 2063. *The Daily*.

12 Conference Board of Canada. (2014). Canadian Outlook Long-Term Economic Forecast: 2014. http://www.conferenceboard.ca/e-library/abstract.aspx?did=6301

13 Wolfson, M. (2011). *Projecting the Adequacy of Canadians' Retirement Incomes*. Montreal: Institute for Research on Public Policy.

14 DeLong, D.W. (2004). *Lost Knowledge: Confronting the Threat of an Aging Workforce*. New York: Oxford University Press.

15 The exception is the federally regulated private sector.

16 Data in this paragraph are from Statistics Canada, CANSIM Table 282-0051. The median age (the midpoint in the distribution of retirement ages) is a more accurate measure of retirement trends than average age.

17 The survey focused on individuals aged 50 to 75 who were still working or had worked in the past 24 months. Pignal, J., Arrowsmith, S., & Ness, A. (2010). *First Results from the Survey of Older Workers, 2008.* Ottawa: Statistics Canada, Catalogue 89-646-X.

18 Uppal, S. (2010). Labour market activity among seniors. *Perspectives on Labour and Income* 22: 5–18; Pignal, J., Arrowsmith, S., & Ness, A. (2010). *First Results from the Survey of Older Workers, 2008.* Ottawa: Statistics Canada, Catalogue 89-646-X.

19 Bialik, C. (4 September 2012). Seven careers in a lifetime? Think twice, researchers say. *Wall Street Journal.* http://blogs.wsj.com/numbers/a-lifetime-of-career-changes-988/

20 Cappelli, P., & Novelli, B. (2010). *Managing the Older Worker.* Cambridge, MA: Harvard Business Review Press, p. 114.

21 Tammy, E. (16 February 2009). The four biggest reasons for generational conflict in teams. *HBR Blog Network, Harvard Business Review.* http://hbr.org/erickson/2009/02/the_four_biggest_reasons_for_i.html

22 Pink, D.H. (2009). *Drive: The Surprising Truth about What Motivates Us.* New York: Riverhead Books, p. 133.

23 Loch, C.H., Sting, F.J., Bauer, N., & Mauermann, H. (March 2010). How BMW is defusing the demographic time bomb. *Harvard Business Review*, pp. 99–102. Also see http://www.impactlab.net/2011/02/19/bmw-opens-new-car-plant-where-the-workforce-is-all-aged-over-50/

24 Dychtwald, K., Erickson, T., & Morison, B. (March 2004). It's time to retire retirement. *Harvard Business Review*, p. 55.

25 Taylor, D. (9 February 2009). Retaining older workers: Is phased retirement the answer? *Canadian HR Reporter*, p. 14.

26 Gutner, T. (2008). *Shifting the Focus: Updating Your Work-Life Approach to Integrate Employee Engagement and Talent Management.* New York: The Conference Board.

27 Lawler, E.E. III. (2008). *Talent: Making People Your Competitive Advantage.* San Francisco: Jossey-Bass.

28 Klie, S. (15 November 2010). Older workers keen on flexibility. *Canadian HR Reporter*. http://www.hrreporter.com/articleview/8459-older-workers-keen-on-flexibility

29 See http://www.aarp.org/work/employee-benefits/info-09-2009/about_the_best_employers_program.html

30 James, J.B., Swanberg, J.E., & McKechnie, S.P. (November 2007). Generational differences in perceptions of older workers' capabilities. Center for Aging and Work/Workplace Flexibility, Boston College. *Flexibility Issue Brief*, No. 12. http://www.bc.edu/content/dam/files/research_sites/agingandwork/pdf/publications/IB12_OlderWorkersCapability.pdf

31 Canadian Chamber of Commerce. (2010). *Canada's Demographic Crunch: Can Underrepresented Workers Save Us?*

32 Ross, D. (2010). Ageing and work: An overview. *Occupational Medicine* 60: 585–8.

33 See https://www.gov.uk/government/collections/age-positive.

34 Hartlapp, M., & Schmid, G. (2008). Labour market policy for "active ageing" in Europe: Expanding the options for retirement transitions. *Journal of Social Policy* 37: 409–31.

35 Tikkanen, T. (2007). *Increasing Employment of Older Workers through Lifelong Learning*. Stavanger, Norway: International Research Institute of Stavanger.

36 Government of Australia. (5 March 2015). *2015 Intergenerational Report: Australia in 2055*. http://www.treasury.gov.au/PublicationsAndMedia/Publications/2015/2015-Intergenerational-Report

37 Australian School of Business. (18 May 2010). Cross-generational workforce: How older workers are learning new tricks. *Knowledge@ Australian School of Business*. http://www.businessthink.unsw.edu.au/Pages/Cross-Generational-Workforce-How-Older-Workers-Are-Learning-New-Tricks.aspx

38 Organisation for Economic Co-operation and Development. (2005). *Ageing and Employment Policies – Canada*. Paris: OECD; Expert Panel on Older Workers. (2008). *Supporting and Engaging Older Workers in the New Economy*. Ottawa, ON: Human Resources and Social Development Canada. http://publications.gc.ca/site/eng/381561/publication.html

39 Alberta Employment and Immigration. (2011). *Engaging the Mature Worker: An Action Plan for Alberta.* http://work.alberta.ca/documents/engaging-the-mature-worker.pdf

6 Cultivating Workers' Capabilities

1 Lynch, K. (4 September 2010). Another new world order. *Globe and Mail.*
2 Conference Board of Canada. (n.d.). *Employability Skills 2000+.* http://www.conferenceboard.ca/topics/education/learning-tools/employability-skills.aspx
3 CBC.ca. (25 November 2015). CIBC CEO Victor Dodig says colleges and universities need to make more innovative grads. http://www.cbc.ca/news/business/cibc-ceo-victor-dodig-1.3336222
4 Canadian Chamber of Commerce. (2012). Canada's skills crisis: What we heard. A Canadian Chamber of Commerce report on cross-country consultations in 2012, p. 7.
5 Cowan, A., & Wright, R. (2010). *Valuing Your Talent: Human Resource Trends and Metrics.* Ottawa: Conference Board of Canada, ch. 5.
6 *Canadian HR Reporter.* (1 October 2013). 74 per cent of employers believe essential skills strategically relevant. http://www.hrreporter.com/articleview/18963-74-per-cent-of-employers-believe-essential-skills-strategically-relevant. The survey was conducted on behalf of ABC Life Literacy Canada.
7 Statistics Canada. (1999). *Workplace and Employee Survey, 1999.* Micro data file.
8 Oxford Economics. (2015). Workforce 2020. http://2020workforce.com/
9 The Institute for Performance and Learning. https://performanceandlearning.ca/awards/
10 Silliker, A. (26 February 2013). 9 in 10 execs say innovation top priority: Survey. *Canadian HR Reporter*, p. 9.
11 Porter, M.E., & Rivkin, J.W. (2014). *An Economy Doing Half Its Job: Findings of Harvard Business School's 2013–14 Survey on U.S. Competitiveness.* Cambridge, MA: Harvard Business School.

12 Dingman, S. (18 July 2015). Waterloo's nest wave. *Globe and Mail*, B6–B7.

13 Brown, P., Lauder, H., & Ashton, D. (2011). *The Global Auction: The Broken Promises of Education, Jobs and Incomes*. New York: Oxford University Press, p. 86.

14 Cooke, G.B., Chowhan, J., & Brown, T. (2011). Declining versus participating in employer-supported training in Canada. *International Journal of Training and Development* 15 (4): 271–89.

15 Direnzo, M.S., & Greenhaus, J.H. (2011). Job search and voluntary turnover in a boundaryless world: A control theory perspective. *Academy of Management Review* 36 (3): 567–89.

16 OECD. (2012). *OECD Skills Strategy, Country Snapshot – Canada*. http://skills.oecd.org/informationbycountry/canada.html. For the full report on skills strategies, see *OECD Skills Strategy: Better Skills, Better Jobs, Better Lives: A Strategic Approach to Skills Policies*. http://skills.oecd.org/documents/oecdskillsstrategy.html

17 Organisation for Economic Co-operation and Development. (9 September 2014). Canada shows highest level of tertiary education attainment, says OECD. http://www.oecd.org/canada/eag2014ca.htm

18 Employment and Social Development Canada. (2016). Canadian occupational projection system: Imbalances between labour demand and supply (2013–2022). http://occupations.esdc.gc.ca/sppc-cops/l.3bd.2t.1ilshtml@-eng.jsp?lid=29&fid=1&lang=en; Statistics Canada. (4 April 2013). Study: Employment changes across industries during the downturn and recovery (correction). *The Daily*. http://www.statcan.gc.ca/daily-quotidien/130404/dq130404a-eng.htm

19 Statistics Canada. (9 November 2014). University tuition fees, 2014/2015. *The Daily*. http://www.statcan.gc.ca/daily-quotidien/140911/dq140911b-eng.htm. Average full-time undergraduate tuition in Canada was about $6,000 in 2014–15.

20 Statistics Canada. (10 July 2015). Labour Force Survey, June 2015. *The Daily*. http://www.statcan.gc.ca/daily-quotidien/150710/dq150710a-eng.htm

21 Statistics Canada. (2015). CANSIM database, Table 282-0087.

22 *Economist*. (8 December 2012). The great mismatch, p. 71.

23 Uppal, S., & Sebastien LaRochelle-Côté. (April 2014). Overqualification among recent university graduates in Canada. *Insights on Canadian Society*. Statistics Canada.

24 *Randstad Workmonitor*. (September 2012). *Results wave 3: Employees feel overqualified for their job*. http://www.ir.randstad.com/news-and-events/press-releases/pr-2012/2012-09-10.aspx

25 Statistics Canada. (12 June 2013). Digital technology and Internet use, 2012. *The Daily*. http://www.statcan.gc.ca/daily-quotidien/130612/dq130612a-eng.htm

26 Wikipedia. (n.d.). *Digital literacy*. https://en.wikipedia.org/wiki/Digital_literacy (accessed 14 June 2013)

27 Gaudin, S. (9 October 2009). Study: 54 percent of companies ban Facebook, Twitter at work. *Wired*. http://www.wired.com/2009/10/study-54-of-companies-ban-facebook-twitter-at-work/

28 *Economist*. (30 January 2010). *A World of Connections: A Special Report on Social Networking*. http://www.economist.com/node/15351002

29 See https://www.capitalone.com/about/; Khanna, S., & New, J.R. (2008). Revolutionizing the workplace: A case study of the future of work program at Capital One. *Human Resource Management* 47: 795–808.

30 Pontefract, D. (15 July 2015). Working anywhere anytime. *Forbes*. http://www.forbes.com/sites/danpontefract/2015/07/09/working-anywhere-anytime/#4c0f3cd40898

31 We tested for statistically significant differences ($p < 0.05$).

32 Statistics Canada. (4 April 2013). Study: Employment changes across industries during the downturn and recovery, (correction). *The Daily*. http://www.statcan.gc.ca/daily-quotidien/130404/dq130404a-eng.htm

33 Statistics Canada. (2015). CANSIM database, Table 282-0010: Labour force survey estimates (LFS), by National Occupational Classification for Statistics (NOC-S) and sex, annual (persons unless otherwise noted). http://www5.statcan.gc.ca/cansim/pick-choisir

34 This paragraph draws on *Economist*. (15 August 2011). Middle managers: Saving David Brent. http://www.economist.com/blogs/schumpeter/2011/08/middle-managers?fsrc=nlw|mgt|08-17-11|management_thinking

35 Buckingham, M., & Coffman, C. (1999). *First, Break All the Rules: What the World's Greatest Managers Do Differently*. New York: Simon & Schuster.

36 Silverman, R.E. (22 June 2012). Who's the boss? There isn't one. *Globe and Mail*, B15.

37 Ton, Z. (2014). *The Good Jobs Strategy: How the Smartest Companies Invest in Employees to Lower Costs & Boost Profits*. Boston: New Harvest, ch. 7.

38 The classic article is Huselid, M.A. (1995). The impact of human resource management practices on turnover, productivity, and corporate financial performance. *Academy of Management Journal* 38: 635–72.

39 Bloom, N., & Van Reenen, J. (2010). Why do management practices differ across firms and countries? *Journal of Economic Perspectives* 24 (1): 203–24.

40 Drucker, P.F. (1993). *Post-Capitalist Society*. New York: Harper Business, p. 8.

7 A Blueprint for Redesigning Work

 1 McAfee, A. (November 2014). Mapping the future: The future of work. World Economic Forum. http://reports.weforum.org/outlook-global-agenda-2015/future-agenda/mapping-the-future-the-future-of-work/

 2 Remarks by Angel Gurría, Secretary-General of the OECD, at the launch of the OECD report, *In It Together: Why Less Inequality Benefits All* (21 May 2015). http://www.oecd.org/social/publication-launch-in-it-together-why-less-inequality-benefits-all.htm

 3 Collins, J. (2001). *Good to Great: Why Some Companies Make the Leap and Others Don't*. New York: Harper Business.

 4 This section draws on EKOS polls that are representative of adult Canadians, or the workforce, conducted between December 2013 and February 2015.

 5 This discussion of the minimum wage draws on Edmonds, S., & Sidhu, N. (2014). *Where Are Minimum Wage Earners in Ontario Working? An Analysis of Minimum Wage Employment and Firm Size*. Toronto: Social Planning Toronto & Campaign to Raise the Minimum Wage; Holpuch, A. (4 December 2014). Fast food and other minimum-wage workers protest in major cities over pay. *Guardian*. http://www.theguardian.com/us-news/2014/dec/04/us-minimum-wage-workers-protest-across-the-us-for-higher-pay; Strike Fast Food website: http://fight for15.org/november10/; Krassa, M., & Radcliff, B. (November 2014).

Evidence that higher minimum wages improve economic well-being: Research brief. Scholars Strategy Network; Statistics Canada. (16 July 2014). Study: The ups and downs of minimum wage, 1975 to 2013. *The Daily*; Finnegan, W. (15 September 2014). Dignity: Fast-food workers and a new form of labor activism. *New Yorker*; Nelson, J. (16 May 2014). Food fight: Rising income disparity and the struggle for higher wages. *Globe and Mail*.

6 Battle, K. (2015). *Canada Social Report Minimum Wage Rates in Canada: 1965–2015*. Ottawa: Caledon Institute of Social Policy.

7 Ontario Ministry of Labour. (16 November 2014). Press release: Province passes legislation to increase minimum wage: Ontario strengthening protections for vulnerable workers. https://news.ontario.ca/mol/en/2014/11/province-passes-legislation-to-increase-minimum-wage.html

8 Vinik, D. (14 April 2015). Low-wage workers deserve predictable work schedules. *New Republic*.

9 Arthurs, H. (2006). *Fairness at Work: Federal Labour Standards for the 21st Century*. Report of the Federal Labour Standards Review. Ottawa: Human Resources and Skills Development Canada.

10 Cowan, J. (April 2014). Time to ban unpaid internships. *Canadian Business*, p. 38.

11 Goodman, L.A. (6 March 2014). Backlash against unpaid internships growing in Canada, called "exploitation." *Canadian Employment Law Today*.

12 Goodman, L.A. (26 January 2015). Unpaid interns on agenda as federal officials meet with youth worker advocates. CBC News. Also see Canadian Intern Association: http://internassociation.ca/

13 Surowiecki, J. (9 February 2015). A fair day's wage. *New Yorker*. http://www.newyorker.com/magazine/2015/02/09/fair-days-wage

14 BBC. (1 April 2015). McDonald's to raise wages for 90,000 US employees; Saft, J. (9 March 2015). Walmart's raises not loved by the markets. *Canadian HR Reporter*, p. 15.

15 Ribeiro, J. (5 October 2014). Google to put guards on payroll, amid concerns about inequality. *PCWorld*.

16 Foulis, P. (2014). Payback time. *The Economist: The World in 2015*, p. 129.

17 Ton, Z. (2014). *The Good Jobs Strategy: How the Smartest Companies Invest in Employees to Lower Costs and Boost Profits*. Boston: New Harvest.

18 https://www.bcorporation.net/what-are-b-corps/why-b-corps-matter; also see Semuels, A. (26 November 2014). A new business strategy: Treating employees well. *Atlantic*. http://www.theatlantic.com/business/archive/2014/11/a-new-business-strategy-treating-employees-well/383192/

19 See https://www.vancity.com/AboutVancity/.

20 https://www.vancity.com/AboutVancity/VisionAndValues/Values BasedBanking/livingwage/. Also see http://livingwagecanada.ca/index.php/living-wage-employers/employer/.

21 Ontario Hospital Association: https://www.oha.com/CurrentIssues/keyinitiatives/QualityHealthCareWorkplaceAwards/Pages/Default.aspx

22 http://fmiosa.com/

23 http://bcsafetycharter.ca/

24 Lowe, G., & Schellenberg, G. (2001). *What's a Good Job: The Importance of Employment Relationships*. Ottawa: Canadian Policy Research Networks.

25 Berg, J.M., Dutton, J.E., & Wrzesniewski, A. (2008). What is job crafting and why does it matter? Centre for Positive Organizational Scholarship. Ross School of Business, University of Michigan.

26 Barry, M., & Wilkinson, A. (2015). Pro-social or pro-management? A critique of the conception of employee voice as a pro-social behaviour in organizational behaviour. *British Journal of Industrial Relations*. http://onlinelibrary.wiley.com/doi/10.1111/bjir.12114/abstract

27 *Economist*. (6 April 2013). Unions, Inc., pp. 68–9.

28 Statistics Canada, Labour Force Survey. CANSIM database Table 282-0223. Labour Force Survey estimates (LFS), employees by union status, North American Industry Classification System (NAICS) and sex, Canada.

29 Bernier, L. (27 January 2014). Ontario public sector execs could see compensation cap. *Canadian HR Reporter*, p. 11.

30 Fiz-Morris, J. (16 January 2015). RCMP officers have right to collective bargaining, Supreme Court rules: Federal government given 1 year to amend law to allow collective bargaining. CBC News. http://www.cbc.ca/news/politics/rcmp-officers-have-right-to-collective-bargaining-supreme-court-rules-1.2912340; Fine, S. (30 January 2015).

Canadian workers have fundamental right to strike, top court rules. *Globe and Mail*. http://www.theglobeandmail.com/news/national/top-court-upholds-canadian-workers-right-to-strike/article22717100/

31 Pugen, D., & Lindner, J. (14 January 2015). Federal labour law amendments: Harder to certify a union (and easier to decertify a union). McCarthy Tetrault LLP. http://www.lexology.com/library/detail.aspx?g=583992e7-7c89-4e8e-9111-ab475c89b2c2

8 Actions to Improve Well-Being and Prosperity

1 Conference Board of Canada: http://www.conferenceboard.ca/conf/betterworkplace/agenda.aspx

2 For the report on the summit, see http://www.unifor.org/en/take-action/good-jobs-summit/gjs-report. Also see Zizys, T. (2014). Better work: The path to good jobs is through employers. Metcalf Foundation. http://metcalffoundation.com/stories/publications/better-work-the-path-to-good-jobs-is-through-employers/

3 Lammam, C. (2014). *The Economic Effects of Living Wage Laws*. Vancouver: Fraser Institute.

4 Clemens, J., Lammam, C., Palacios, M., & Ren, F. (2015). *Comparing Government and Private Sector Compensation in British Columbia*. Vancouver: Fraser Institute.

5 *Economist*. (9 August 2014). In search of the good business, pp. 55–6.

6 McGugan, I. (21 July 2014). Like the sound of a 3-day work week? Billionaire Carlos Slim does. *Globe and Mail*.

7 Giang, V. (12 January 2015). What will work look like in 2030? *Fast Company*. http://www.fastcompany.com/3040701/what-will-work-look-like-in-2030

About the Authors

Graham Lowe is president of the Graham Lowe Group Inc., a workplace consulting and research firm. He also is a professor emeritus at the University of Alberta, where he had a distinguished academic career. Graham has three decades of organizational, labour market, and employment policy consulting experience. He has advised numerous employers on how to create healthier and more productive workplaces. His books include *The Quality of Work: A People-Centered Agenda* and *Creating Healthy Organizations: How Vibrant Workplaces Inspire Employees to Achieve Sustainable Success.* He regularly contributes articles to practitioner publications such as *Canadian HR Reporter, Canadian Business, Health & Productivity Management, HR Professional,* and *Healthcare Quarterly.* As a "thought leader" on work issues, Graham has given hundreds of conference talks and workshops across Canada and internationally. He is a recipient of the Canadian Workplace Wellness Pioneer Award and holds a PhD in sociology from the University of Toronto.

Frank Graves is one of Canada's leading public opinion, social policy, and public policy experts, as well as one of its leading applied social researchers. In 1980, he founded EKOS Research Associates Inc., an applied social and economic research firm. Under the leadership of Graves, EKOS has earned a reputation for creative and rigorous research in the areas of public policy, social policy, and program evaluation and as a leader in innovative survey techniques and methodology. During his career he has directed hundreds of large-scale studies of Canadian attitudes to a vast array of issues. Graves has conducted several major evaluations of the effectiveness of labour market interventions and has been studying changes in Canadian workplaces for the past 20 years. Graves was named a Fellow of the Marketing Research and Intelligence Association (MRIA), the highest professional designation in the marketing research industry in Canada.

Index

The letter *f* following a page number denotes a figure.

Lightning Source UK Ltd.
Milton Keynes UK
UKHW01n0620040518

322101UK00007B/540/P